Tattoo Models

Timothy Remus & Ákos Bánfalvi

Published by:

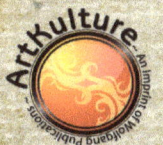

PO Box 223
Stillwater, MN 55082
www.wolfpub.com

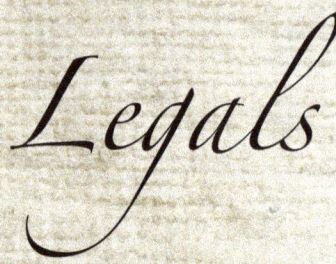

Legals

2021 reprint and resize of the original book:
The Colorful World of Tattoo Models.

First published in 2012 by Wolfgang Publications Inc.,
P.O. Box 223, Stillwater MN 55082

© Timothy Remus, 2012

All rights reserved. With the exception of quoting brief passages for the purposes of review no part of this publication may be reproduced without prior written permission from the publisher.

The information in this book is true and complete to the best of our knowledge. All recommendations are made without any guarantee on the part of the author or publisher, who also disclaim any liability incurred in connection with the use of this data or specific details.

We recognize that some words, model names and designations, for example, mentioned herein are the property of the trademark holder. We use them for identification purposes only. This is not an official publication.

ISBN 13: 978-1-941064-68-9

Printed and bound in U.S.A.

Tattoo Models

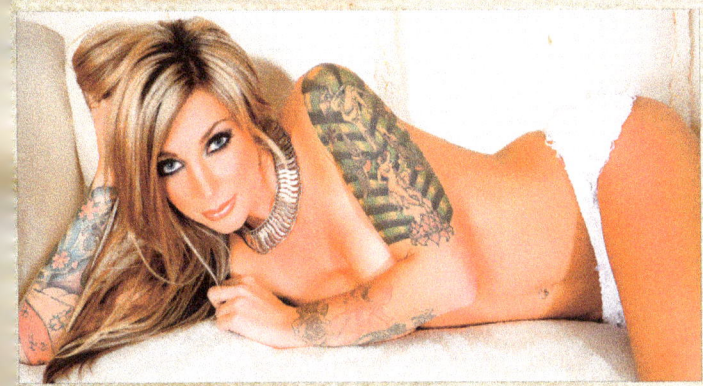

Kali Ann Harris	Page 6
Jen Ashton	Page 10
Bridget Blonde	Page 14
Brittany Casualty	Page 18
Angie Collord	Page 22
Amy DeLaCroux	Page 28
Jessie DeVille	Page 32
Stephanie Fleischman	Page 36
Suzanne Franco	Page 40
Dejah Garcia	Page 44
Lala Hartline	Page 50
Kandy	Page 54
Demanda Lavette	Page 58
Bernadette Macias	Page 64
Malice McMunn	Page 68
Heather Moss	Page 72
Niki Nix	Page 76
Katie Omand	Page 80
Megan Renee	Page 84
Monica Renee	Page 88
Ruca	Page 96
Kristeen St. Pierre	Page 102

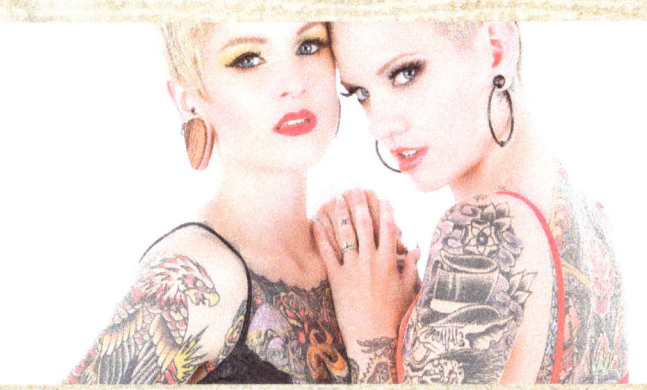

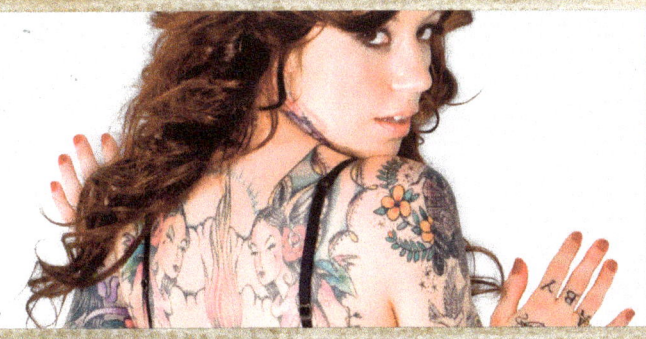

Crystal Wyatt	Page 106
Yeonji	Page 110
Lacy Dupras	Page 114
Jennifer Groblebe	Page 118
Krissy Logan	Page 124
Sarah Mudle	Page 130
Jacque Oh	Page 134
Lexington	Page 138
Photographers	Page 142

Introduction

I like to think that *Tattoo Models* is the perfect melding of three art forms. The first is obvious — tattoos. The Art of Tattoo gets better and better, the creativity exhibited by the various artists knows no bounds. When you think it can't get any better, it does. Again, and again. The second art form is modeling. Anyone who has ever tried to take a picture of their significant other, or some cute hottie, soon realizes that there's more to it than just, "stand over there and look pretty." The Art of Modeling is an expressive art form all its own. The third art form captured here is the Art of Photography. Every photo in this book is technically perfect. The images are correctly exposed, everything is in sharp focus — except for those cases where the artist wanted parts of the images to be soft and out of focus. But like the tattoo artists, the shutter bugs did more than just take a correctly exposed and focused photo. The use of props and backgrounds, the pose and placement of the model within that setting, the lighting and the camera angle, all work together to create images as creative and compelling as the tattoos themselves. There's more here than just a collection of photos. More than just a book about pretty girls. We've created a package that celebrates three art forms. Call it synergy - the total package is more than just the sum of its parts.

The issue you hold in your hands is a revised and resized version of the original book — *The Colorful World of Tattoo Models*. We've reduced the size to fit the requirements of our new distribution system, Lightning Source. Though the distribution — and printer — have changed, all the photos and text of the original book are right here.

Acknowledgements

This book came about with an email from some guy in Hungary, inquiring as to whether I would like to buy a group of tattoo-model photos and interviews. That guy's name was Ákos, and despite my initial skepticism, he convinced me that it was a straight up deal, no hidden agendas, no problem getting the models and photographers to sign off on the rights, and no problems with the quality of the images. I can only say that Ákos made good on all his promises. Thus my "thank yous" start with Ákos.

I have to express my gratitude to all the models for allowing us to use their images on these pages. I hope each and every one takes pleasure in seeing their images in this new book. The images themselves are the work of a very talented group of artists, I can only say I stand in awe at the quality and creativity of each and every photo in this book, thank you. Finally, the look of the book and the design of the cover is the work of another talented artist — Jacki Mitchell — the art director at Wolfgang Publications.

— *Timothy Remus*

I would like to say thank you for the following persons for their help. Without you this book wouldn't be real:

My friends and family:
Boldizsár Laki-Lukács (www.diffikult.com), Timothy Remus and the Wolfgang Publications staff, Barna Bartha and the Hungarian Tattoo Magazine (www.tattoomania.hu), Matthias Reuss and the Edition Reuss, Angelika Bánfalviné Szőke, Sándor Bánfalvi, Éva Bánfalviné Kokovai, Éda Bánfalvi, Péter Ágoston, Ferenc Mida, Ákos Horváth, Viktor Szilágyi, Krisztián Szász, Gábor Mélypataki, Attila Kajtor, Péter Bana

— *Ákos Bánfalvi*

Authors

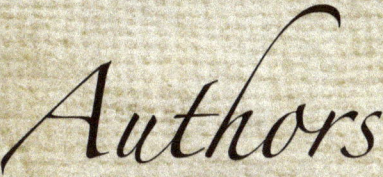

Timothy Remus

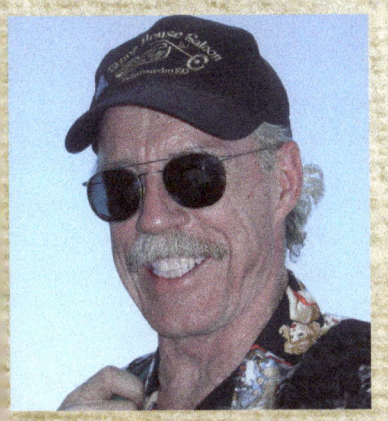

Author of over 30 books, Timothy Remus from Stillwater, Minnesota began his adult life as an automotive mechanic. A back injury brought that career to an end some fifteen years later, and began a second career – writing how-to books. After writing a number of books as an author for a big publisher, Timothy took the leap and began to publish the books he wrote. Publishing for other authors was only a short step, and today Wolfgang Publications publishes eight to twelve new titles each year.

Though Tim's first books concerned themselves with automotive and motorcycle subjects, more recently he's branched out into new territory. Currently there are eight Tattoo books on the Wolfgang web site, with two more already in the works. Those titles include two flash books, Tattoo Bible One and Two; as well as Tattoo Sketch Book; and Into the Skin, a How-To-Tattoo book offered with a companion DVD.

www.wolfpub.com
www.artkulture.com
info@wolfpub.com

Ákos Bánfalvi

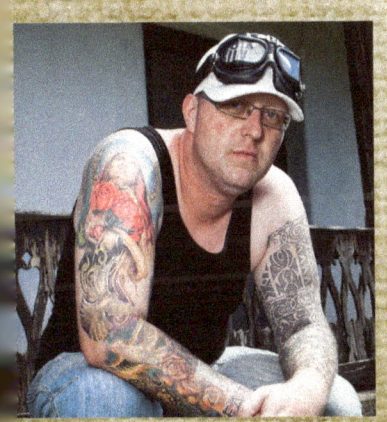

For well-known Hungarian journalist Ákos Bánfalvi, his career really started with his love for rock music during his teens. Before long he became the principal contributor of Hungarian RockinforM Magazine. That association lasted for more than 15 years, and during this period he wrote four successful books about bands like Marilyn Manson, Limp Bizkit, and the most famous Hungarian punk 'n' roll band, Junkies. If that weren't enough, Ákos also worked for years as a host and editor for different rock/metal radio and television programs.

In more recent times, Ákos turned his attention to tattoos and now makes a living writing about skin art. In 2007 he began working for Hungarian Tattoo Magazine, and since then Ákos has kept busy interviewing tattooed bands, photographers, artists, and models from around the world. In fact, Ákos just started a brand new, 160 page monthly digital magazine called Tattoo Slide filled with tattoos, tattooed girls, art, and underground fashion – currently available in English and German.

www.facebook.com/akos.banfalvi
www.myspace.com/banfalviakos

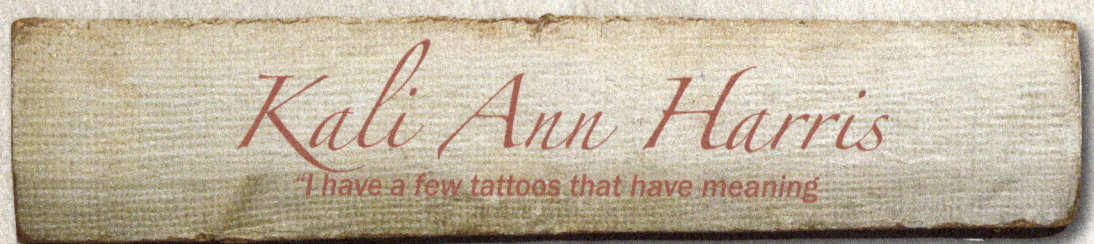
Kali Ann Harris
"I have a few tattoos that have meaning"

I am Kali Ann, a lady with many hats. I am a body piercer, model, pit bull activist, crafter and a wife. Body Piercing is my full time job. I have been piercing at Fine Line Tattoo in Garland, Texas going on six years. Modeling is more for fun and crafting is what I do in my free time. I make jewelry, knit hats and scarves and anything else my nibble fingers can do.

What kind of modeling do you do? And what made you get into modeling?

I'm open to trying new things. I don't want to single myself into a single form of modeling. I like glamour, high fashion, and pin-up, but do not want to limit myself to that. My good friend Phoenix Taylor is a photographer. I started shooting with him every once in a while and then worked to make it a career.

How did you started to collecting tattoos?

I have always been the type of person that if you are going to do something then you might as well go big. I had a few because my older sister was tattooed and I admired them on her. But I didn't get heavily tattooed until I started working at the shop. If you work in a shop and you are surrounded by tattoos you are going to get tatted. And that's what happened. I started to know other artists in the industry and started getting tattooed by them. I like to have several different artists tattoo me.

Which was your first one? And why did you choose it?

My first one was a kanji that meant "art" because I was just accepted into art school. I was there because of my sister and was just looking on the walls and I saw it. That small Chinese symbol summed up my whole life and I had to get it. I got it covered by a panther by Casey Cokrlic because I wanted a bigger tattoo on my foot.

Please talk us through some of your tattoos and the reasons behind them.

I have my grandmothers' names on my shoulders. I have a couple that are jokes between friends and I. But the majority of my tattoos are there cause I think they look cool. I don't think that everything has to have a meaning. It's okay to get a tattoo just 'cause it looks cool.

Please go through your main pieces, where they are on your body, who did them, what shop, and the meaning behind any of them you'd like to share.

There's my back piece, my tiger knee cap, Indian pin-up by Casey Cokrlic at Fine Line Tattoo, no meaning just cool tattoos. My chest piece, peacock, and battle royale on my left forearm by Richard Stell, no meaning just cool tats. I have my right side of my ribs by Oliver Peck of Elm Street Tattoo, just a pretty lady head and roses – no meaning. My favorite tattoo is my back piece. I have had a lot of work go into it and it's so solid. I also love the design. It was inspired by a painting by Ed Hardy.

Have you gotten any new work done?

My back piece has been a work in progress for the past couple of years. I also got my lone wolf done on my left arm which finished that arm off. That was done by Will Card at Saints and Sinners in Texas. I have an appointment in October to get tattooed by Jason Brooks at Great Wave in Austin, Texas. I'm getting my stomach tattooed.

Do you have any funny/weird stories about a tattoo experience?

Two weeks after meeting my husband, tattooer Mike "Jesus" Harris, we were hanging out after hours at the shop where he worked. We both tattooed "Jesus loves Kali" and "Kali loves you" on each other. It was pretty silly 'cause we only knew each other for two weeks. Who knew that three years later we would be married. So, I don't believe in the curse of getting each other's names tattooed on each other.

Any final words?

Peace. Love. And tattoos.

www.facebook.com/kaliannharris
www.facebook.com/kaliann13
www.myspace.com/kalixoxo

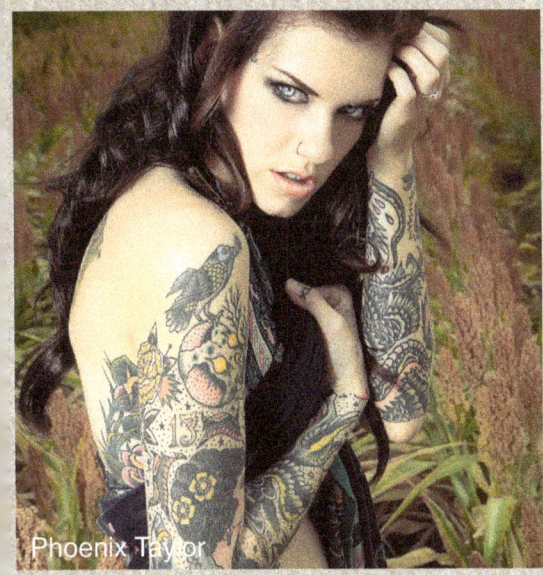
Phoenix Taylor

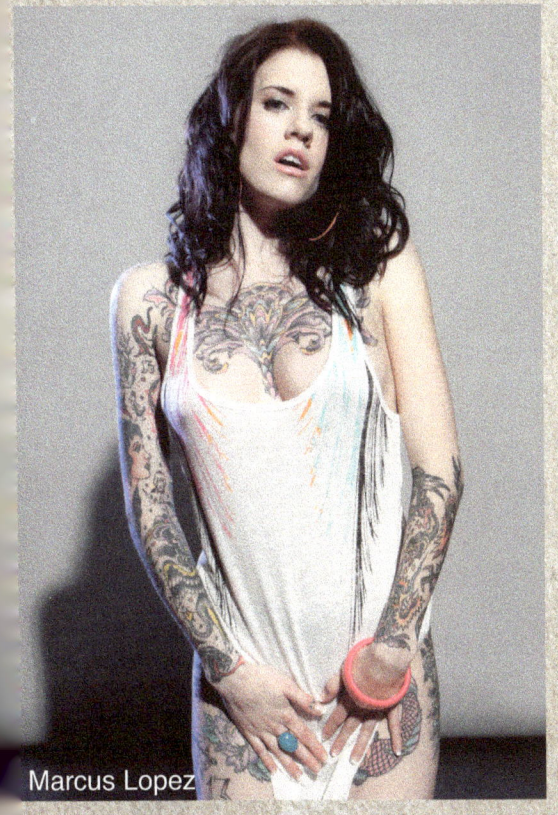
Marcus Lopez

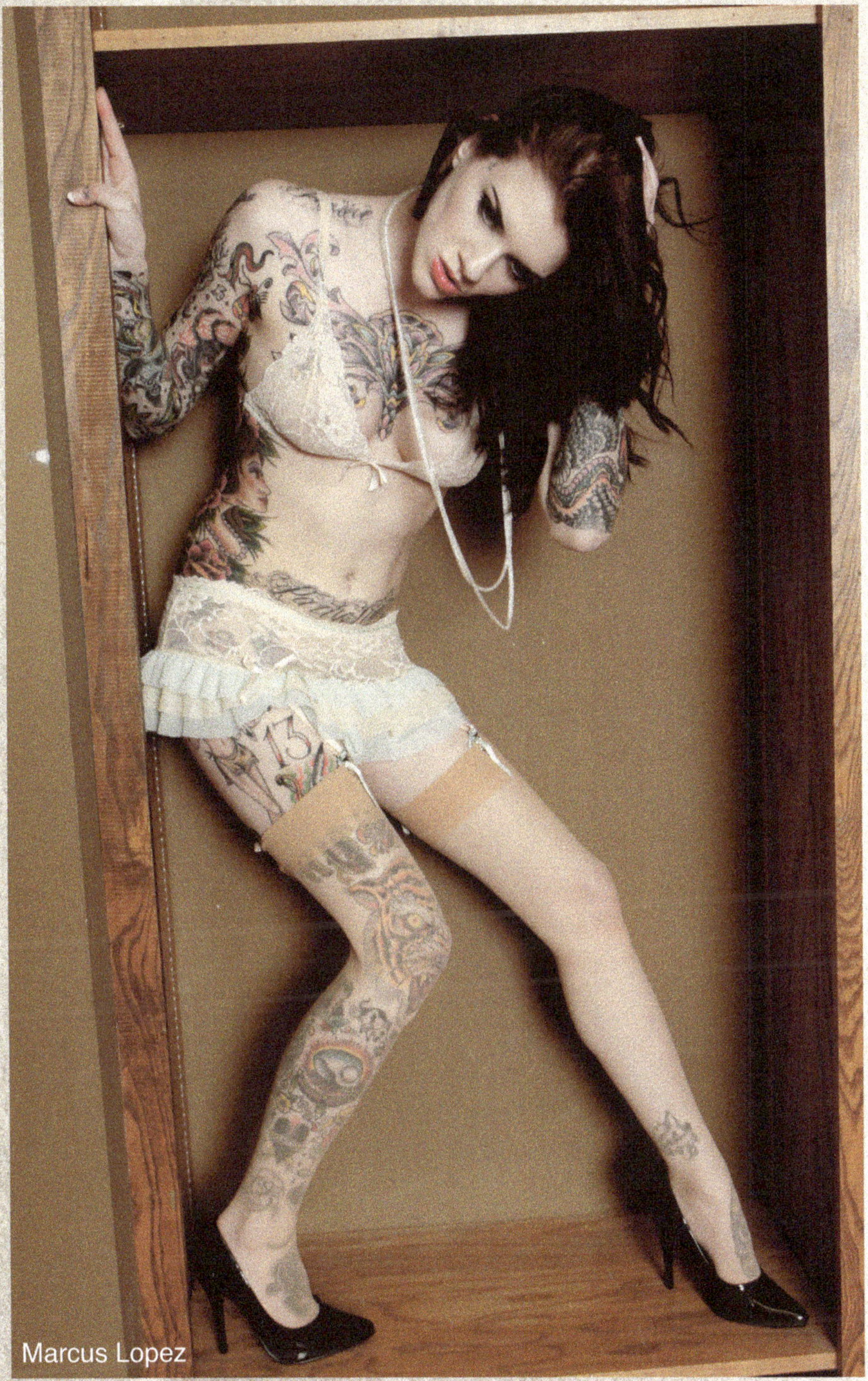

Marcus Lopez

Kali Ann Harris

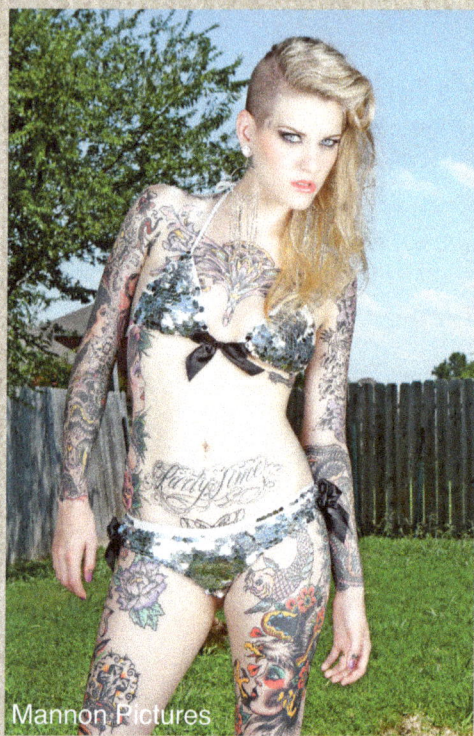
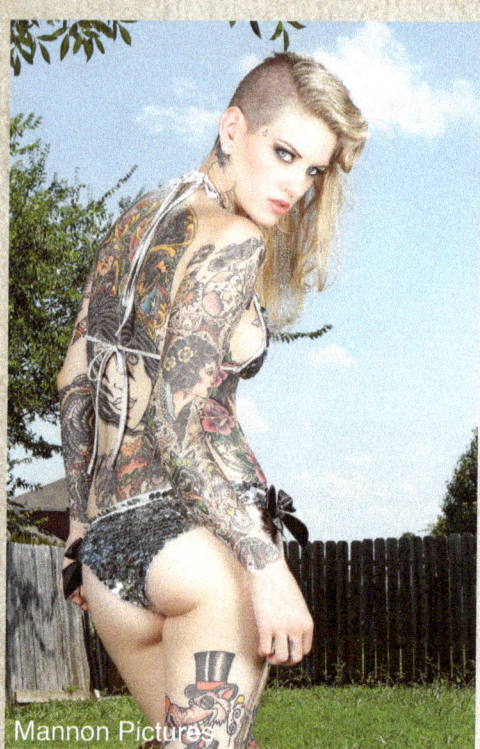
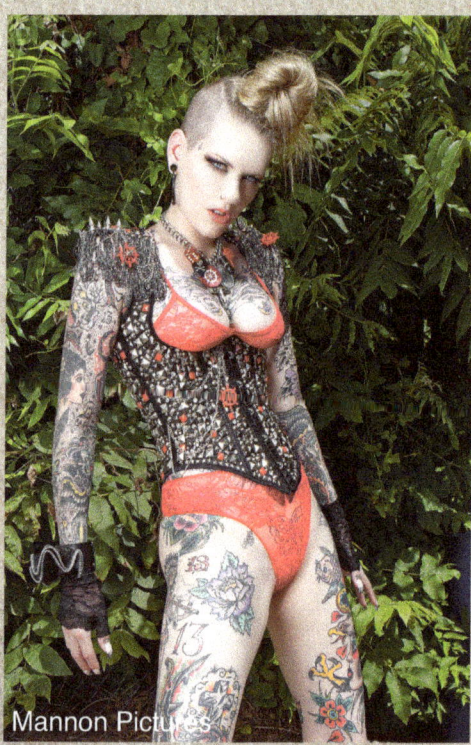
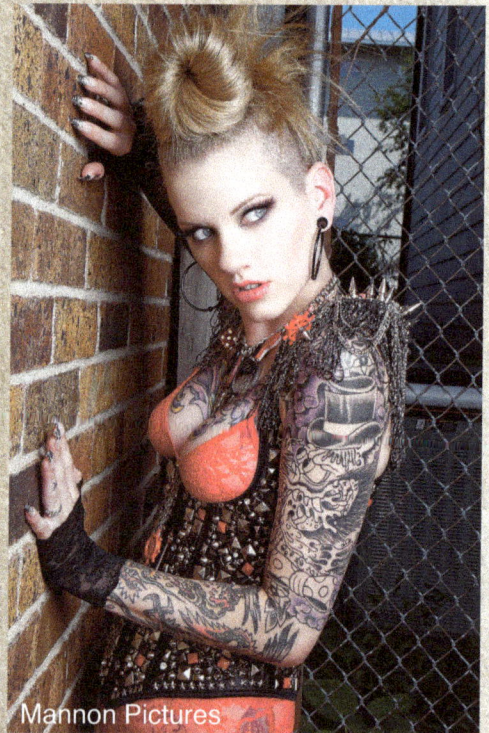

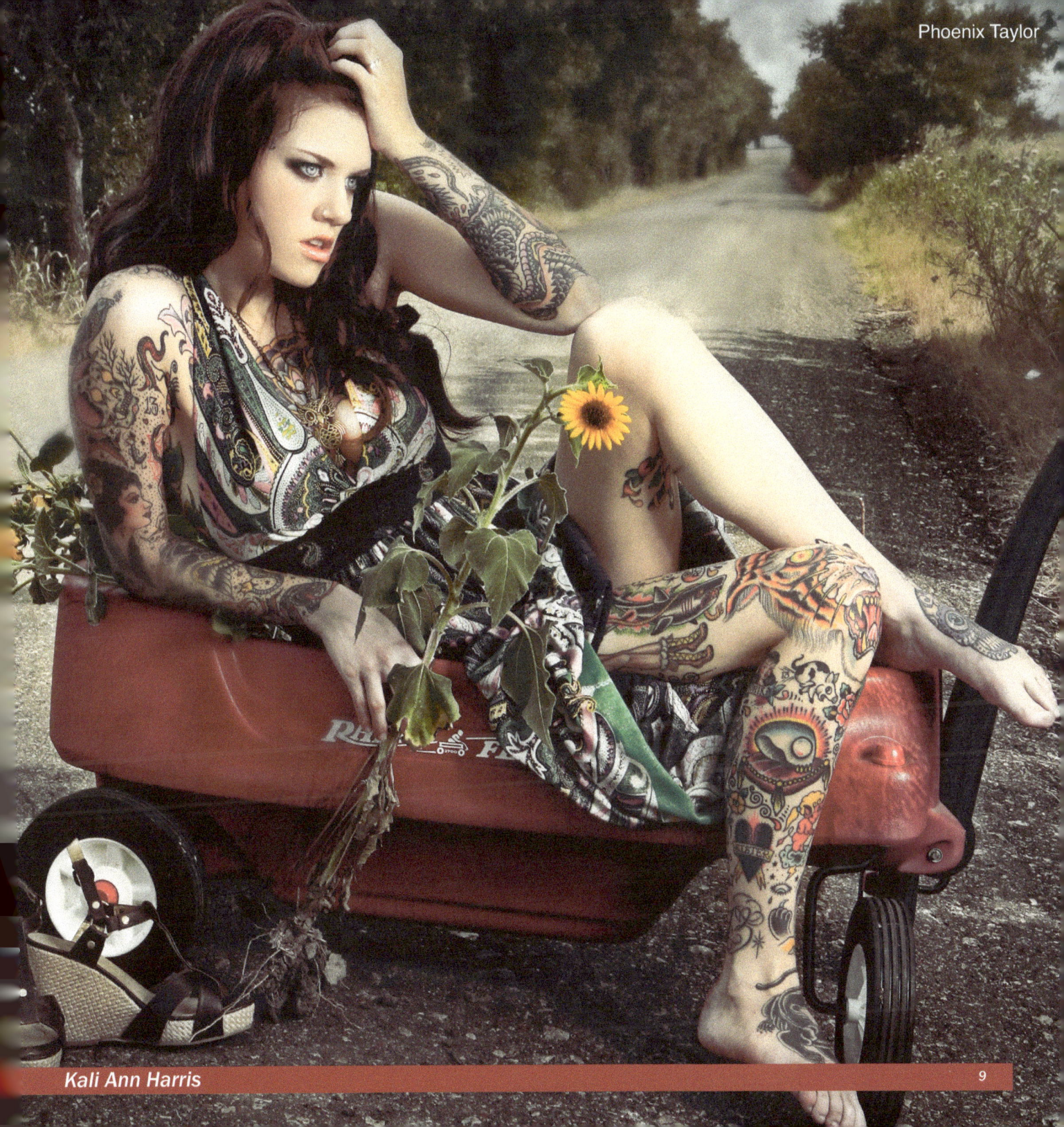
Phoenix Taylor

Kali Ann Harris

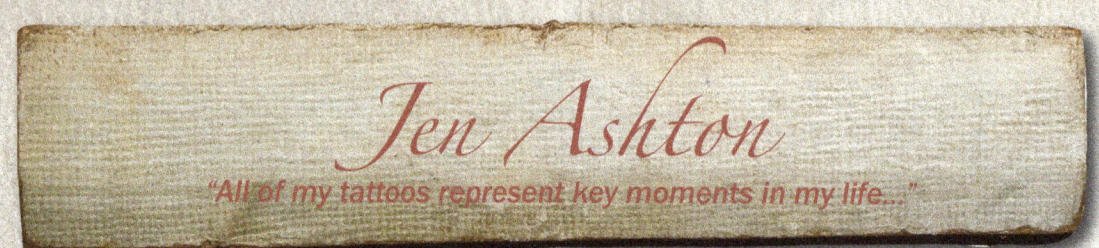

Jen Ashton
"All of my tattoos represent key moments in my life..."

I am Jen Ashton, born and raised in the American Midwest, but from an early age I knew I didn't belong there. I was an artist growing up in the confines of a conservative community. I ended up moving to Southern California on a one-way ticket when I was seventeen years old to pursue my dreams. In my early twenties I took up acting, modeling and music in Hollywood. Success came easy for me. It was a dream come true to be a model in one of the magazines I read as a young girl. Not to mention success in movies and commercials. Still, there was a yearning inside my soul. I am an artist through and through, classically trained in fine art and I decided it was time to get more serious about my talent. Over the next decade, I built a solid career as a professional painter, sculptor and bodypainter. Again, success came easy for me. In 2010, I decided to add to my ever-expanding creative empire and published my first book. Writing quickly became my new love. Today, I am best known for being a bestselling Kindle author, successful artist, entrepreneur and proud mother of my handsome young son. I live at the beach and continually strive to inspire my close friends and family.

How did you come to tattoo?

I apprenticed in a tattoo shop in Orange, California when I was eighteen. Everyone around me had tattoos and they were kind of a prerequisite for working in a shop. It was easy to recognize tattooing as its own form of art and my body quickly became a canvas.

Which is your first one? And why did you choose it?

My first tattoo was on my bum. It's a traditional heart with a banner that reads "MOM." I chose it first because I figured my mom would completely freak that I marked my body. My rationalization was that if I got it as a tribute to her, she couldn't really say anything. My plan didn't necessarily work out, but years later she came to her senses and asked me to take her to get her first tattoo. Unfortunately, it doesn't say "Jen."

Among all your tattoos, which one do you prefer and why?

My favorite tattoo is definitely the one on my left arm. It's sort of a balance of things. I started with the wrench which signifies good luck in American history, with an angel cradled in the top and a devil wrapped around the base. A classic symbols of good and evil. Later I decided to add to the design. The two Chinese characters stand for power and pride, and the two song birds represent peace and harmony. The lotus flower, the symbol of zen, supports the entire design, depicting the childlike happiness of birth.

Which is the last one?

My last tattoo was about 10 years ago, and ironically, it is also my smallest. It's the Kanji symbol for "best friends." It was a tribute to my three best friends from childhood. All four of us got the same tattoo on the day of one of their mothers' funeral. It marked a memorable moment in my life, one that I'll never forget.

What are the meanings of your tattoos?

All of my tattoos represent key moments in my life. I chose to use artwork that has cultural meaning, derived from American history, Japan, China, etc. They stand for things like loyalty, religion, tranquility, independence, strength, and honor.

Do you have a message for kids who would like to be tattooed?

Honestly, I would just advise them to think through their decisions about the art they choose. You're not ever going to be able to talk someone out of getting a tattoo... once they get the itch, they've got the itch, ya know? But it is important to consider what you put on your body. Be weary of trends and symbolism of a fanatic belief when you're young. Life is a journey and we all evolve. Growth is a part of the human process. For this reason, it's probably wise to choose imagery that will stand the test of time.

www.jenashton.com
www.twitter.com/jenashtonart
www.facebook.com/jenashtonauthor

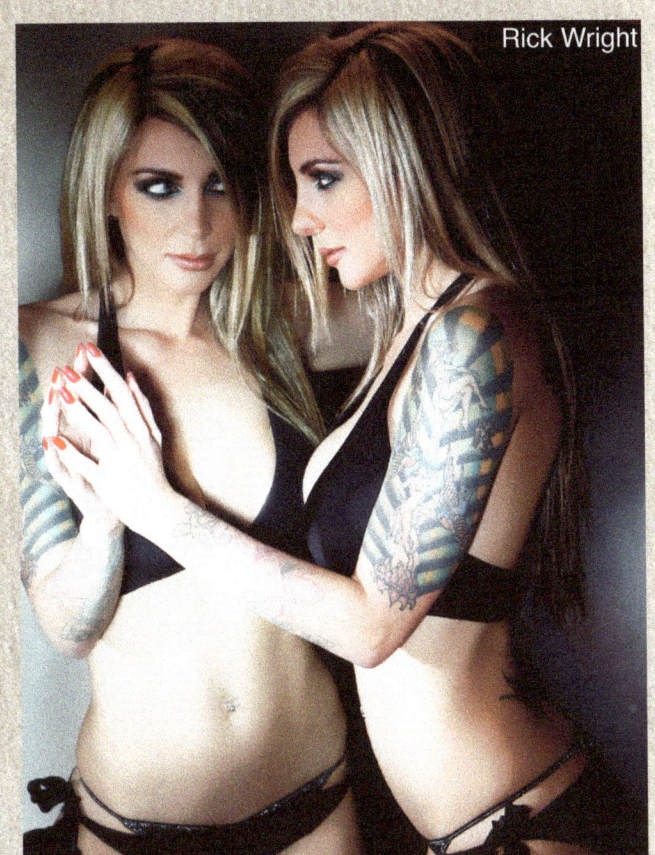
Rick Wright

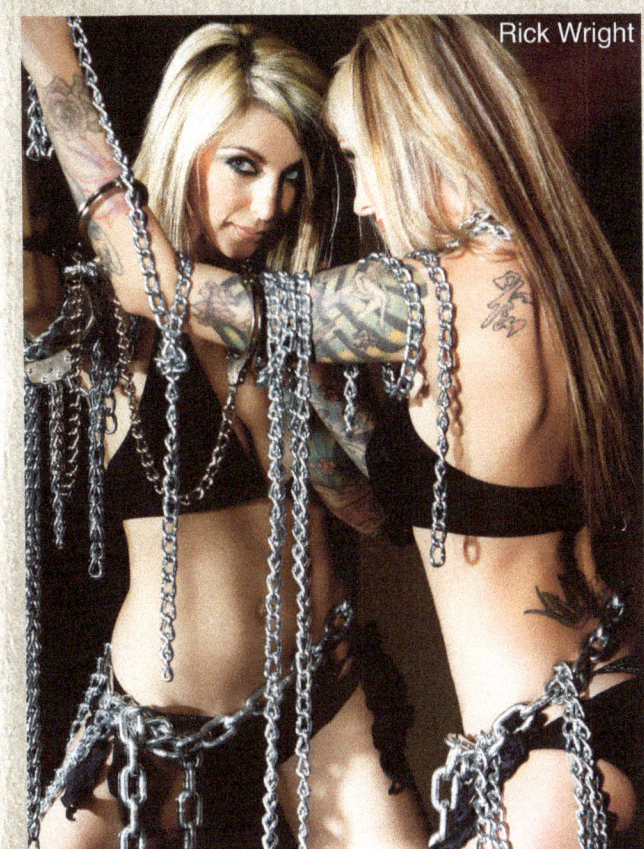
Rick Wright

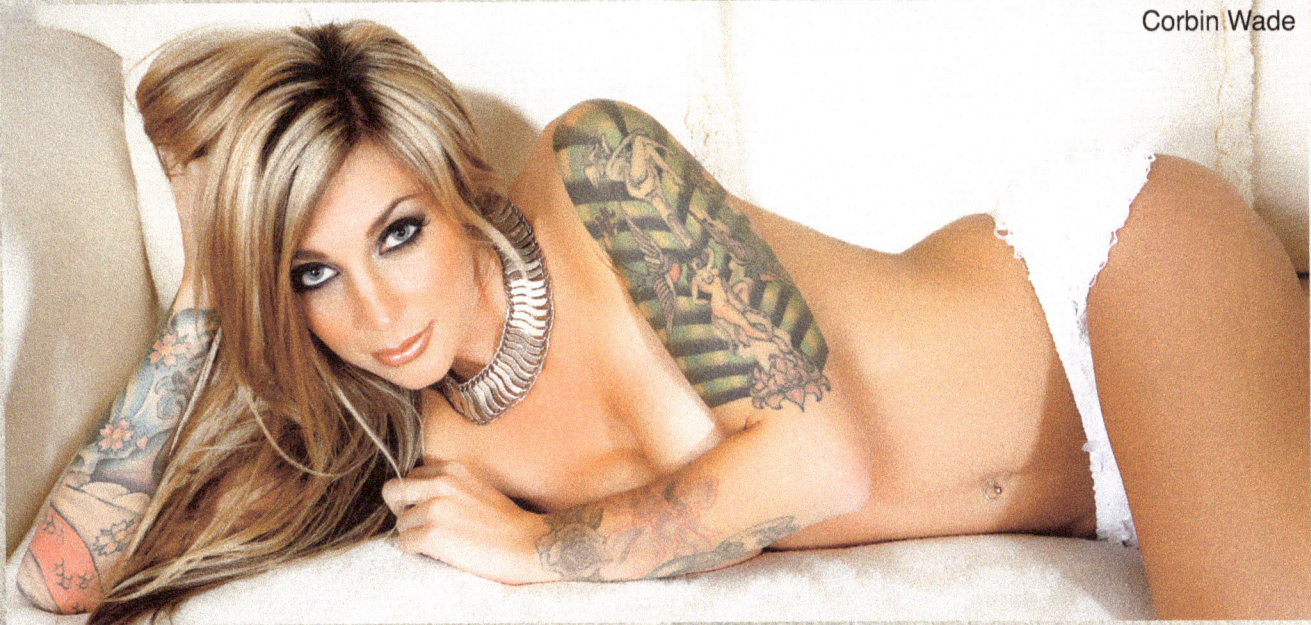
Corbin Wade

Jen Ashton

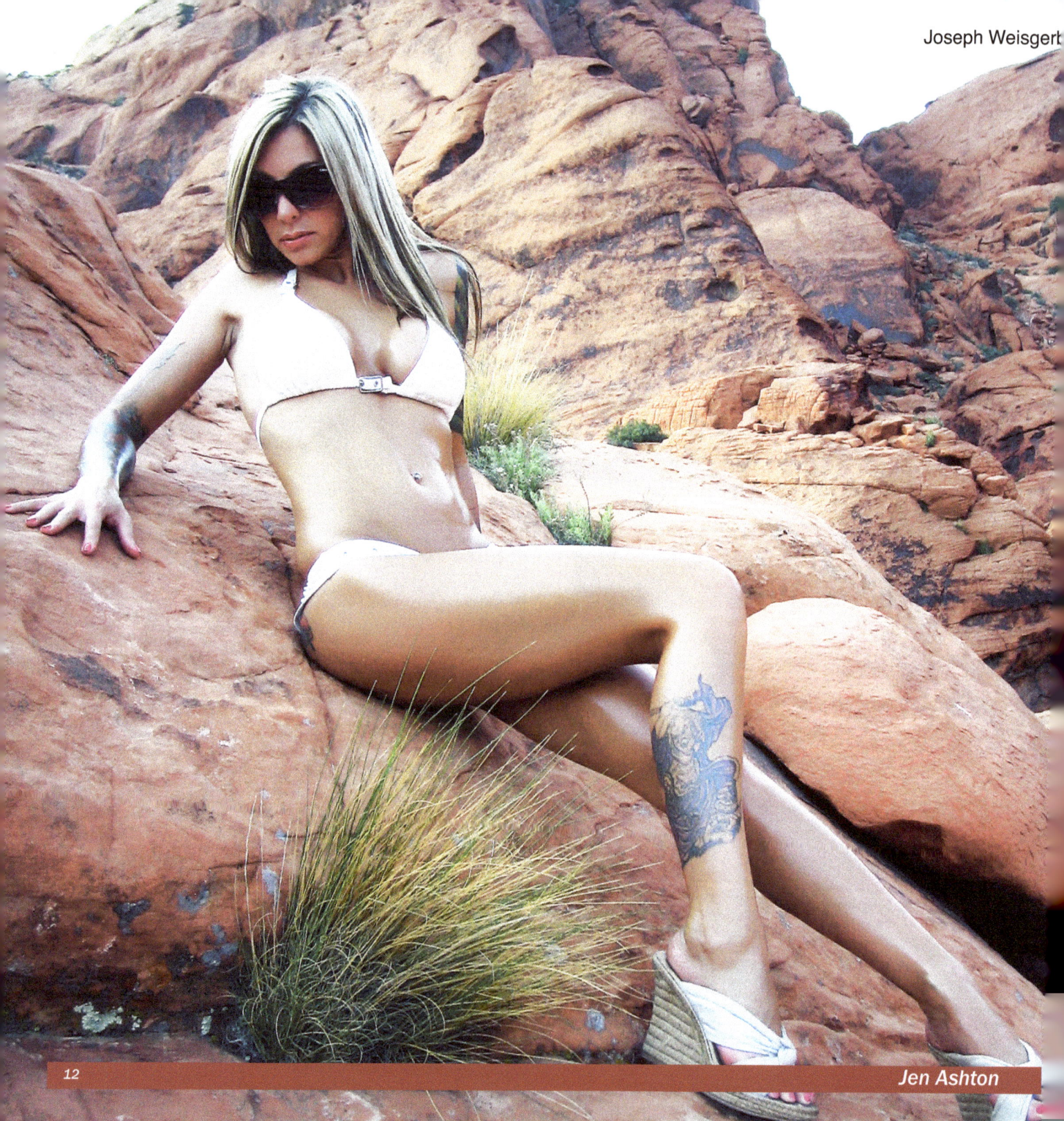

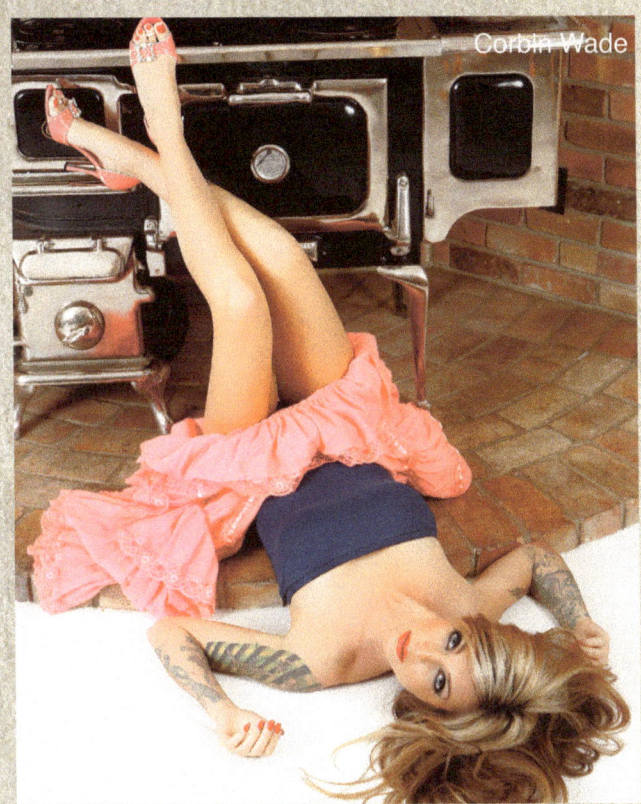
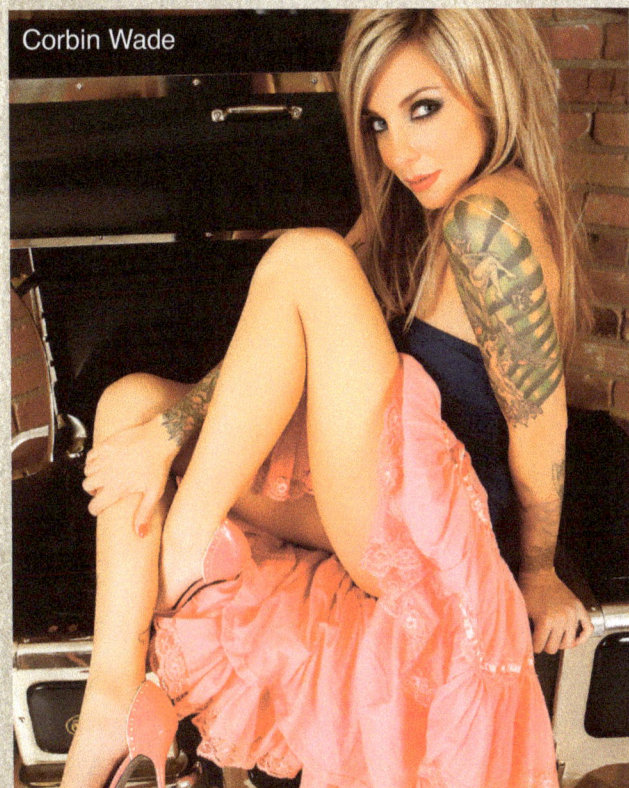

Jen Ashton

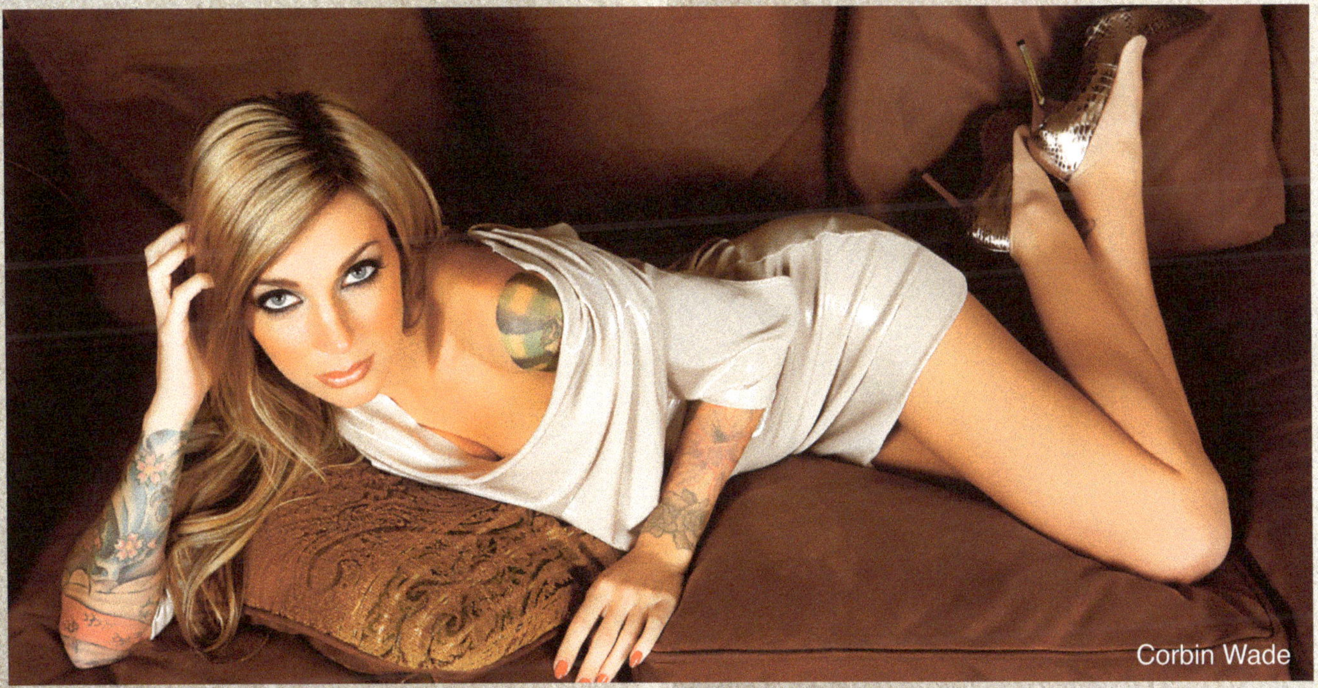

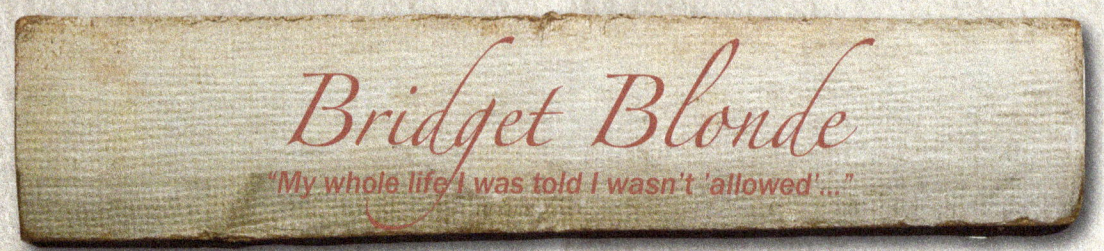

Bridget Blonde
"My whole life I was told I wasn't 'allowed'..."

I am Bridget Blonde, a TEXAS girl loving life in California!

Have you ever had a job or experience that made you think "maybe this isn't for me"?
NEVER! I made the decision to run with this career choice and never looked back.

What do you enjoy the most about modelling?
Taking an idea out of my head and making it come to life on film.

What would you say, in your opinion, is the biggest misconception about modelling?
Some of us models LOVE to eat!!

It's obvious that you're a beautiful and attractive woman. Do you often receive fan mails from different men? Which was the most bizarre offer you ever received?
Hahaha... lots of marriage proposals!

You already worked with a lot of great photographers. Who are your favorites and why?
Steve Prue, WOLF189, Julian Humphries, Simon Gentry, and Dont Ask Photography... because for some reason these particular people make me feel alive and it shows through their camera.

How was the shooting with Greg Truelove?
Super fun! He is awesomely talented in an insanely creative way!

You've done like hundreds of photo shoots, but which photo shoot did you have the most fun doing?
Last year I shot in Hawaii... definitely my favorite shoot! Who doesn't want to lay on a beach for a week?!

When did your interest in tattoos begin? And how long was it from then until you got your first one?
I have been interested in tattoos since before I can remember.

Which is your first one? And why did you make it?
Oh gosh... I was 17 using my older friends I.D. My first tattoo was the tribal on my lower back... it was spur of the moment straight off the wall hahaha... good times!

What is it about tattoos that appeals to you?
My whole life I was told I wasnt "ALLOWED"... so of course I was going to get them!

What do your tattoos mean to you? Are they symbolic or do you just dig the art?
Little bit of both.

Among all your tattoos, which one do you prefer and why?
P R I N C E S S on my knuckles... it's my favorite! I love it because it describes me without me having to tell someone to "GO AWAY"!

Have you got an idea of the next one?
Next I am finishing the vintage barbie portrait on my forearm and I am going to tattoo my clothing lines logo on me somewhere.

Of all above mentioned things that you've accomplished in your relatively short career what would you pick as your biggest achievements in your career?
Building myself as a brand and using that to create something bigger, my clothing line THE BLONDE LOCKS!!!

Is there anything else you would like to add?
Check out my new clothing line THE BLONDE LOCKS!

www.theblondelocks.com
www.twitter.com/theblondelocks
www.facebook.com/theblondelocks

www.bridgetblonde.com
www.facebook.com/thebridgetblonde

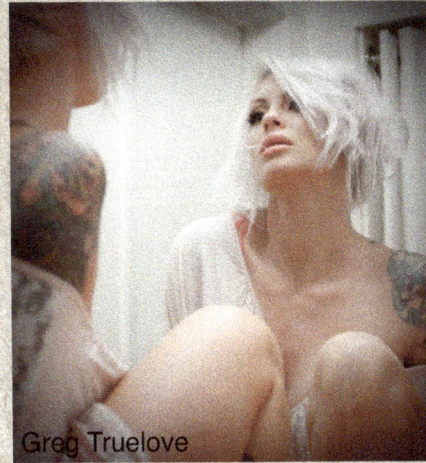
Greg Truelove

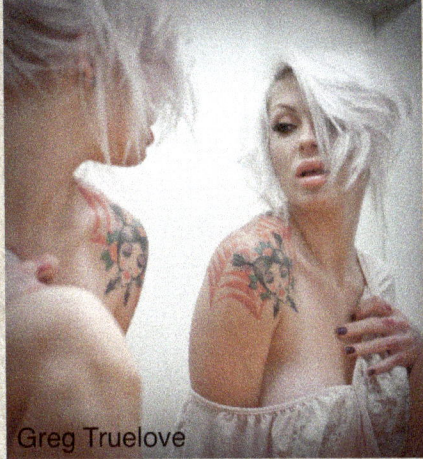
Greg Truelove

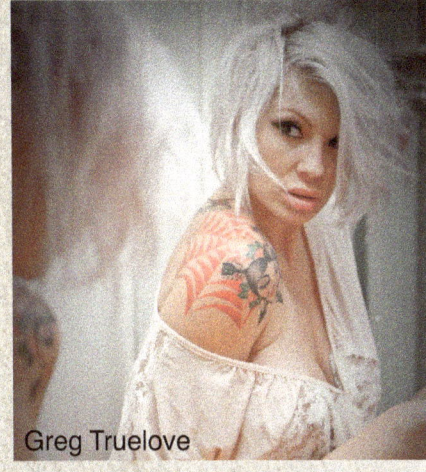
Greg Truelove

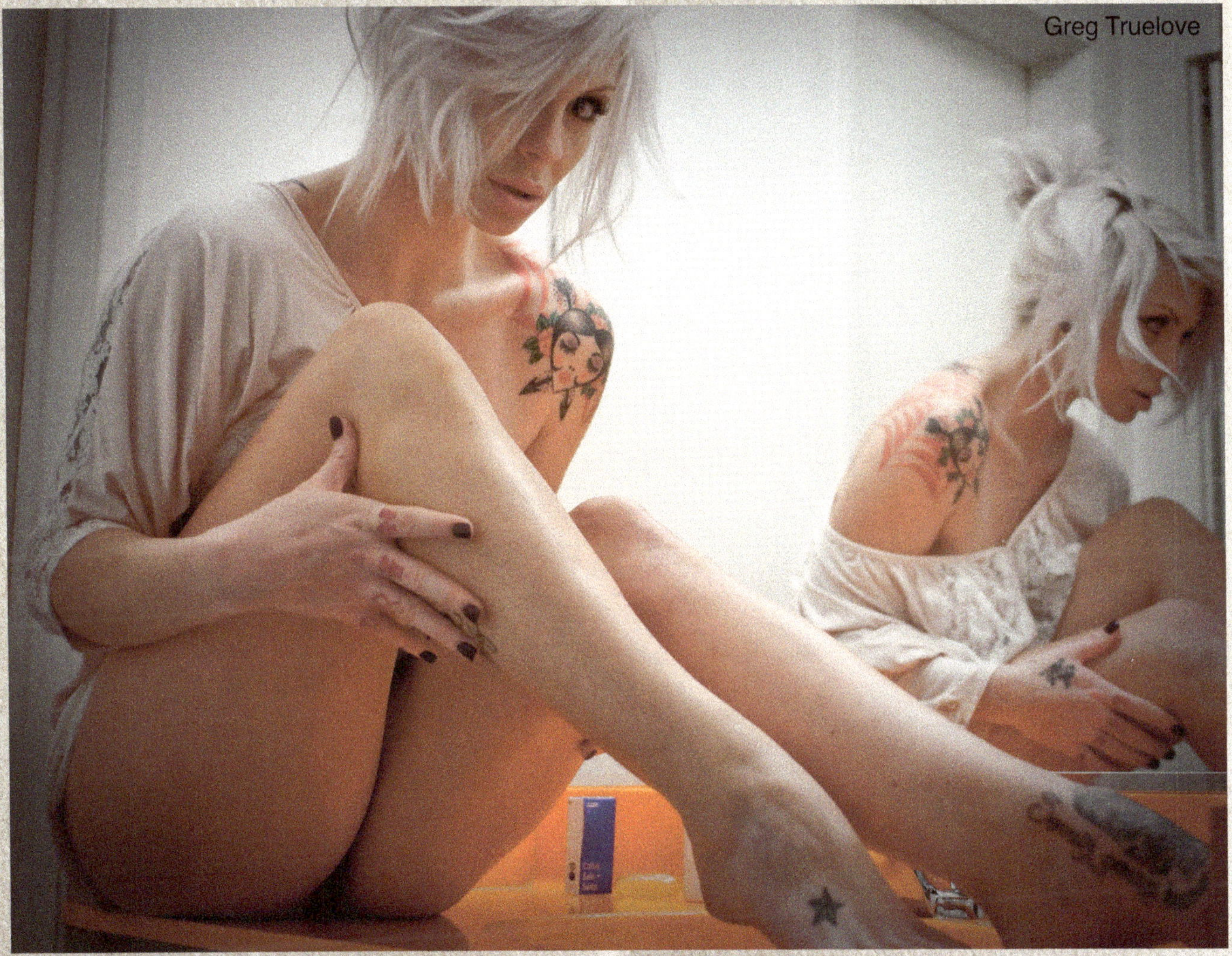

Greg Truelove

Bridget Blonde

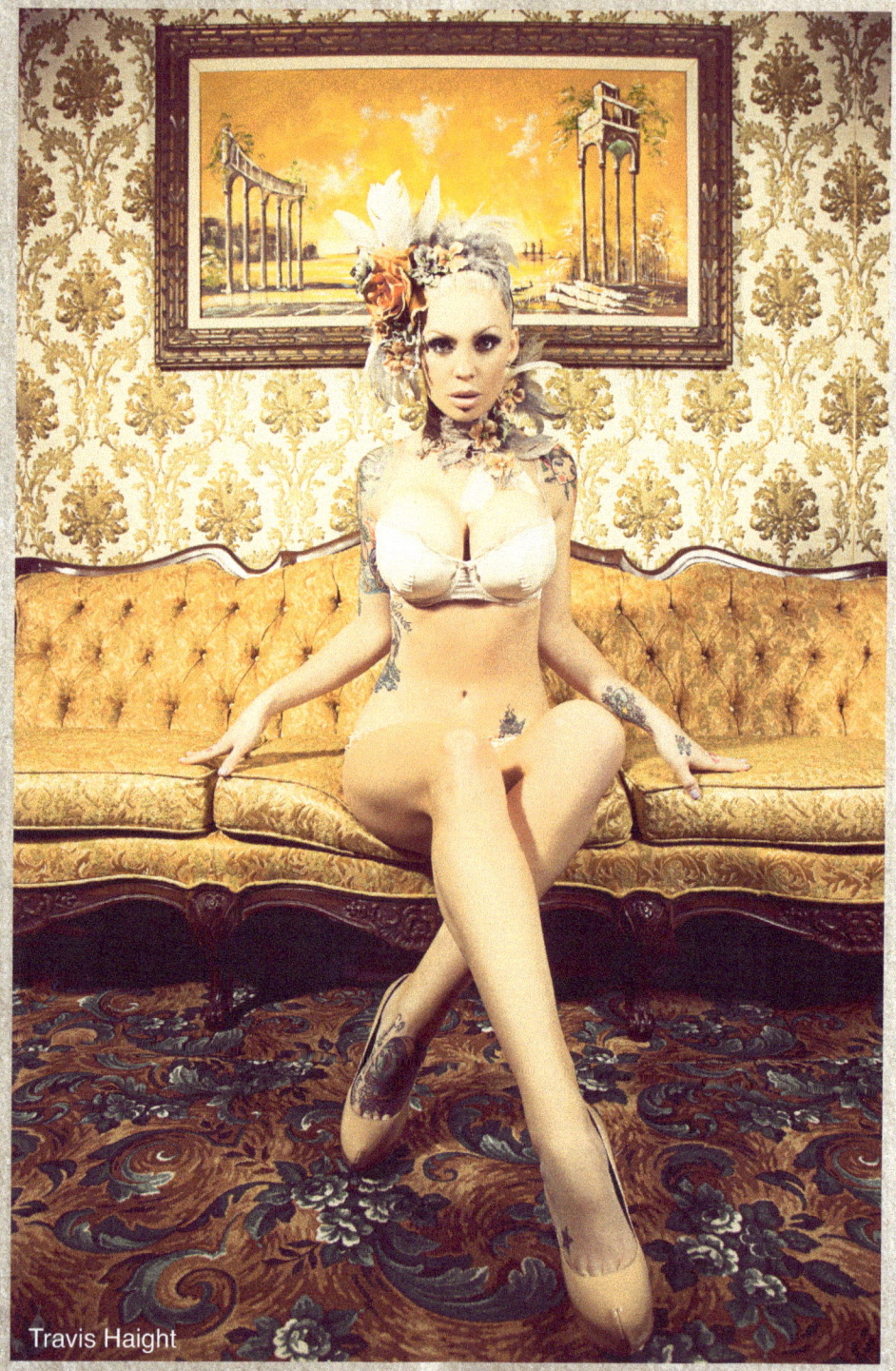

Travis Haight

Bridget Blonde

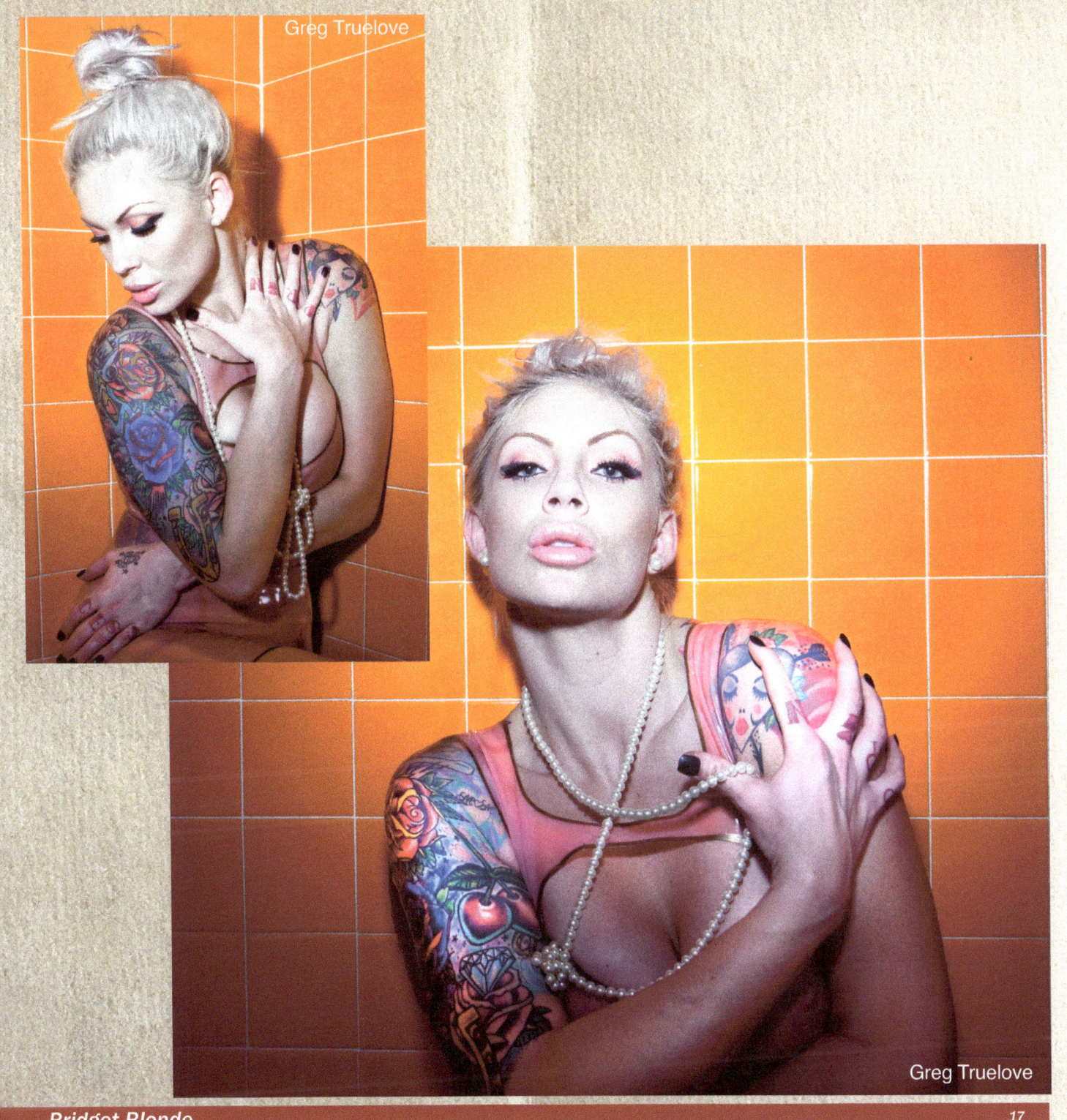

Bridget Blonde

Brittany Casualty

"I've always thought tattoos were rad..."

I am Brittanhy Casualty, an old-fashioned housewife. My family is my whole world.

What kind of modeling do you do?

I don't really consider myself a model. I've done a couple of magazines, a calendar and work for some clothing companies, those photos were used on their websites. They are all things I've been asked to do. To be a real model, I think it has to be your job and/or your passion.

Tell us a little about your interests and about your favorite bands.

I'm a total Sci-Fi geek. I LOVE Stargate!!! I also love video games, cooking, crafting and writing. I listen to a wide variety of music, depending on my mood.

How did you come to tattoo?

I've always thought tattoos were rad. When I was a small child, I used to draw tattoos all over myself and my mom with a sharpie.

Which is your first tattoo? And why did you make it?

My first tattoos were the swallows on my lower stomach. I got them 10 years ago! I guess I just really liked them at the time.

Among all your tattoos, which one do you prefer and why?

Probably my hip piece, it's just huge and very colorful. I wish I could show it off more!

Which is the last one?

I've just been trying to finish up some old work. I have a lot of pieces that I started with various tattoo artists and never finished.

Have you got an idea of the next one?

I'm planning to get a traditional piece on the side of my neck with my kid's names. Also, a huge Star Wars piece on my other hip and thigh.

What do you think about the rise of tattoo, is it a fashion or a new breath for the body culture?

I think it's a little of both. It's definitely a fad right now with the all of the reality shows and tattoo artists starting clothing lines, but I think those things have helped tattoos become more accepted. Now, instead of getting dirty looks, I'm getting people stopping me, asking who does my work, commenting on how beautiful it all is.

Do you have a message for kids who would like to be tattooed?

Stop getting tattooed out of people's garages, you get what you pay for! Save your money for a real tattoo!

What's the next step for Brittany Casualty?

I've been focusing on my writing. I'm hoping to be published by the time I'm 30, that's not too far off!

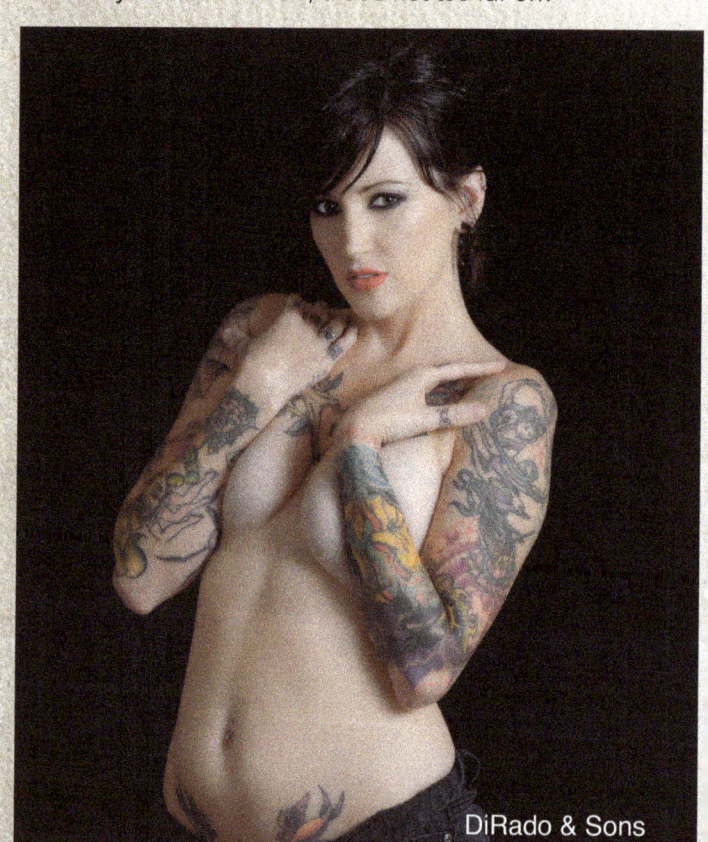

DiRado & Sons

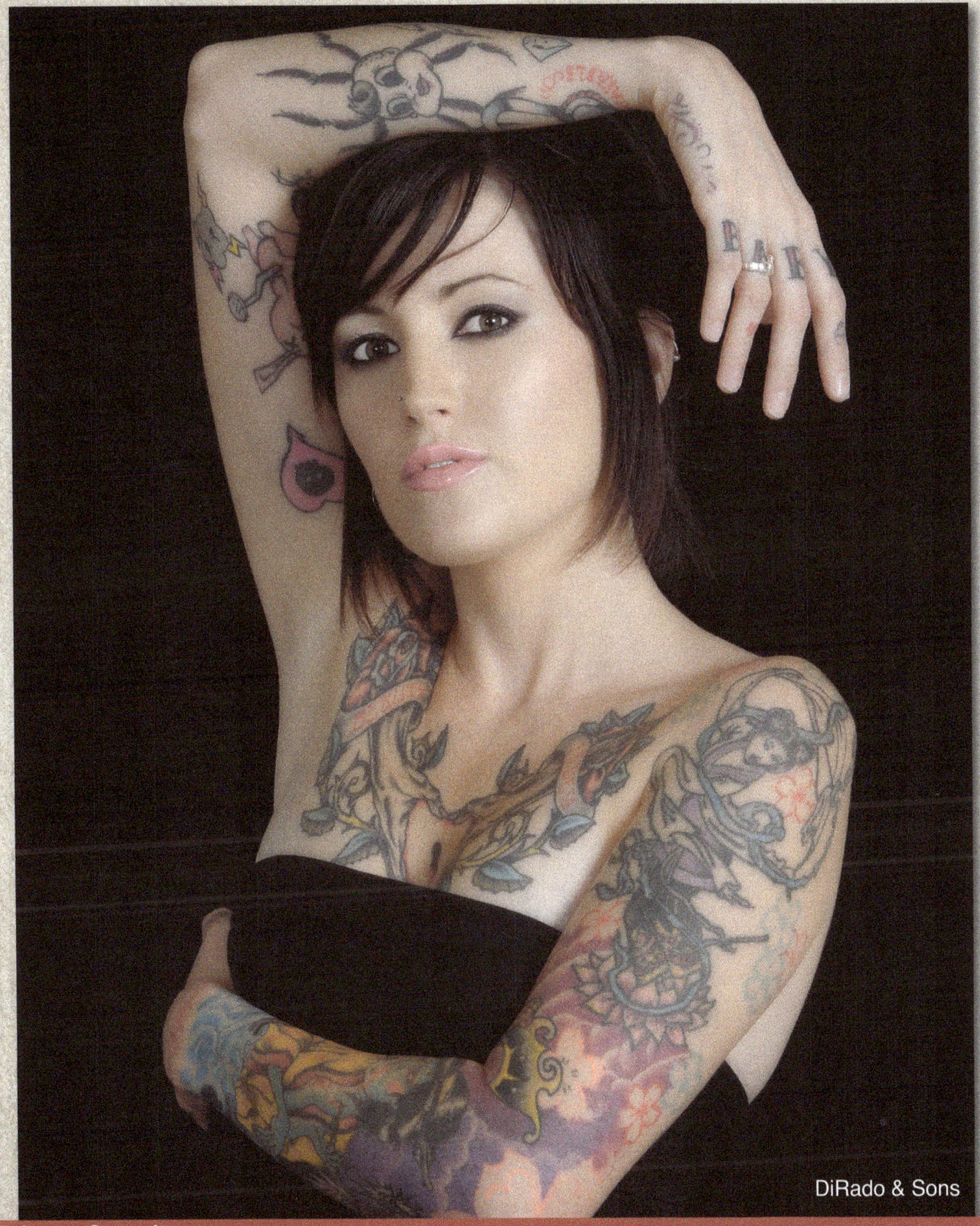

DiRado & Sons

Brittany Casualty

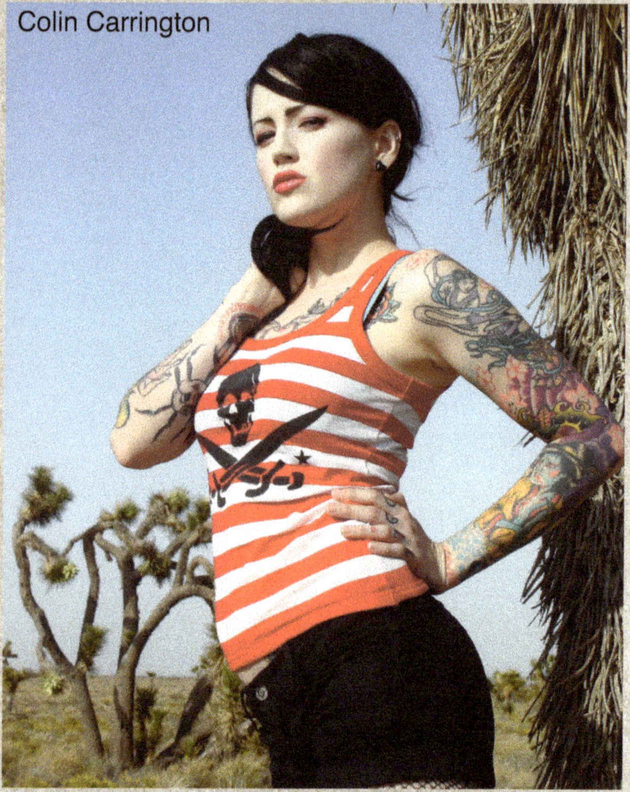

Colin Carrington

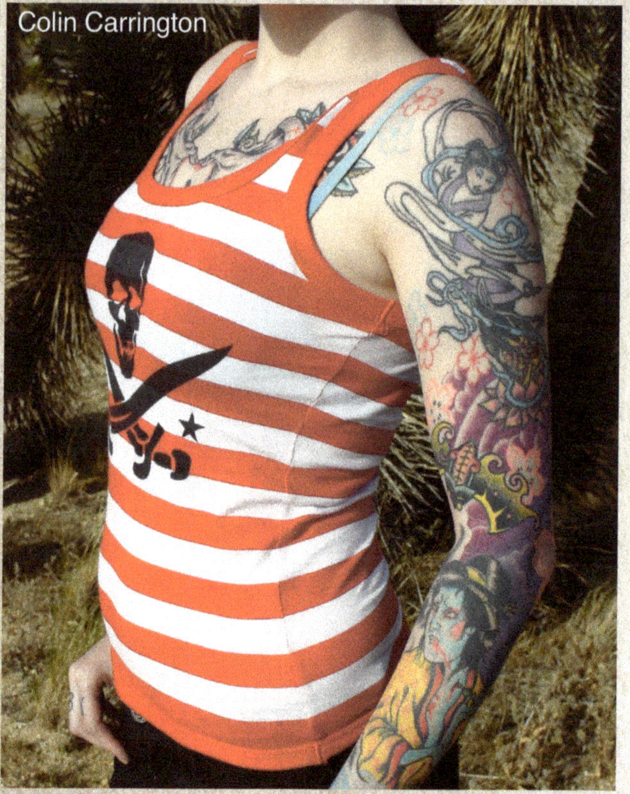

Colin Carrington

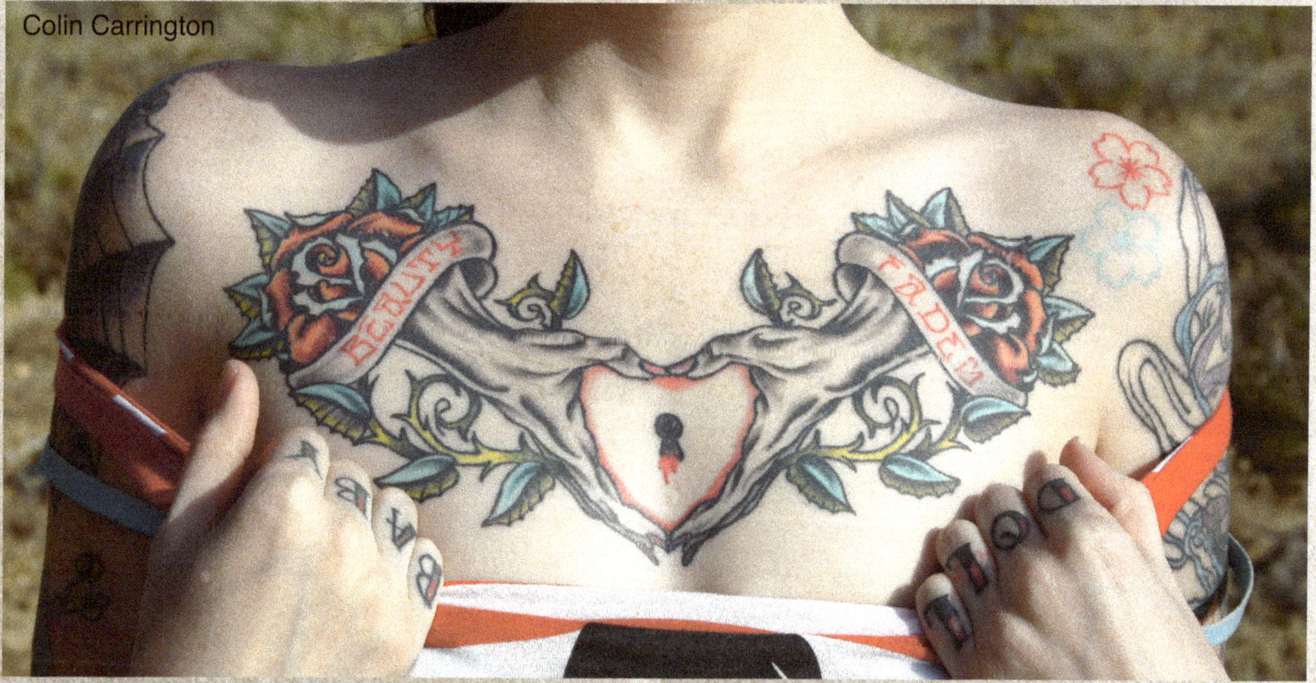

Colin Carrington

Brittany Casualty

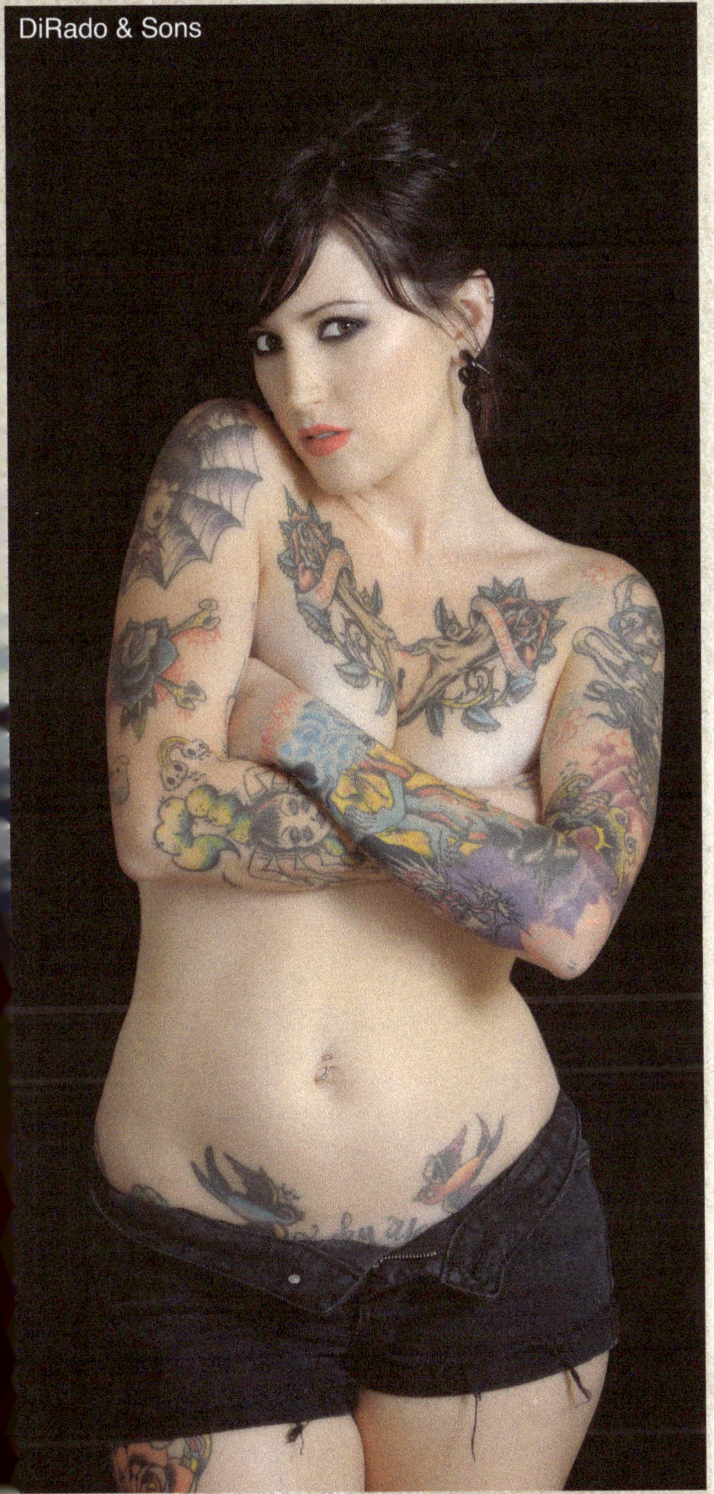

DiRado & Sons

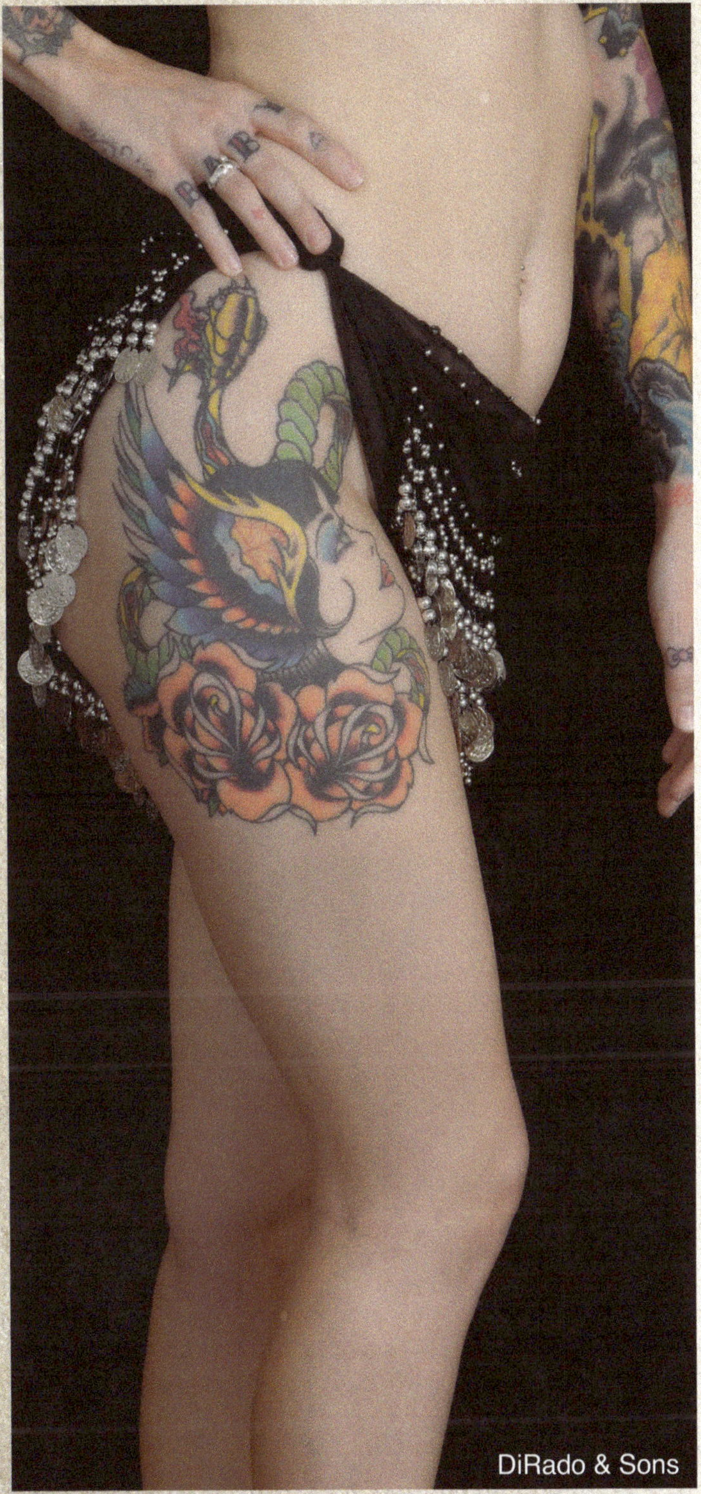

DiRado & Sons

Brittany Casualty

Angie Collord

"Most of my influences come from starlets like Bettie Page and Marilyn Monroe."

My name is Angie Collord. I am an exotic dancer and model. It's the ultimate way to express and transform yourself and shock the world! I will try anything once and love most anything! Don't let this crazy exterior fool ya, I like nothing more than coming home and cooking dinner for my family, watching movies or reading a good book!

Which tattoo style do you like best? And how would you describe your style?

When it comes to a style of tattooing I am a huge fan of bright, solid color pieces that are realistic. A true artist can take the concept you give them and create a vibrant masterpiece full of life! My body is a mix of unique colorful pieces done by different artist and styles that flow together perfectly.

Please tell us about your most important or meaningful tattoo.

My Dia de los Muertos sleeve, done by Clae Welch, is dear to my heart. It represents me and my daughter celebrating our favorite holiday and our heritage. It also includes a very small skull that she designed just for me.

How did you get your start in modeling?

Modeling started for me in my early 20's, but it was more of a fun hobby. When I started working for H2 Ocean, traveling and selling product at tattoo conventions, that's when people started noticing little ol' me. Magazines, posters, calendars, commercials... you name it, I have done it and loved every second of it.

Where do you draw your influences from? Who are your role models?

Most of my influences come from fifties starlets like Bettie Page and Marilyn Monroe. Their classic beauty shines above any other and they have truly set the standard high! My current role models would have to be Elvira and Micheline Pitt. These woman are so strong, smart, independent, and wickedly sexy, it is all I can do to not stalk their every move!

How did your love for tattoos start?

My love for tattoos started when I was a child, always drawing on my skin, pants, and shoes. I loved art and was captivated by all the adults with their tattoos, good and bad.

How old were you when you got your first tattoo?

I was 17, my parents co-signed for me and watched while I sat for over two hours for my sunflower tattoo. That was all I wanted for my high school graduation present. Now all my pre-age-22 tattoos are covered up! Sometimes I wonder what the hell I was thinking back then, or was I?

Please talk us through some of your tattoos and the reason behind them.

I have a traditional Japanese back piece that is being done by Jess Yun. I followed his work for a year at the conventions as we worked together. After two years of building a friendship he finally agreed to tattoo me. My first session was in Providence, Rhode Island; second L.A.; third, Miami, Florida. Who knows when or where my next one will be. We have 36 hours invested in it so far and around 108 more to go!

Do you have any funny/weird stories about a tattoo experience?

When I got the top of both of my feet done at the same time my feet turned to huge jello molds! I couldn't wear shoes for 3 weeks and my feet jiggled when I walked! So GROSS!

Do you think people treat you differently for being heavily tattooed?

Yes. People used to be very judgmental and look down on me for "ruining" my body. Now tattoos have become trendy and living in Portland, Oregon it seems like everyone has them, so I guess it's kinda the thing to do!

www.facebook.com/profile.php?id=100000771151217
www.pinuplifestyle.com/photo/love-angie

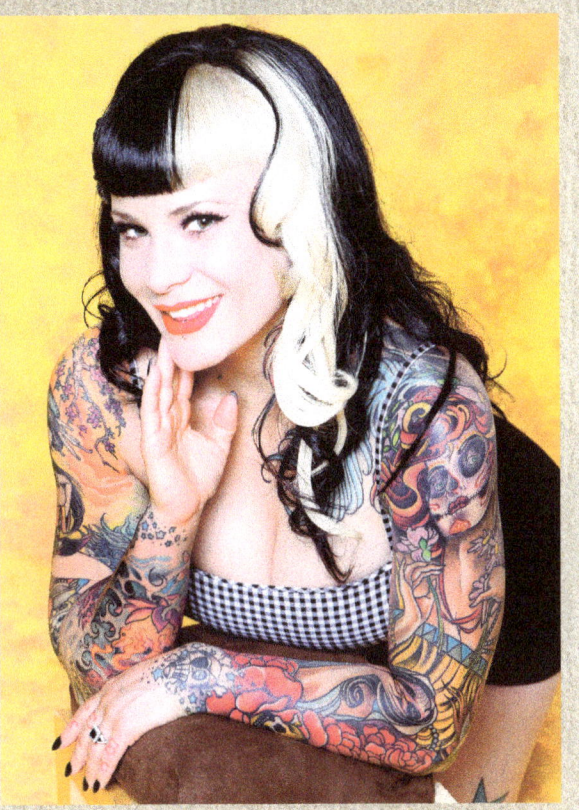
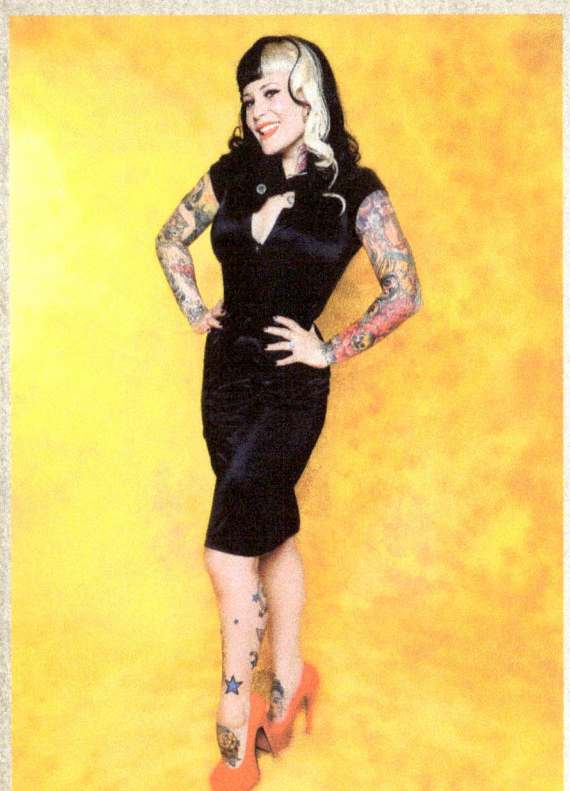

All photos by Justice Howard

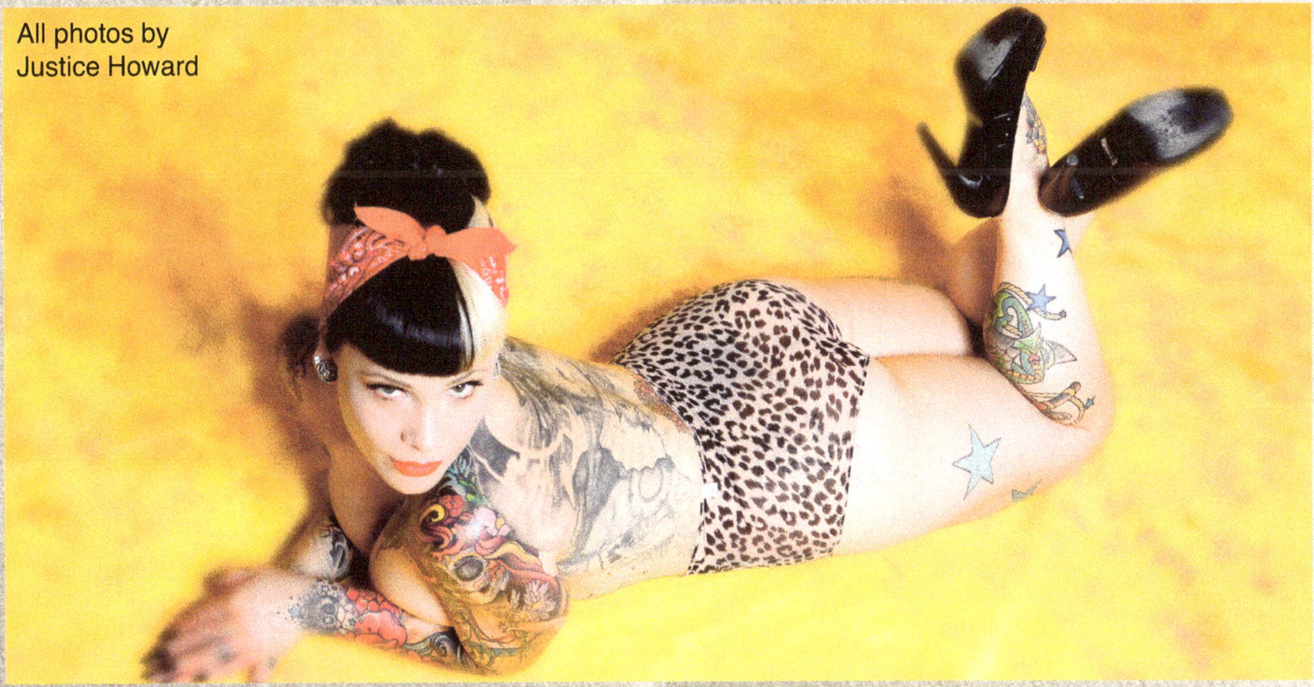

Angie Collord

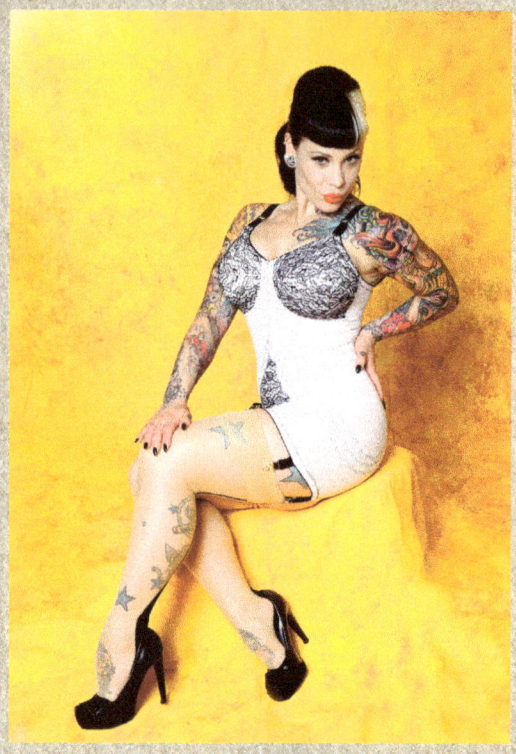
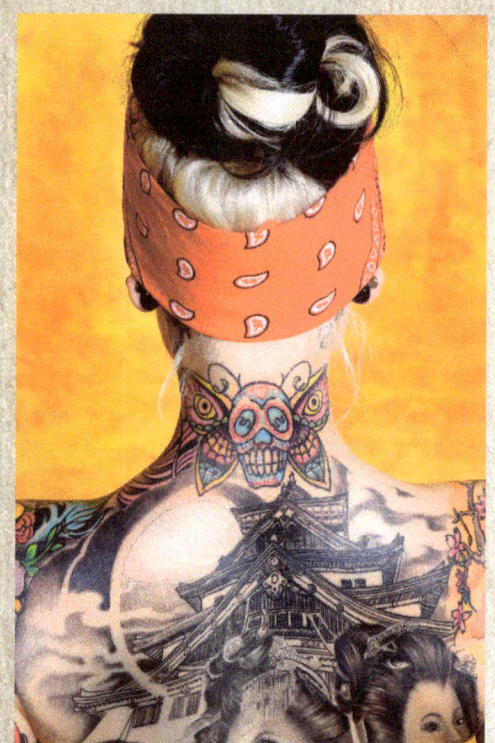
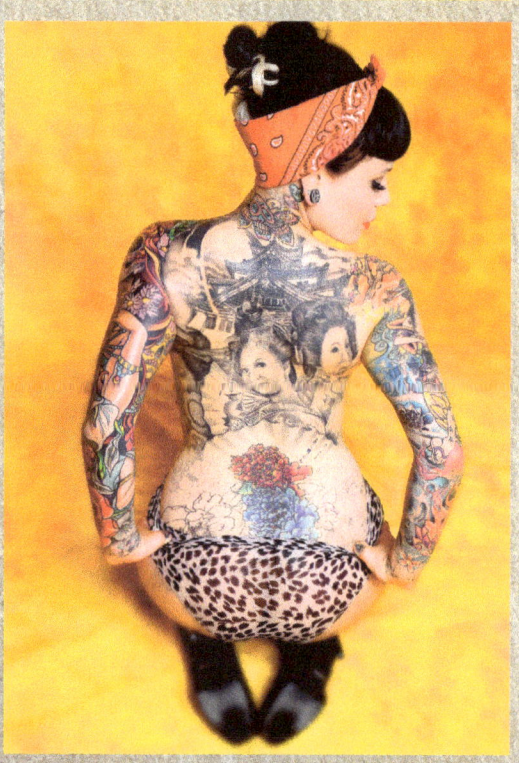
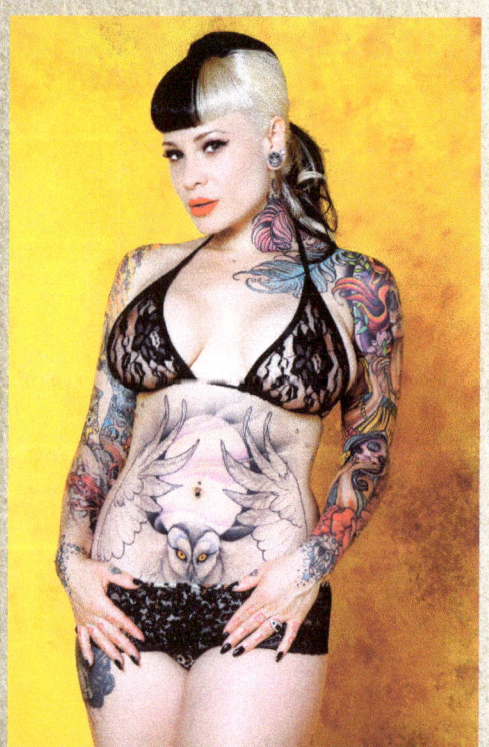

Angie Collord

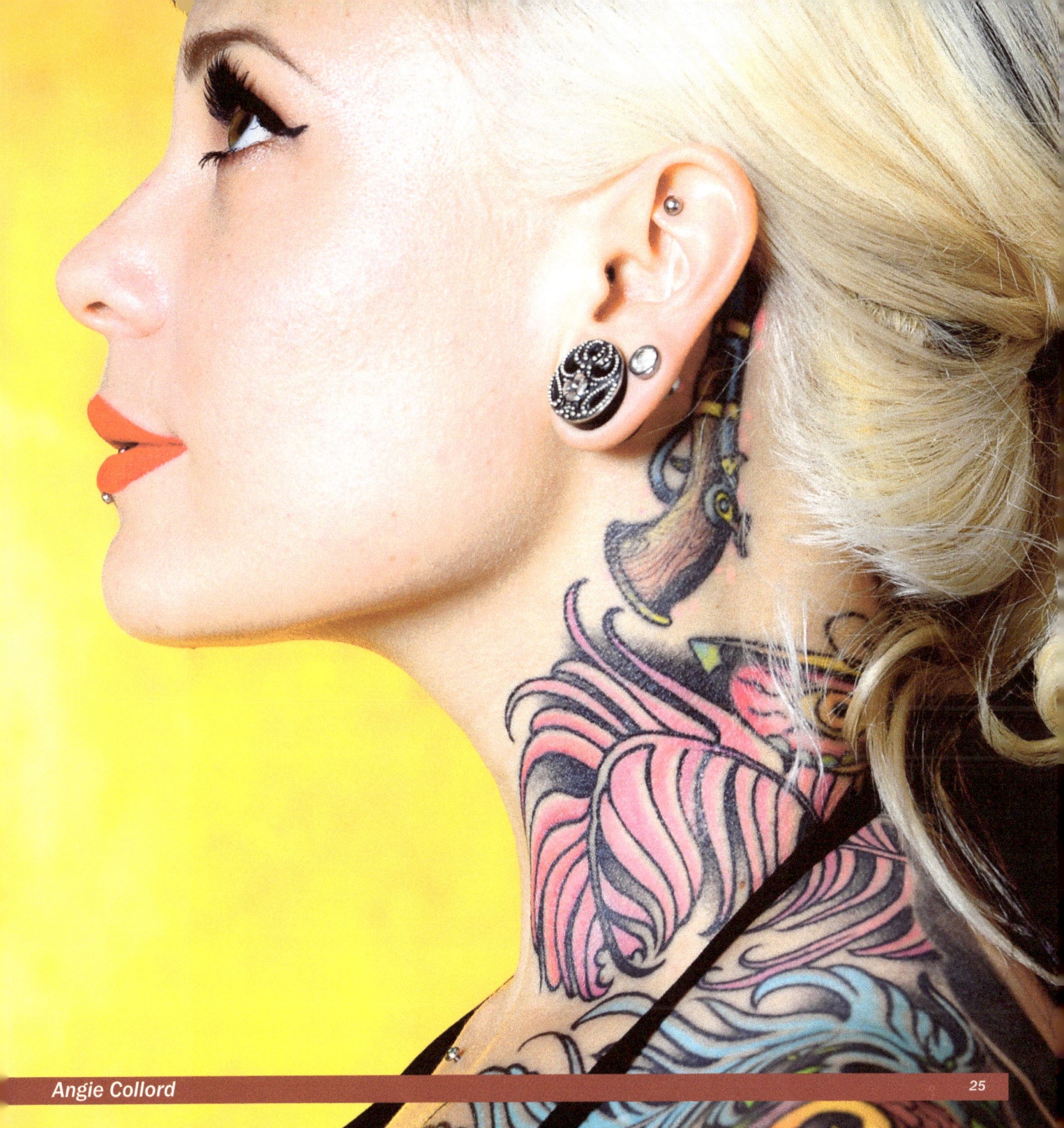
Angie Collord

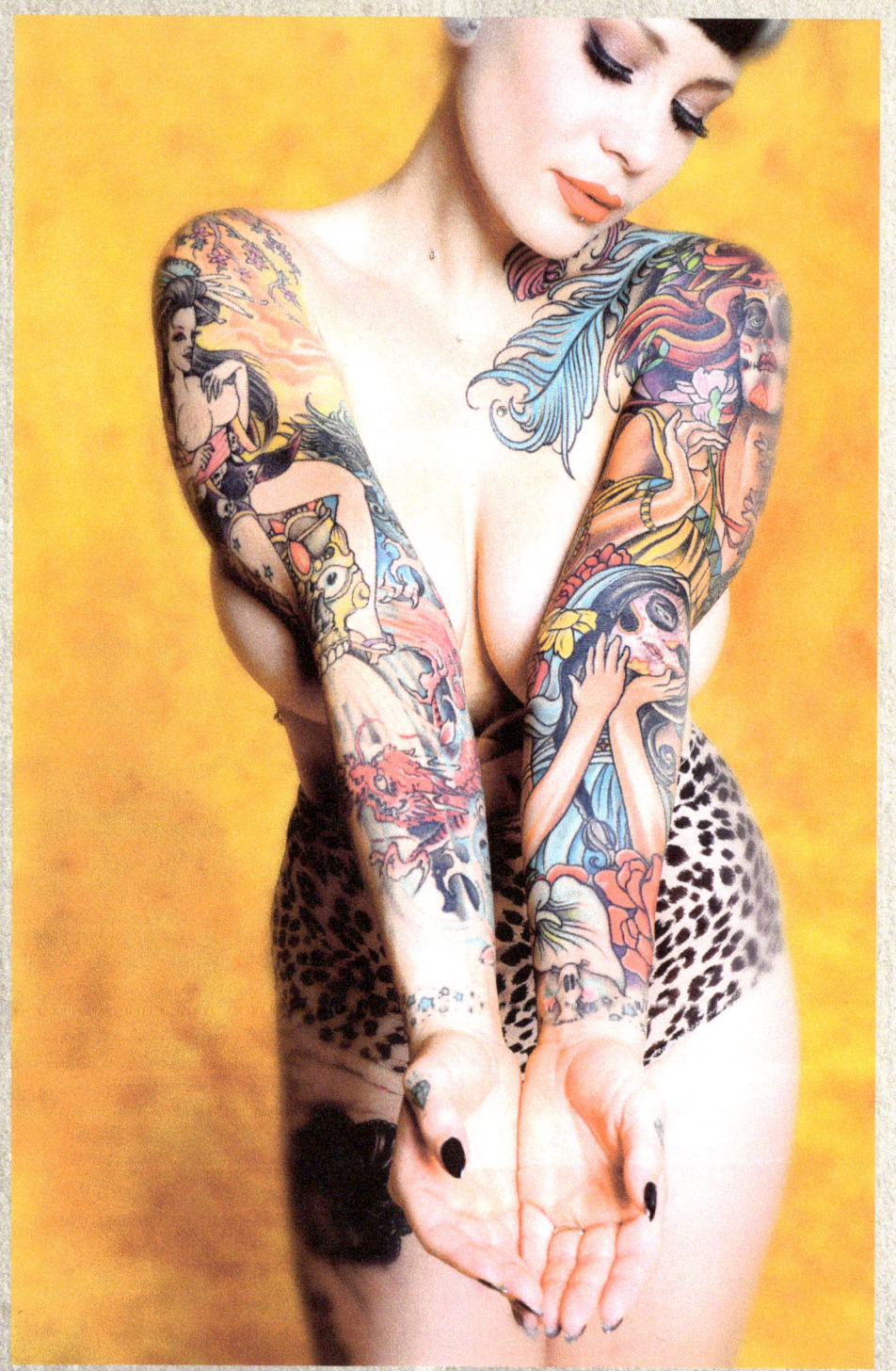

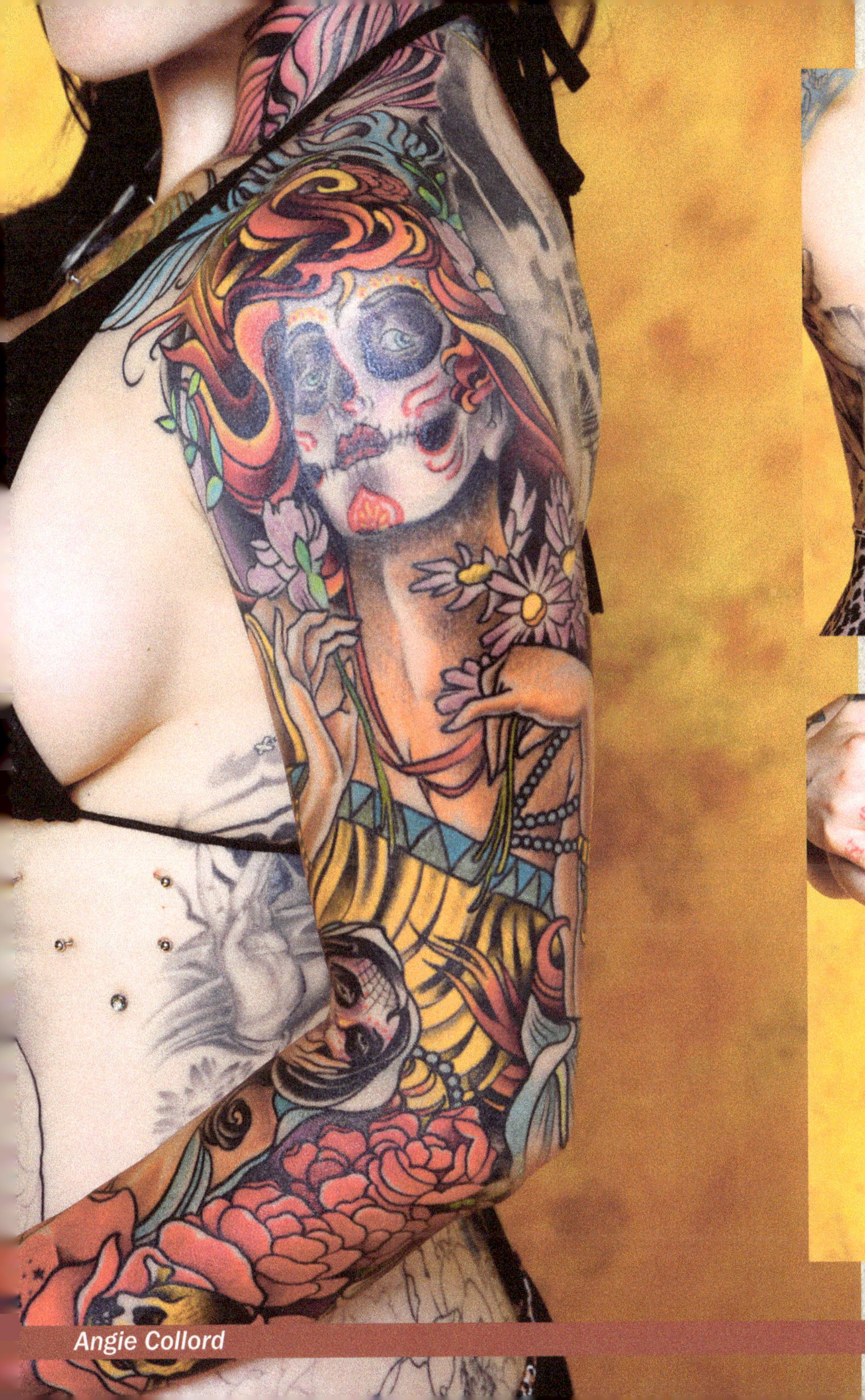

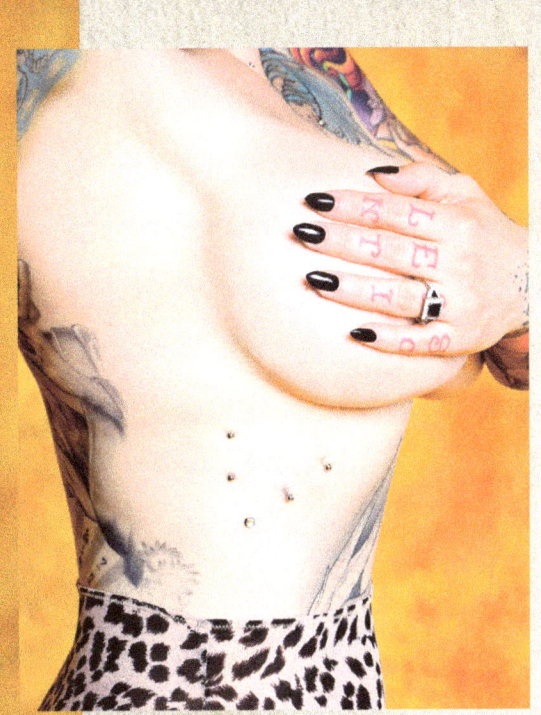
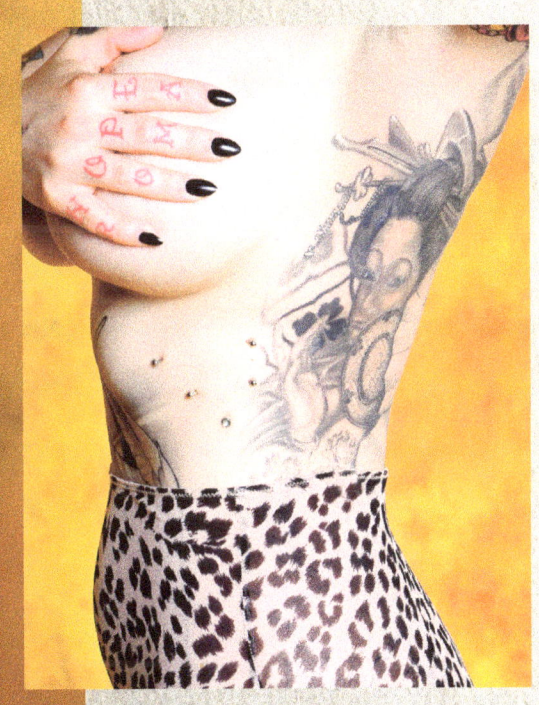

Angie Collord

Amy DeLaCroux

"I don't know what I would do without my tattoos..."

My name is Amy DeLaCroux, I'm an internationally published pin-up and tattoo model.

How did you get your start in modeling?

A friend at the time was a make up artist and needed a model to build her portfolio. I had zero modeling experience and was really skeptical. I reluctantly agreed and ended up having a great time shooting. I continued to pursue photo shoots after that and wanted to get on the cover of one, just ONE, tattoo magazine. The rest is pretty much history.

What did your family and friends think about you getting into the business?

My sister gives me a lot of grief, asking if I get paid for every shoot and why I wear skimpy clothing. I don't know if she's simply curious or fishing for something. My friends are supportive. I try not to talk about my modeling with my friends a whole lot... I don't want to come off as self absorbed.

Tell us about your first photo shoot. Were you nervous?

I was very nervous. I had a girlfriend go with me, and I didn't know what to do with my hands when I was posing. Luckily the photographer was really easy going.

How did your love for tattoos start?

I always wanted a tattoo but never knew what. My mom had a few tattoos. I love the fact that it's permanent art on your body. When I got my first tattoo at age 19 I was instantly addicted.

Which tattoo style do you like best? And how would you describe the style of your tattoos?

I like traditional tattoos the best: bold black outlines and bright colors, and that's what I get.

Please talk us through some of your tattoos and the reason behind them.

Not all of my tattoos have meanings, but the ones that do have meanings are about my parents and they all happen to be on the left side of my body. I have "Imperial" on my left forearm because that is the street both of my parents are buried on. The sunset and cross on my left shoulder is a tribute to my mother after she passed away. The blue sparrow on my left shoulder blade was my first tattoo, my mom and I got matching tattoos after she finished her first round of chemotherapy. The one tattoo that means something silly to me is the leg lamp on my left tricep. I love the movie "A Christmas Story."

What is your favorite tattoo so far, and why?

One of my favorites is the horse shoe and diamond on my left wrist. I really like the placement. I love my chest piece too.

Do you have any funny/weird stories about a tattoo experience?

I love getting tattooed by Jen Davis. She works at Outer Limits in Orange, California and she did the roses on my right side and back. Getting tattooed by her is like seeing a therapist. I open up to her about all my drama and life issues and she gives me good advice. Kind of weird the conversations we end up having over the buzz of the needle!

Do you think people treat you differently for being heavily tattooed?

Yes, I get a lot of stares. Disapproval from old people, gawking from men, jealous looks from women, curious looks from children. I actually hate to be the center of attention believe it or not and a lot of the time when I go out I'll wear something to cover my tattoos so I won't get stared at. It makes me uncomfortable.

Any final words?

No, I let my work speak for itself.

www.facebook.com/AmyDeLaCroux
www.facebook.com/pages/Amy-DeLaCroux/133292293378607
www.modelmayhem.com/1220685
www.53deluxe.com/everything-else/2456/amy-delacroux/
www.tumblr.com/tagged/amy-delacroux

All photos by Keith Selle

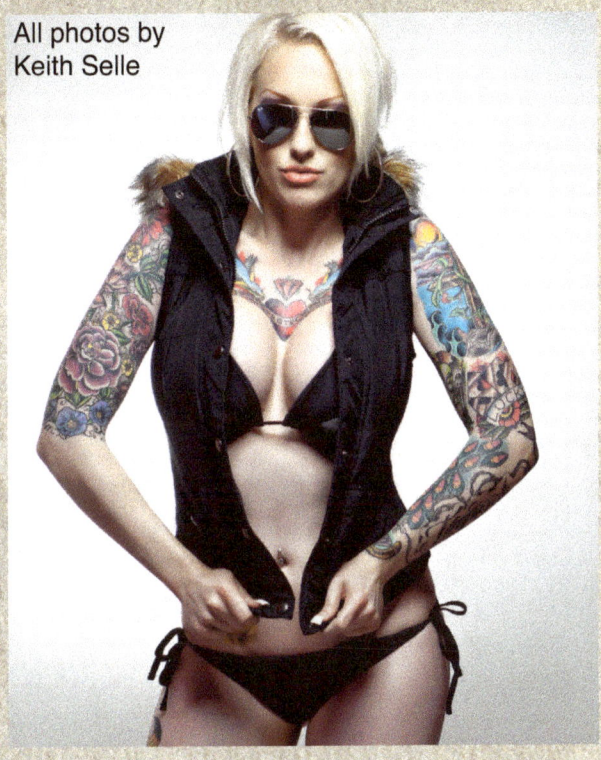
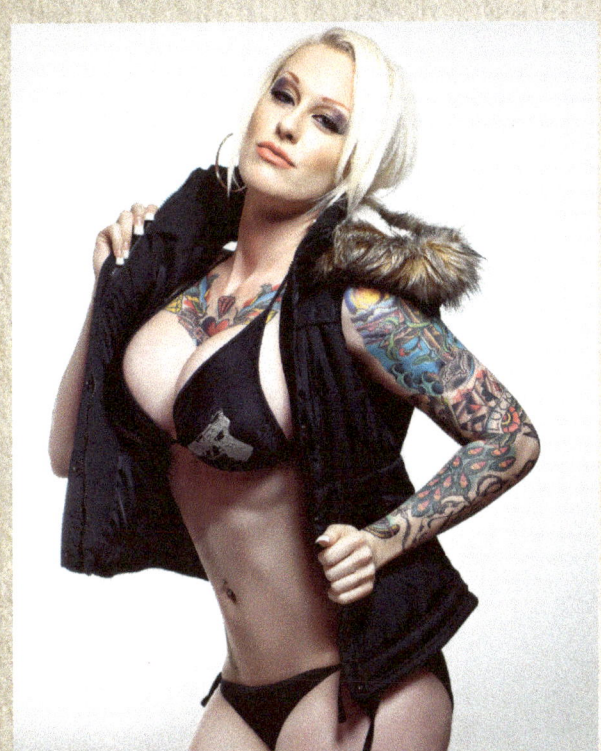
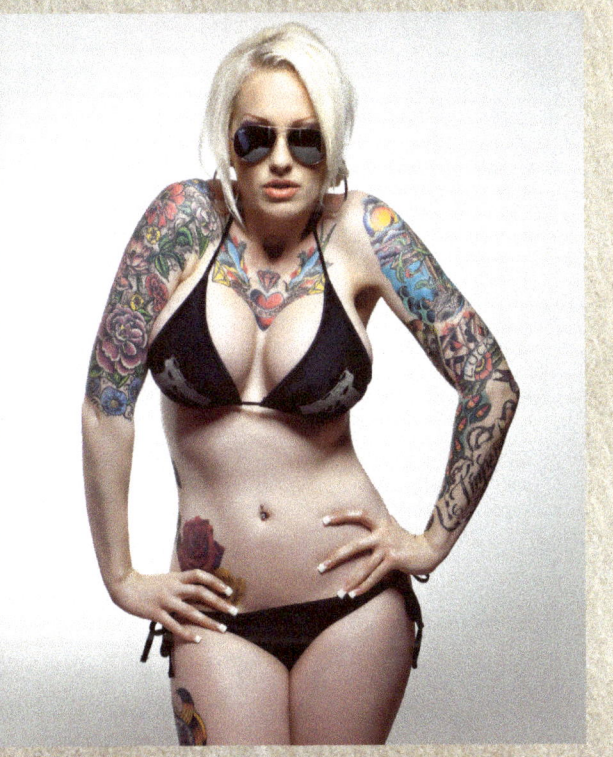
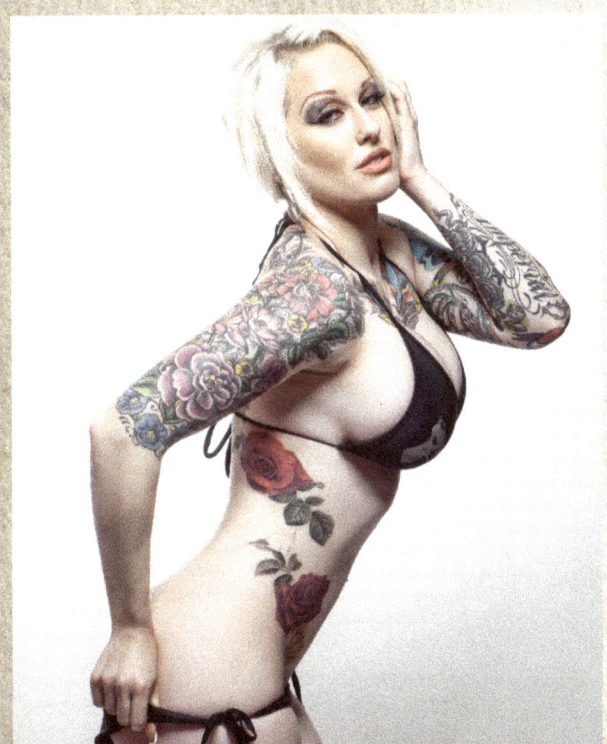

Amy DeLaCroux

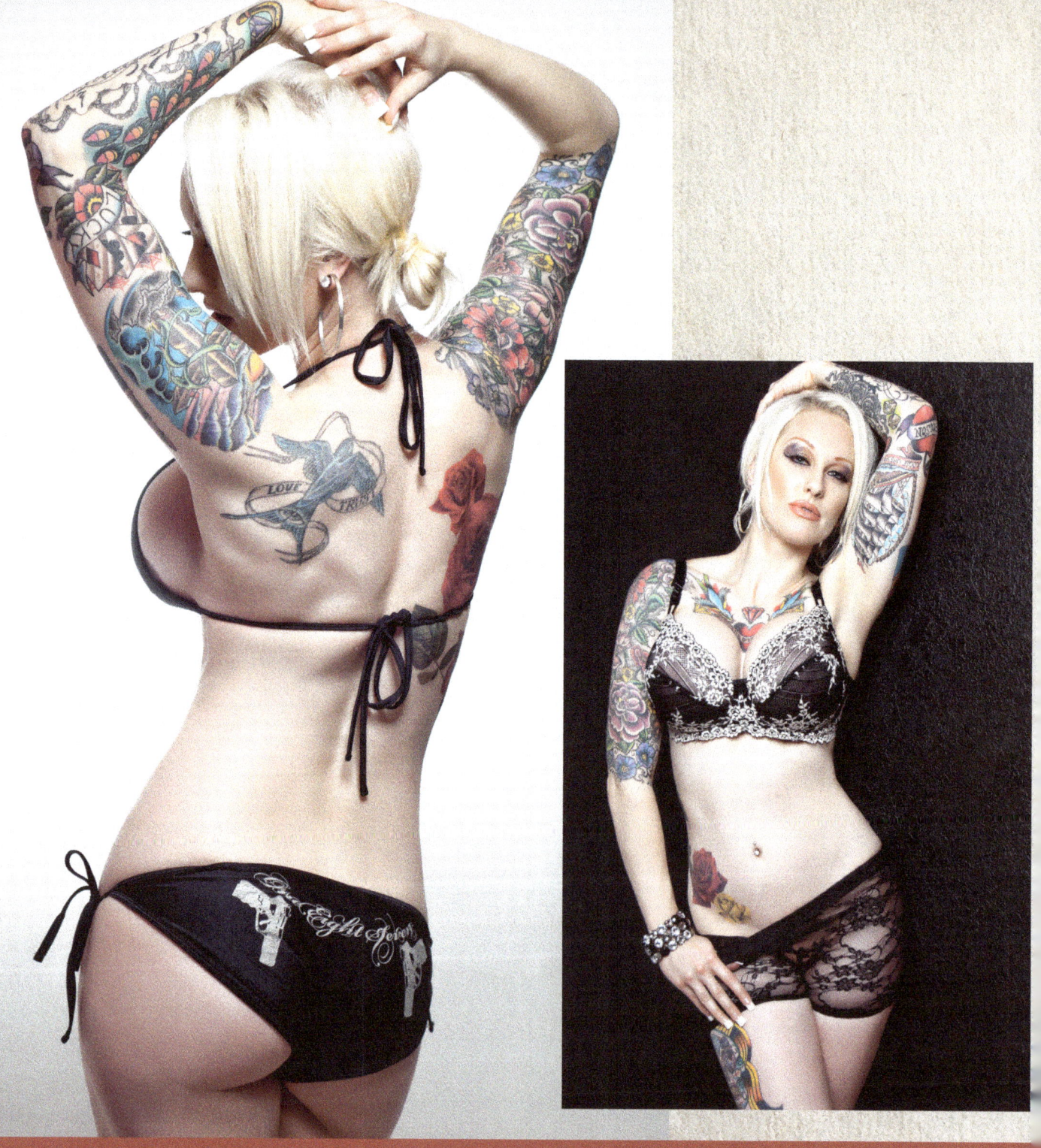

Amy DeLaCroux

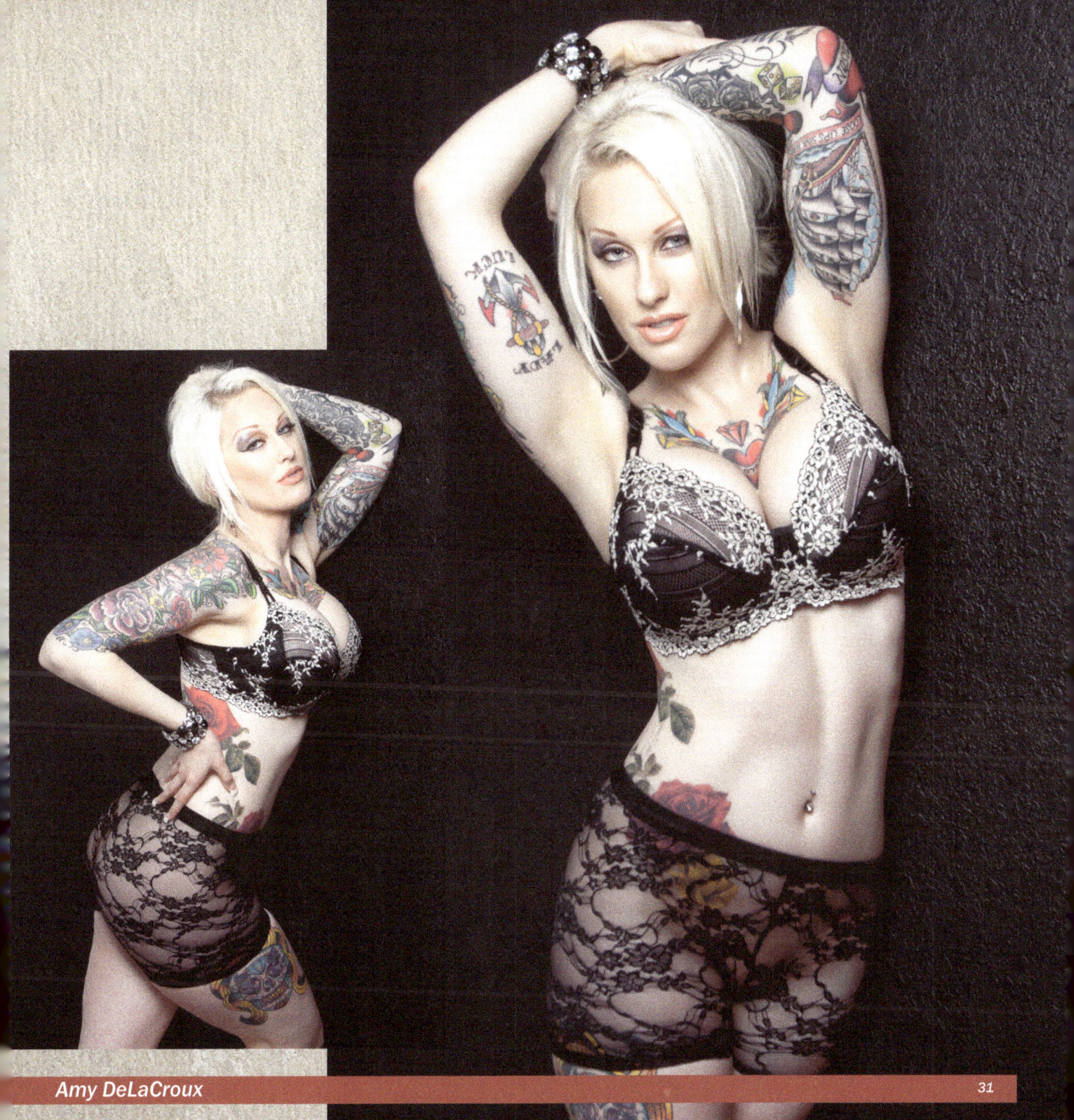
Amy DeLaCroux

Jessie DeVille

"I hate to call myself a 'pin-up' model, my style is a little more alternative…"

I am Jesses DeVille, 25 years old and I live in Northern California. I'm happily married and run a Rock N' Roll bar with my husband. I also do hair and make up, but right now my major focus is my bar.

Did you ever think you would be a model?
I was a model for a short period of time when I was a child. I started modeling again a few years ago for a friend's clothing company. Looking back I would never thought I would have more than 20 magazine covers to my credit!

What is your definition of beauty?
Inner beauty. To feel beautiful on the outside you have to feel beautiful on the inside. A good personality and inner beauty goes a long way in this industry.

What is your favorite photo set?
Everything I shoot with Keith Selle is truly amazing and always ends up getting published. I am so happy I have had the last year to work with him on different projects before he moves to L.A.

Which was your first tattoo? And why did you make it?
My first tattoo is covered with Cherries on my chest now. I got a matching heart tattoo with two of my girlfriends, it was so bad, it looked like a rotten tomato!

Among all your tattoos, which one do you prefer and why?
I love all of my tattoos. But, I guess you could say I favor my Virgin Mary on my right arm.

Please talk us through some of your tattoos and the reasons behind them.
I have a matching lock and key tattoo with my husband on my inner right arm, and his name on my hip. I have a matching poison girl tattoo on my hand with my friend Annastasia, there's really no reason behind it we just wanted the same tattoo. Lol. My left sleeve is traditional roses, stars and butterflies - done by Brent Patten at Forever Tattoo Sac Ca. I just picked out things I liked and put them all together. Top of my right arm is a Virgin Mary, I'm not super religious, I just love religious art. If you came into my house you would think we were hardcore Catholics, this one was also done by Bent Patten. The bottom part of my right arm is a collaboration of a bunch of different artists, and still not finished. My thigh is Japanese flowers, water, and clouds. It is a cover up done by Eddy Jullian at Something Wicked in Roseville CA, he did an amazing job.

Have you got an idea of the next tattoo?
I just had my inner arm worked on, and I'm still trying to fill in my right arm and finish up my back. I want to cover my entire back someday.

Who is your favorite tattoo artist and why?
I have many favorites, I really love Nikko Huratados portraits and would love to get something done by him. I also really love Steve Stotos work, I got to meet him in Ohio at The Hell City Tattoo convention this year, he really kicks ass!

Do you regret any of your tattoos?
I have had laser on the lettering on the front of my neck twice, it's not fun and I don't know if I will ever remove it completely.

Do you think people treat you differently for being heavily tattooed?
Yes! Usually people are pretty nice, just really curious and want to ask me questions. Every once in awhile comcone will state opinions and be hateful, but they are just jealous. Lol.

What's the next step for Jessie DeVille?
I'm unpredictable… you never know!

www.jessiedeville.com
http://www.facebook.com/diamonddolljessiedeville
www.facebook.com/pages/Jessie-DeVille/364873176897080
www.h2oceanmodels.com/jessie/
www.tumblr.com/tagged/jessie-deville

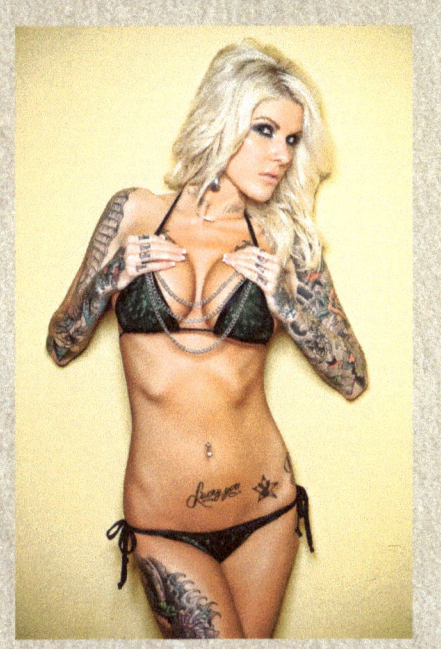
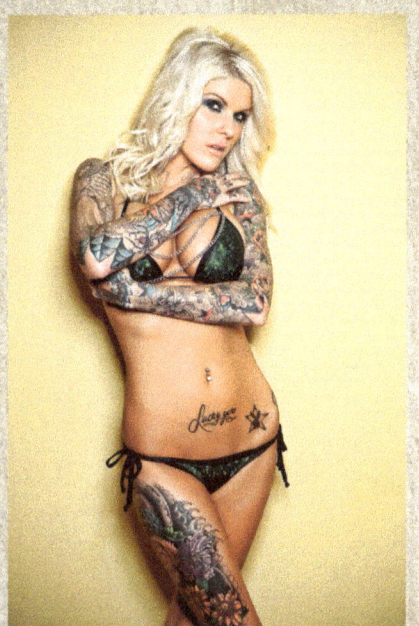
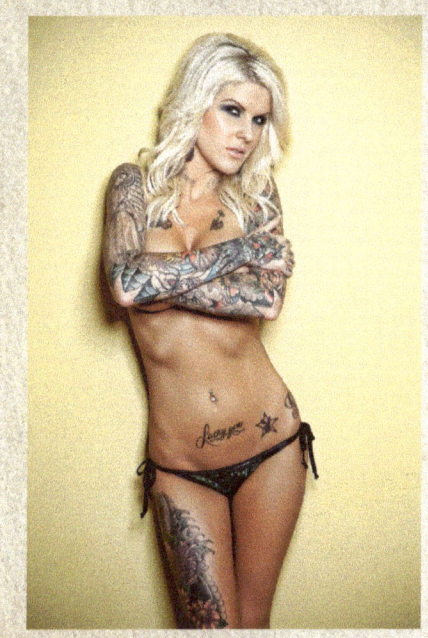

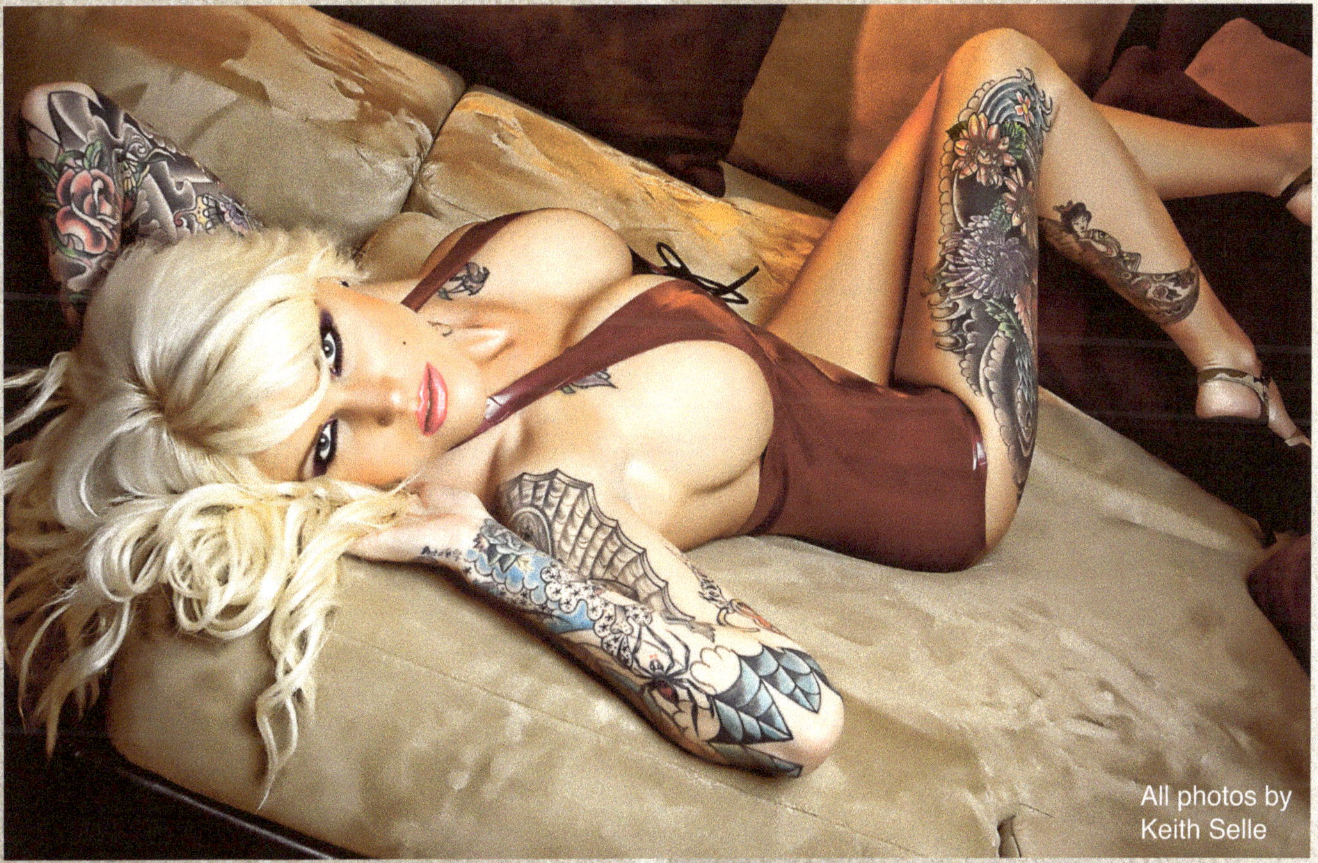

All photos by Keith Selle

Jessie DeVille

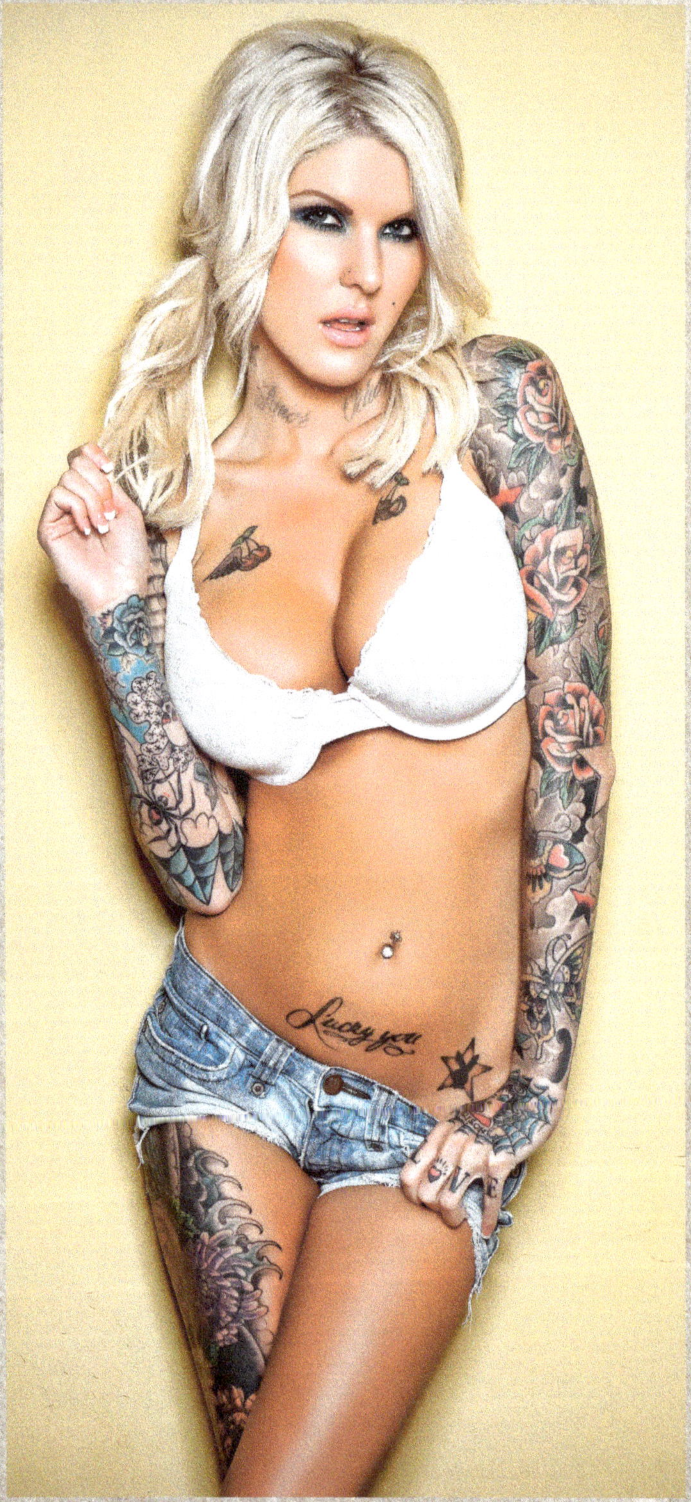

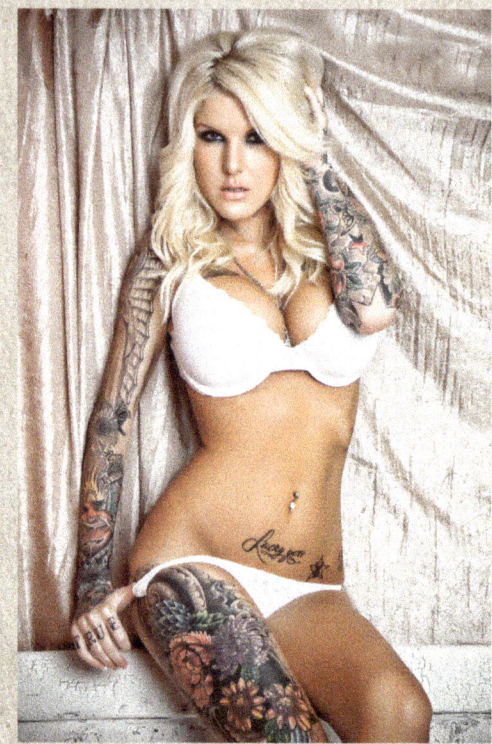
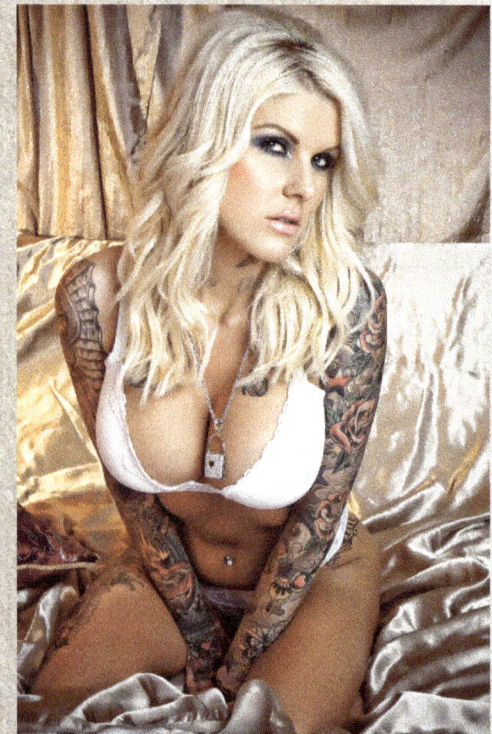

Jessie DeVille

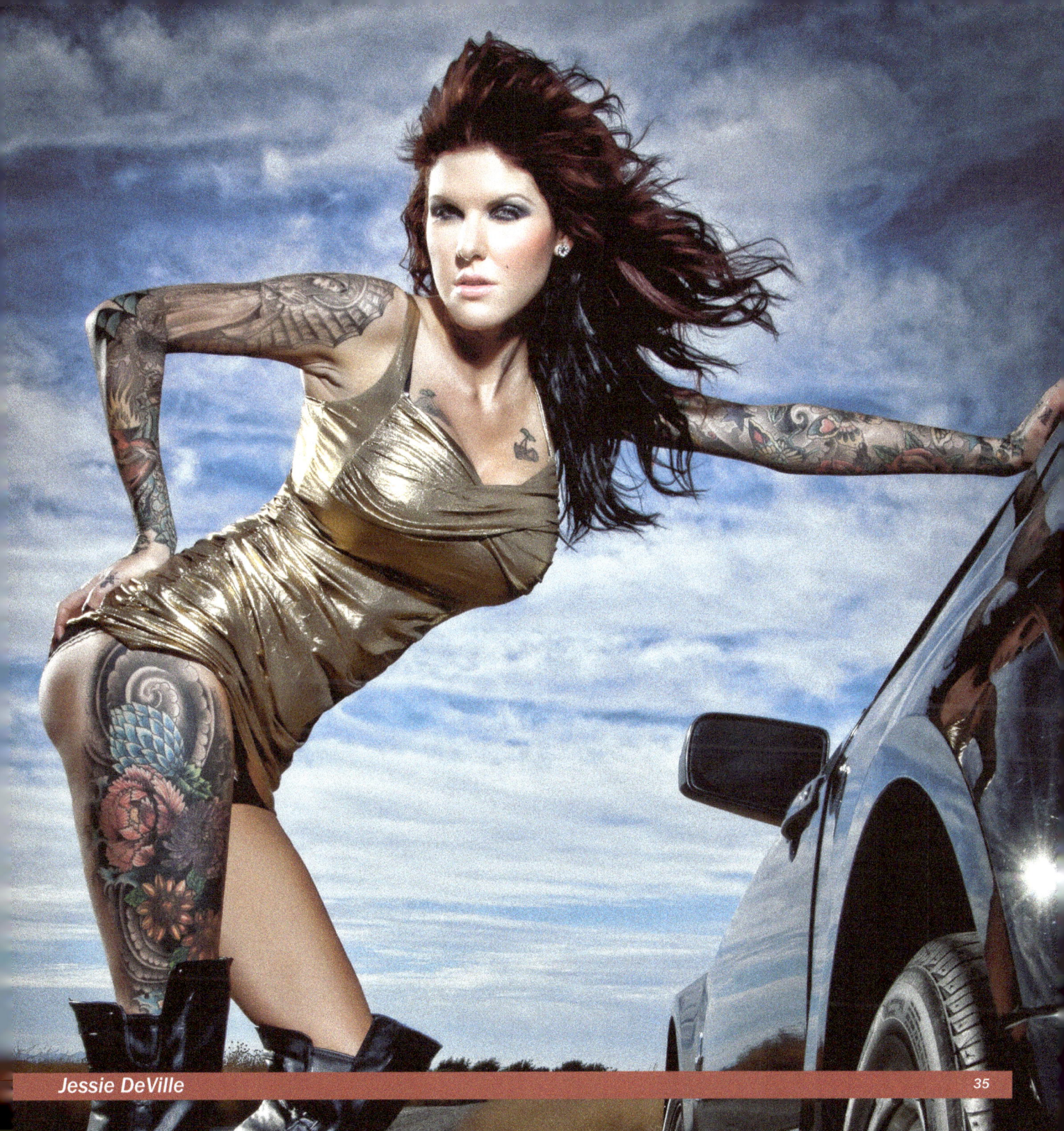

Stephanie Fleischman

"Being involved in the tattoo industry has opened many doorways for me..."

My name is Stephanie Fleischman, I'm a nice Jewish girl in disguise, 27 years old, originally from Long Island, New York. I have been living in Florida for about 16 years now, all over Florida but currently living in Orlando. I am a professional body piercer working at Atomic Tattoos. I have 90% of my body tattooed, and I'm still going.

How did you get your start in modeling?

It's kind of weird, the more I covered my body with tattoos, the more photographers wanted to do photo shoots. In 2005 I met a man, Max Brand, who worked for Prick magazine, and landed the cover with an inside interview. Right after that I had an opportunity to work with Steadfast Brand, I was their first successful model, and currently still am. I just kept marketing after that and traveling all over the united states meeting photographers like Sean Hartgrove, and Greg Truelove, to mention a few. I guess you can say it just happened.

How long have you been a model, and what do you enjoy the most about it?

I have been a successful model since 2005, I enjoy modeling because it is the best way to market myself as a body piercer. I believe it provides a lot of opportunities for me.

You were one of the first tattoo models Greg Truelove shot with and is a big part of how he got to shoot so many other inked models. When and how did that friendship begin?

Greg found me through a Playboy model, Kristen Leigh, who I did a photo shoot with. I remember her being so excited that Greg contacted her until she found out it was for me. Kristen gave me Greg's number and it was love at first sight. Greg paid for my trip from Florida to Atlanta and we just hit it off. He is amazing.

Could you tell us some details about those photo sessions? What is it like to work with a great photographer like Greg?

Well, Greg's studio is actually where he lives, which I might say, is really badass. He makes you feel really comfortable, I had no problem getting naked, LOL. Greg is not just my photographer, he became a great friend.

When did your interest in tattoos begin? And how long was it from then until you got your first one?

I waited until I was 18 to get my first tattoo, which was my full back. I always knew I wanted to be covered. I feel like I will never be done, even though I am running out of space.

Which was your first one? And why did you make it?

My first tattoo was my back piece.

What do your tattoos mean to you? Are they symbolic or do you just dig the art?

My tattoos really do mean the world to me, all of them mean something to me. It's not just the art, but the artists who have worked on me.

Among all your tattoos, which one do you prefer and why?

I don't have one favorite, I love them all.

Please talk us through some of your tattoos and the reason behind them.

Originally I started with a Japanese theme, but as I started to meet artists around the world, I wanted whatever they wanted to do. My upper right leg is all portraits. My lower right leg is dedicated to my favorite band, Mr. Bungle. On my left lower leg I have a lot of fun pieces just of things I love, like Red Bull or Mountain Dew, kind of funny. My left upper leg is a traditional Japanese folklore story. My stomach has my favorite quote from the Bible which says, "An honest answer is the same as a kiss on the lips." I have a full back piece of Japanese paradise.

Do you regret any of your tattoos?

No never.

www.myspace.com/oncelostnowfound
www.modelmayhem.com/StephanieFleischman
www.facebook.com/profile.php?id=1108140239
steadfastbrand.com/Stephanie-Fleischman.html

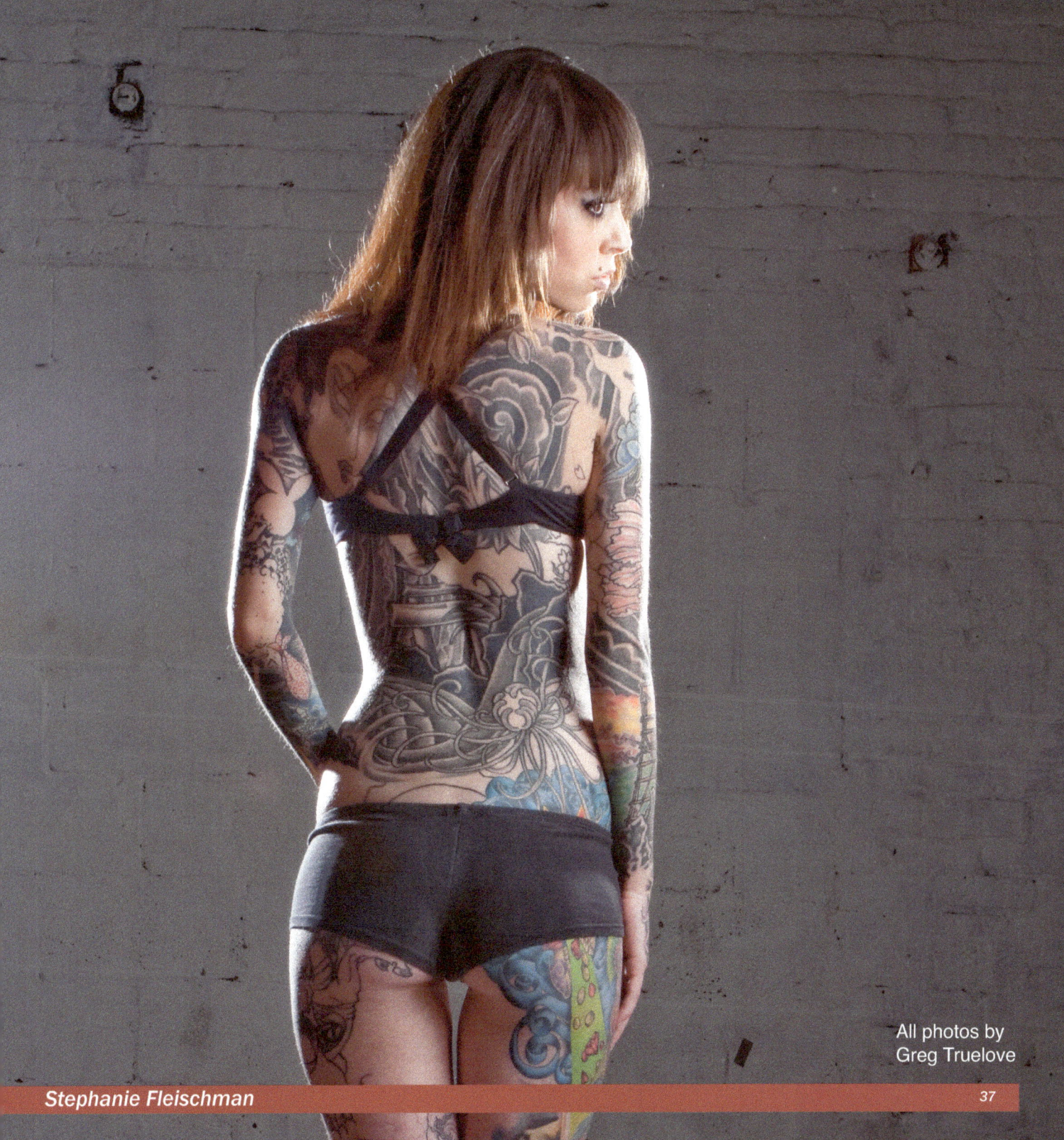

All photos by Greg Truelove

Stephanie Fleischman

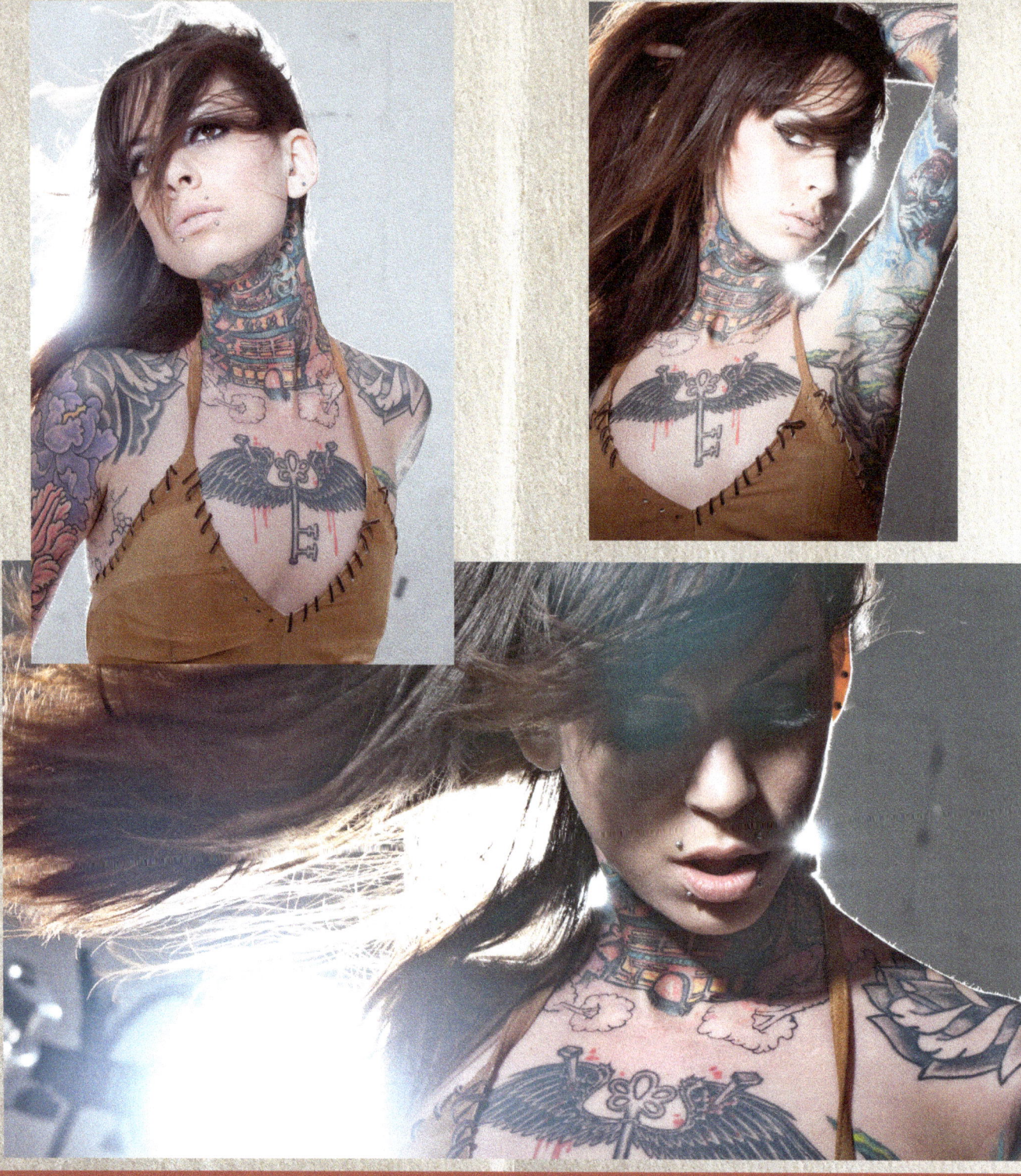

Stephanie Fleischman

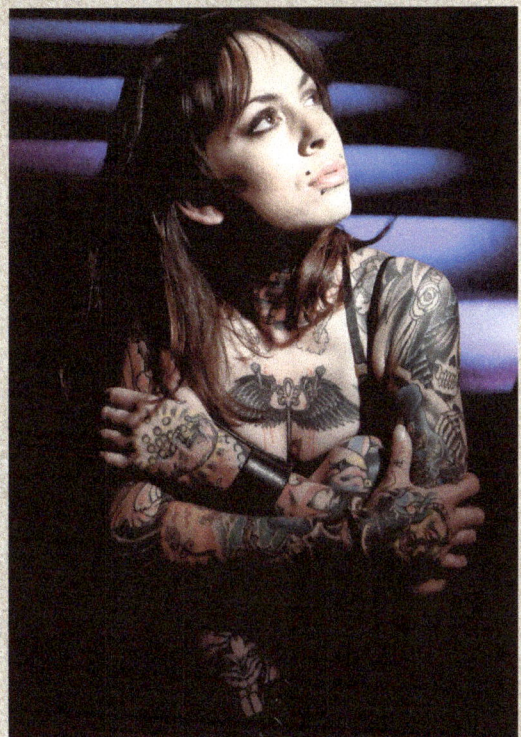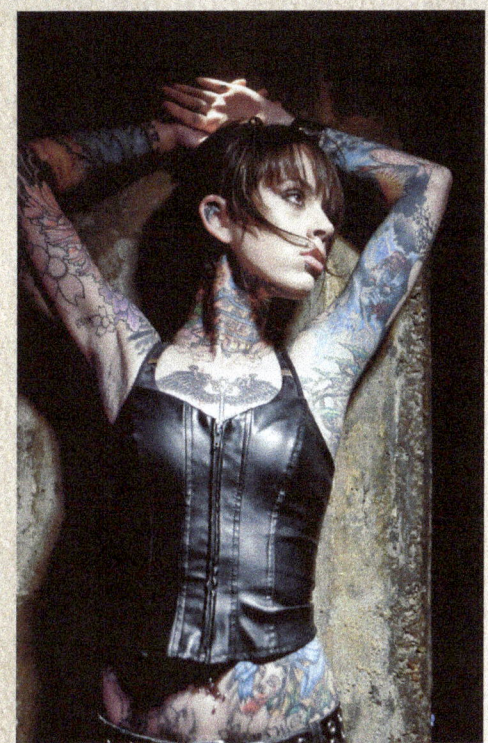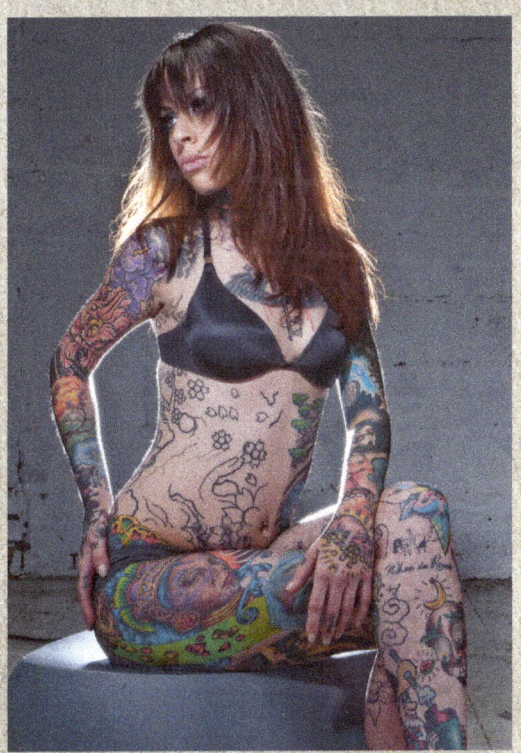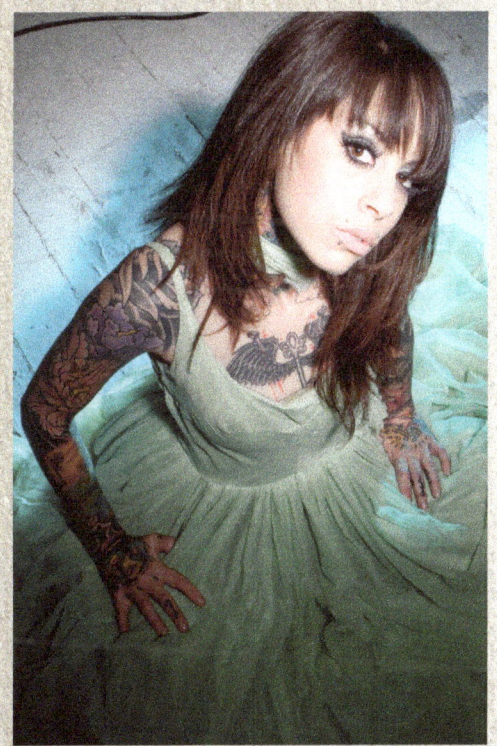

Stephanie Fleischman

Suzanne Franco

"Sometimes I do get treated differently because of my tattoos..."

My name is Suzanne Franco and I'm a tattoo model and occasional ring girl. I live in Northern California and belong to the model and promotional group, Diamond Dolls Ink.

Which tattoo style do you like best? And how would you describe your style?

I love Japanese art and religious art.

How did you get your start in modeling?

I started doing photo shoots almost two years ago here and there, but I didn't dedicate any real effort to it because I didn't think I could cut it as a model. I finally got over that negative thinking and said screw it, let's give it a shot or I'll regret not trying to later. I put my photos out there and started networking myself this past six or eight months. I got picked to be an MMA-KO babe of the month and became a part of Diamond Dolls Ink.

Do you work with any special photographers on a regular basis?

I love to work with Keith Selle and Casper Munoz, they always make me look beautiful.

What would you say, in your opinion, is the biggest misconception about modeling?

That modeling makes me A LOT of money. I wish it did, in reality I still have a day job and career goals outside of modeling.

How did your love for tattoos start?

I was really intrigued by the tattoo culture around the age of 15 or 16. They were a symbol of rebellion to me and I so wanted to rebel against my parents. As I got older they became more of a symbol of individuality, depending on the pieces of course, and the art.

How old were you when you got your first tattoo?

I was around 19 or 20 years old when I first started getting tattooed and if had been up to me I would have gotten my first one at 16. Thank god I didn't because at that age you really have no idea what's really art.

What is your favorite tattoo so far, and why?

My favorite so far is the geisha fan on my left hand, my artist drew it free-hand. I had no idea the hand was going to hurt so bad! A few times I wanted to call it quits while he was tattooing, but it was coming along so amazingly well that I forced myself to sit through it for seven hours.

What do your tattoos mean to you?

They are a symbol of encouragement and faith to me, tied in with a few pieces I just think are beautiful.

As we know tattoos are addictive. Is that what drives you to get more?

I think I'm taking a break from getting tattooed for a while after I finish up my right arm. I have a few ideas in mind though so we'll see.

Do you like to stick to one artist, or try a number of different ones?

I like to stick with just one, my artist, Beau McCoy, in Sacramento is an amazing artist and the only one I'll let work on me.

Do you have any funny/weird stories about a tattoo experience?

It's always funny when my boyfriend and I get stopped by people and they start commenting on my tattoos and then they look at my him and ask him where all of his are.

Do you think people treat you differently for being heavily tattooed?

Sometimes I do get treated differently because of my tattoos. People sometimes tell me they thought I was going to be mean, or that I look intimidating. Once they actually meet me and get to know me, they realize I'm a nice girl and I'm so far from what they thought I was going to be like.

www.facebook.com/profile.php?id=100003005681986
beta.inkfreakz.com/suzanne0015
www.tumblr.com/tagged/suzanne-franco

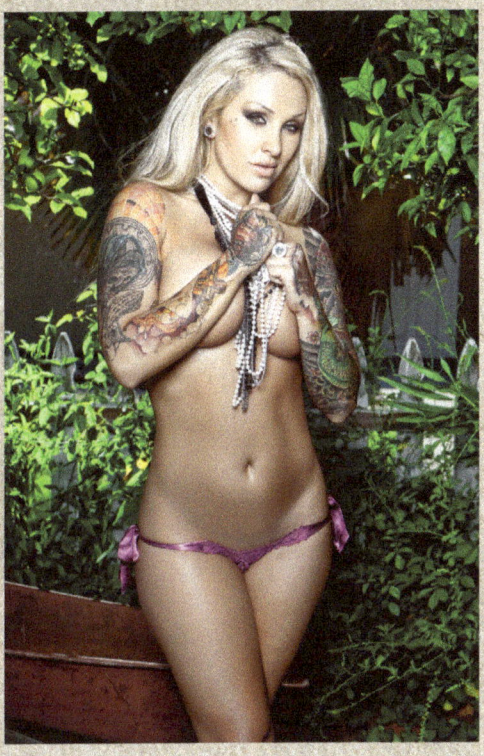
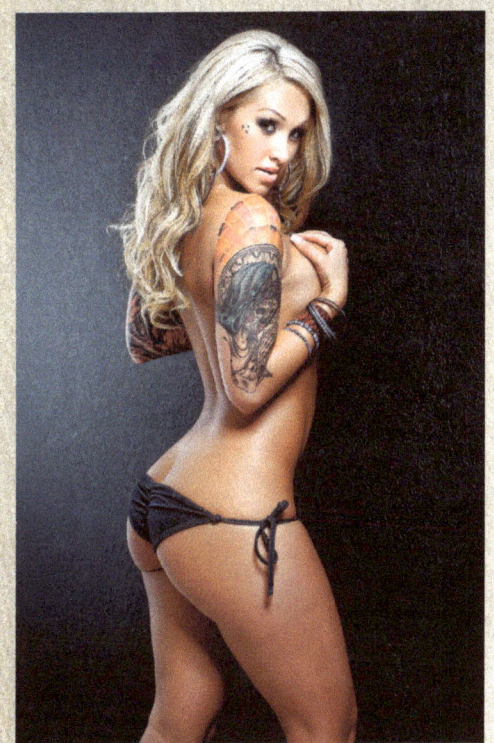
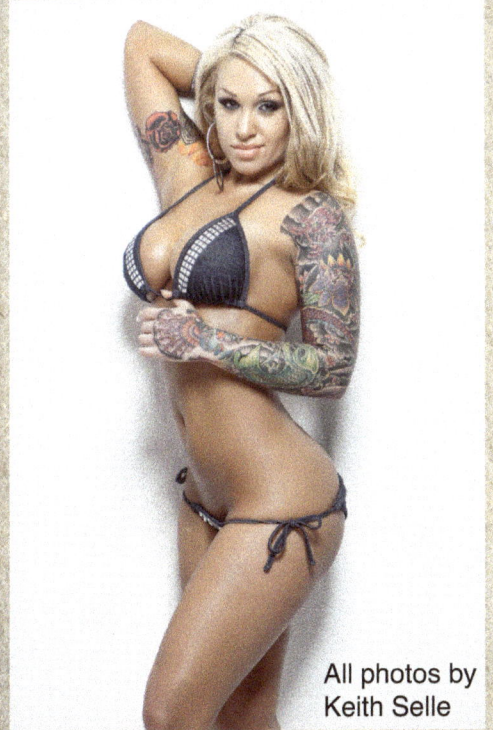
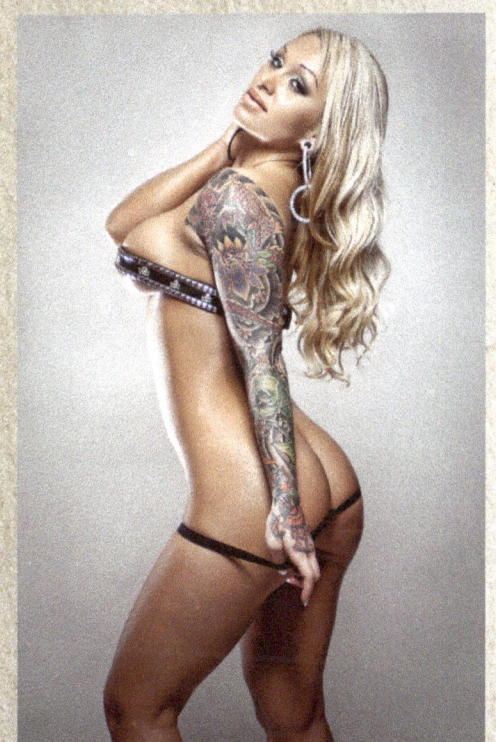

All photos by Keith Selle

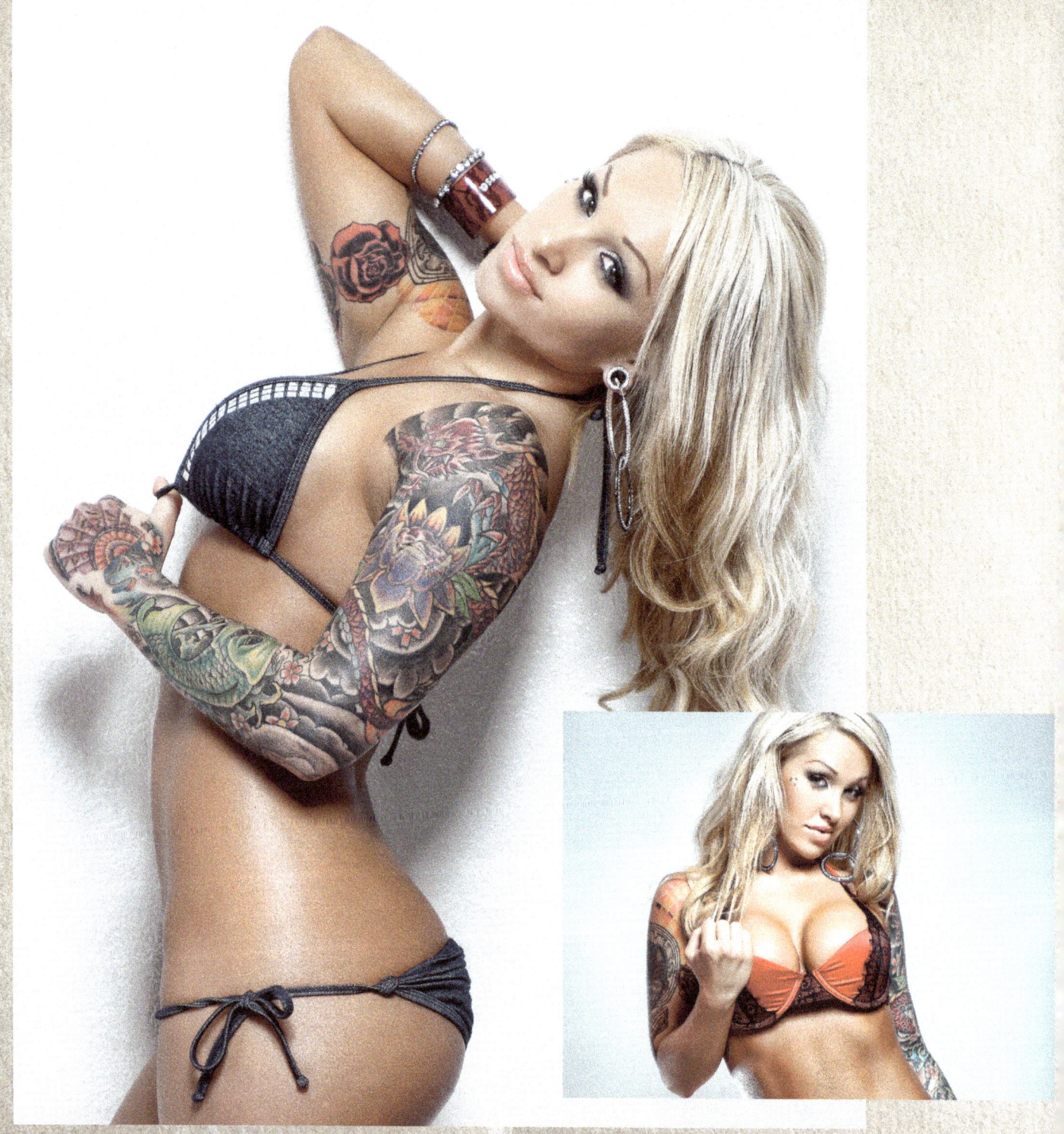

Suzanne Franco

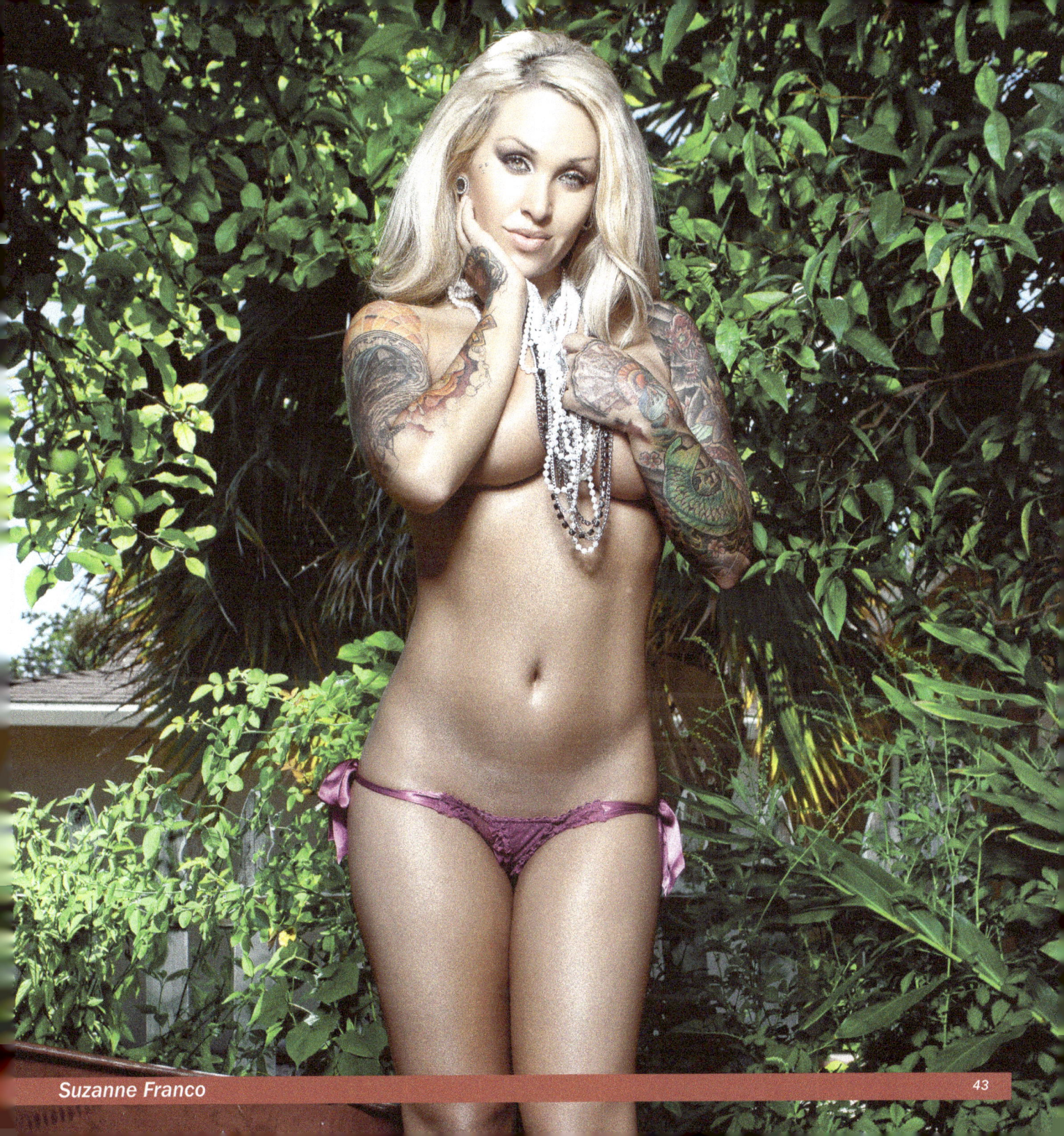

Dejah Garcia

"I have always felt empowered by my tattoos..."

My name is Dejah Garcia, I am from a small town called Bullhead City, AZ. That is where I did my tattoo apprenticeship. I moved to Las Vegas, NV in 1997 where I got my first professional job as a tattooer. I now live in Southern California where I own a shop called Trusted Tattoo.

What made you want to become a tattoo artist?

I have been drawing for as long as I can remember, My grandfather was in the Navy and had the Popeye tattoos on his forearms, I always loved them. I was lucky enough to know what I wanted to do at a young age!

What did your family and friends think about you getting into the business?

When I first started tattooing my parents didn't approve, they kicked me out of the house when I was 15. As adults, though, they are fully supportive, they know how hard I've worked and how much I've sacrificed for my trade.

Which tattoo style do you like best? And how would you describe your style?

I try to be well rounded in all styles of tattooing. I like to mix black and grey with color, the black really makes the color pop. I respect the technique of Japanese tattooing and try to use some of those principals in my tattooing.

What would you say is the biggest misconception about modeling?

The biggest misconception about modeling for me is that I am a model. I'm actually a full-time tattooer who is lucky to have artistic friends!

Do you work with any special photographers on a regular basis?

I usually work with the amazing Justice Howard. I met her when I was 18 and I feel comfortable with her, not only do we work well together I consider her one of my closest friends. She can make any girl feel empowered and sexy.

How old were you when you got your first tattoo?

I was probably about 15 or 16 when I got my first tattoo. It is covered now, I really wish I would have waited.

Please talk us through some of your tattoos and the reason behind them.

My left sleeve was all stuff I got before I turned 18 and I have been getting it lasered off and now I'm working on it getting it covered up. My right arm I call my "good arm." Guy Aitchison did the pumpkins on my hand. Tim Hendricks did the David Bowie portrait, most of that arm has a Halloween theme. I was born on Oct. 27 so that is a significant time of year for me.

What is your favorite tattoo so far, and why?

My back piece was done by Ben Corn, that has been my favorite tattoo thus far! It is laid out like a Japanese tattoo but has a Mexican theme it is a Santa Muerte skull holding a human heart with a sprout growing out of one of the valves. It represents life and rebirth to me. I love it.

What do your tattoos mean to you?

Tattoos mean everything to me, they're a way to provide for myself and express myself through my art and the tattoos I collect.

Have you gotten any new work done?

I have just started working on my legs. Clark North did a snake on my right thigh. I consider myself to be a desert dweller and love reptiles, in the future I will get a scorpion on my left thigh.

Do you like to stick to one artist, or try a number of different ones?

I consider myself to be a tattoo collector so I like to get tattooed by different people, although the majority of my tattoo work has been done by Ben Corn.

Any final words?

Don't forget to tip your artist!

www.facebook.com/profile.php?id=620303568
www.myspace.com/trustedtattoo
www.skinink.com/dejah-garcia– slingin-beauty/
www.tumblr.com/tagged/dejah-garcia

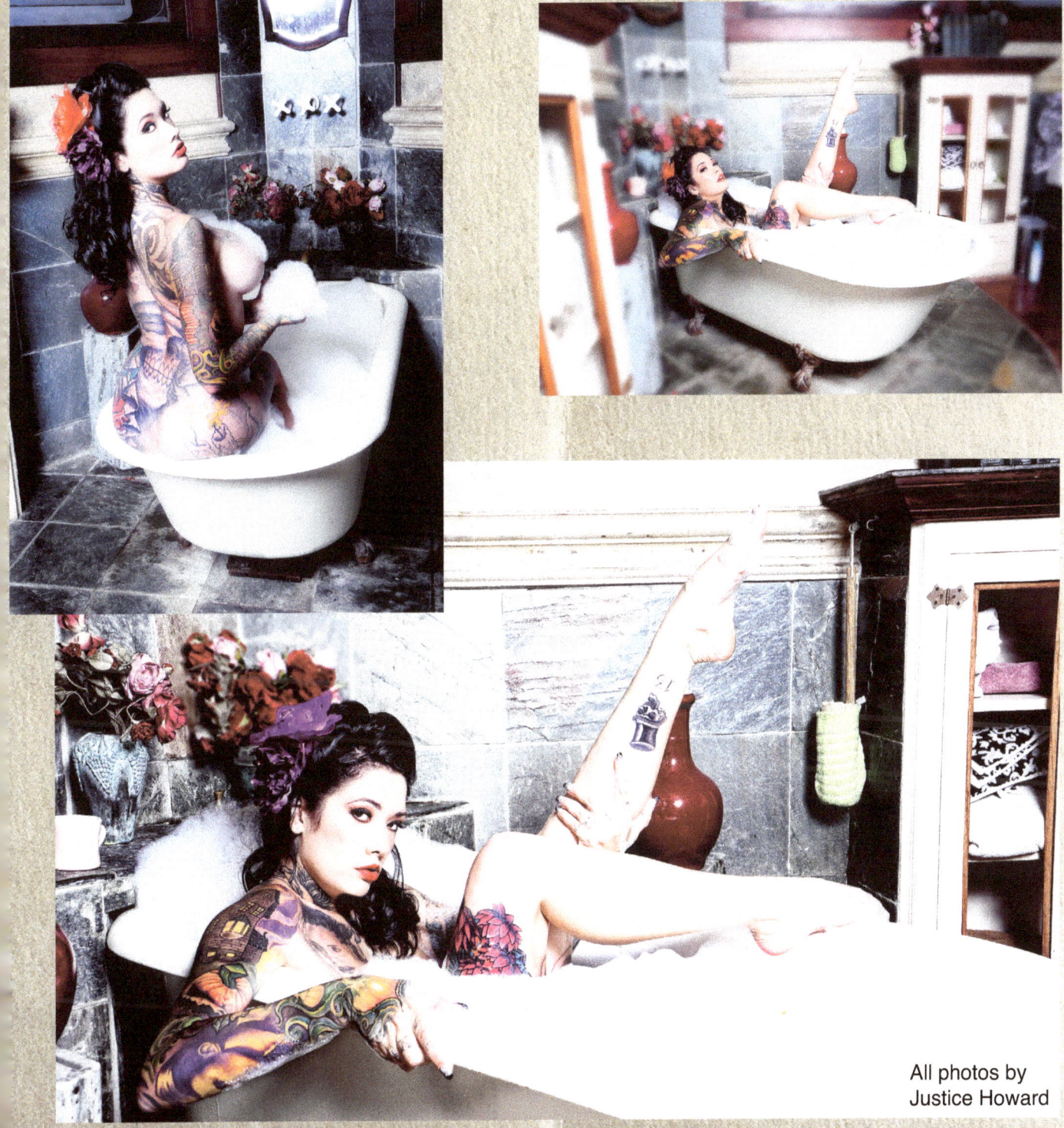

All photos by Justice Howard

Dejah Garcia

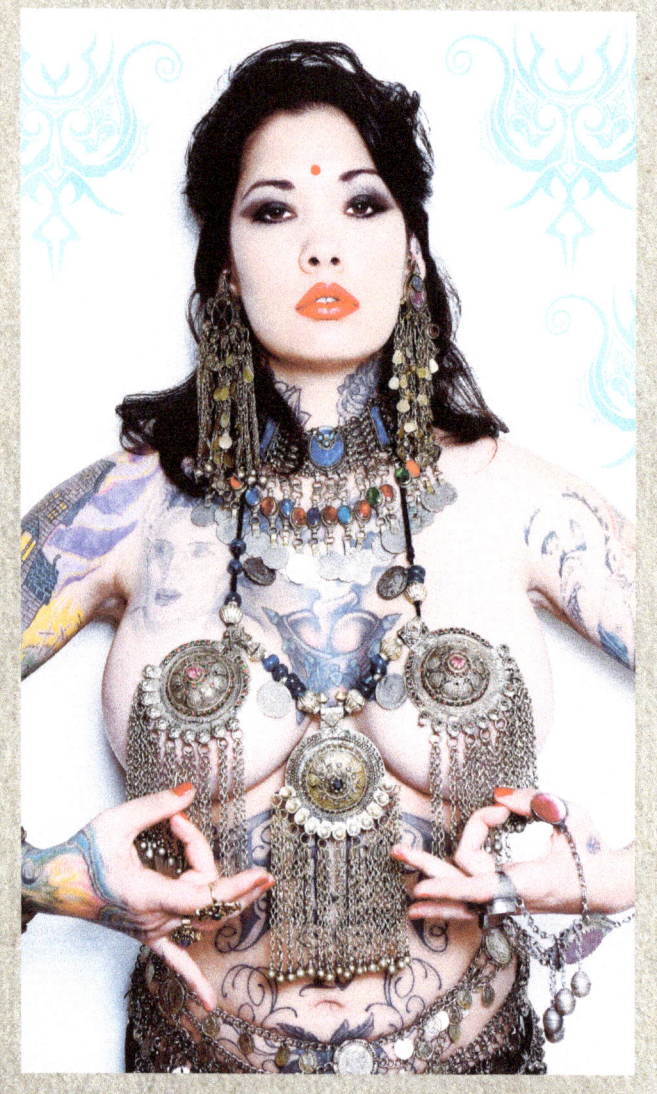

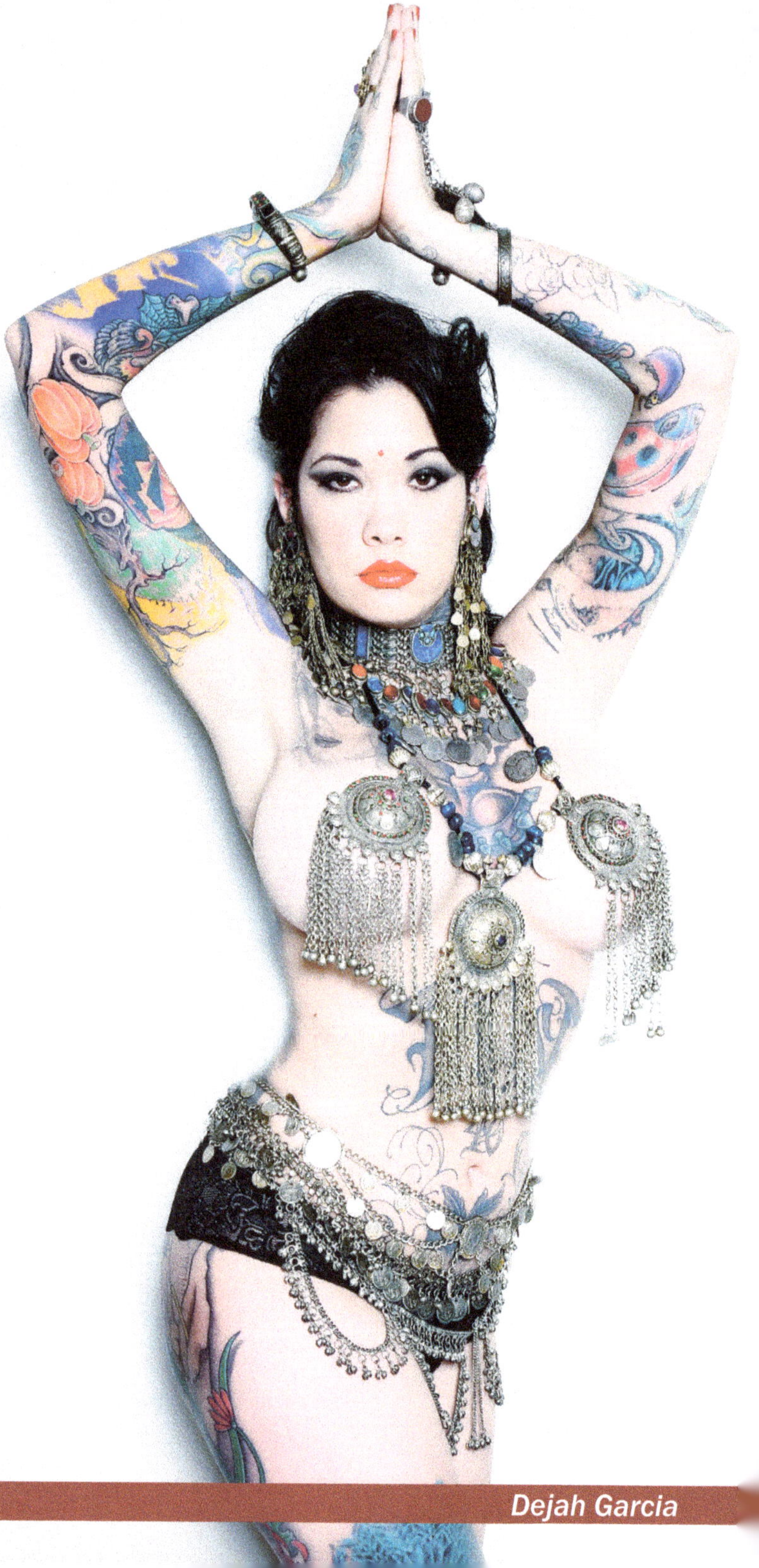

Dejah Garcia

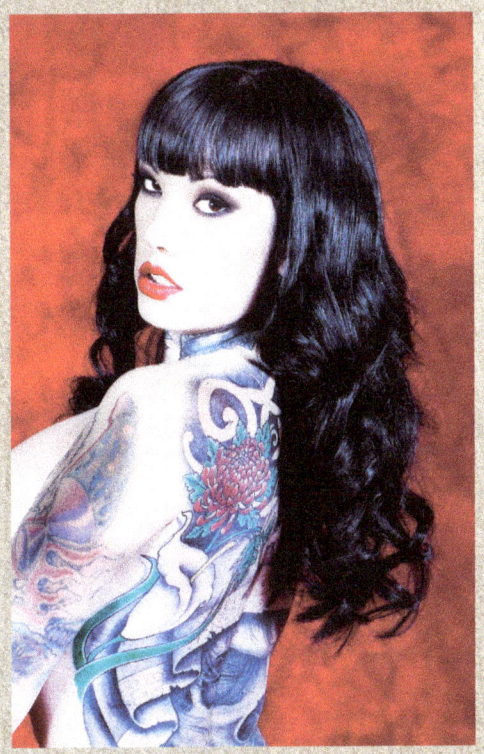
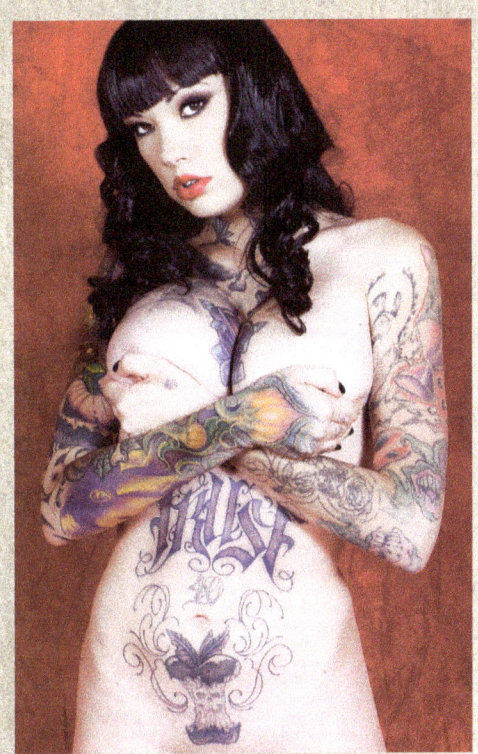
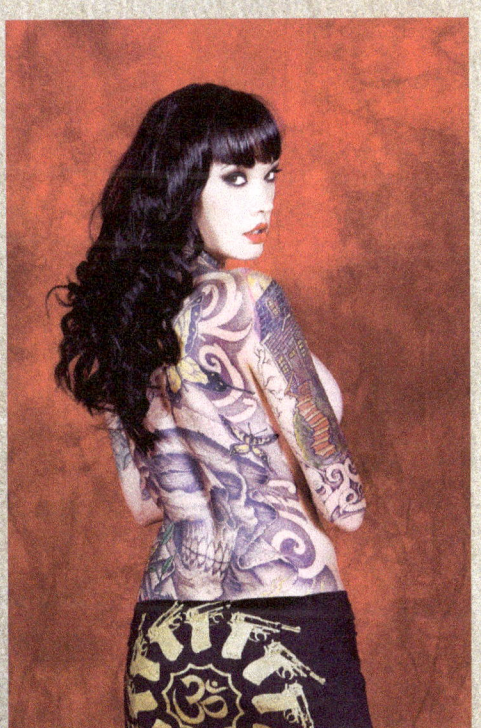
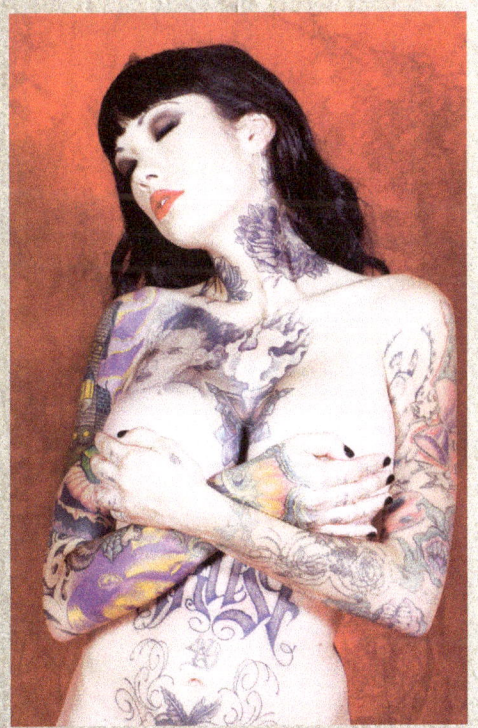

Dejah Garcia

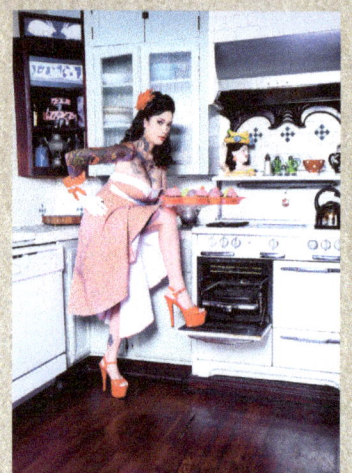
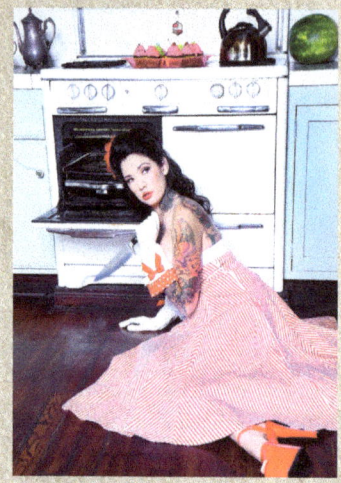
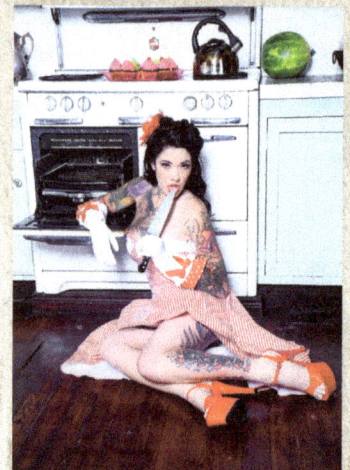
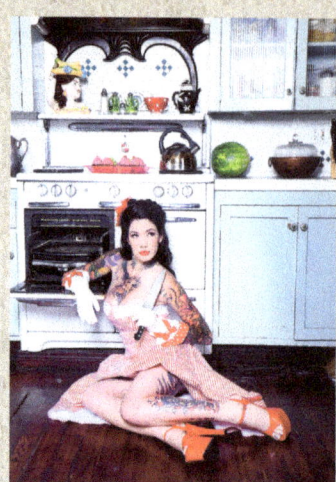

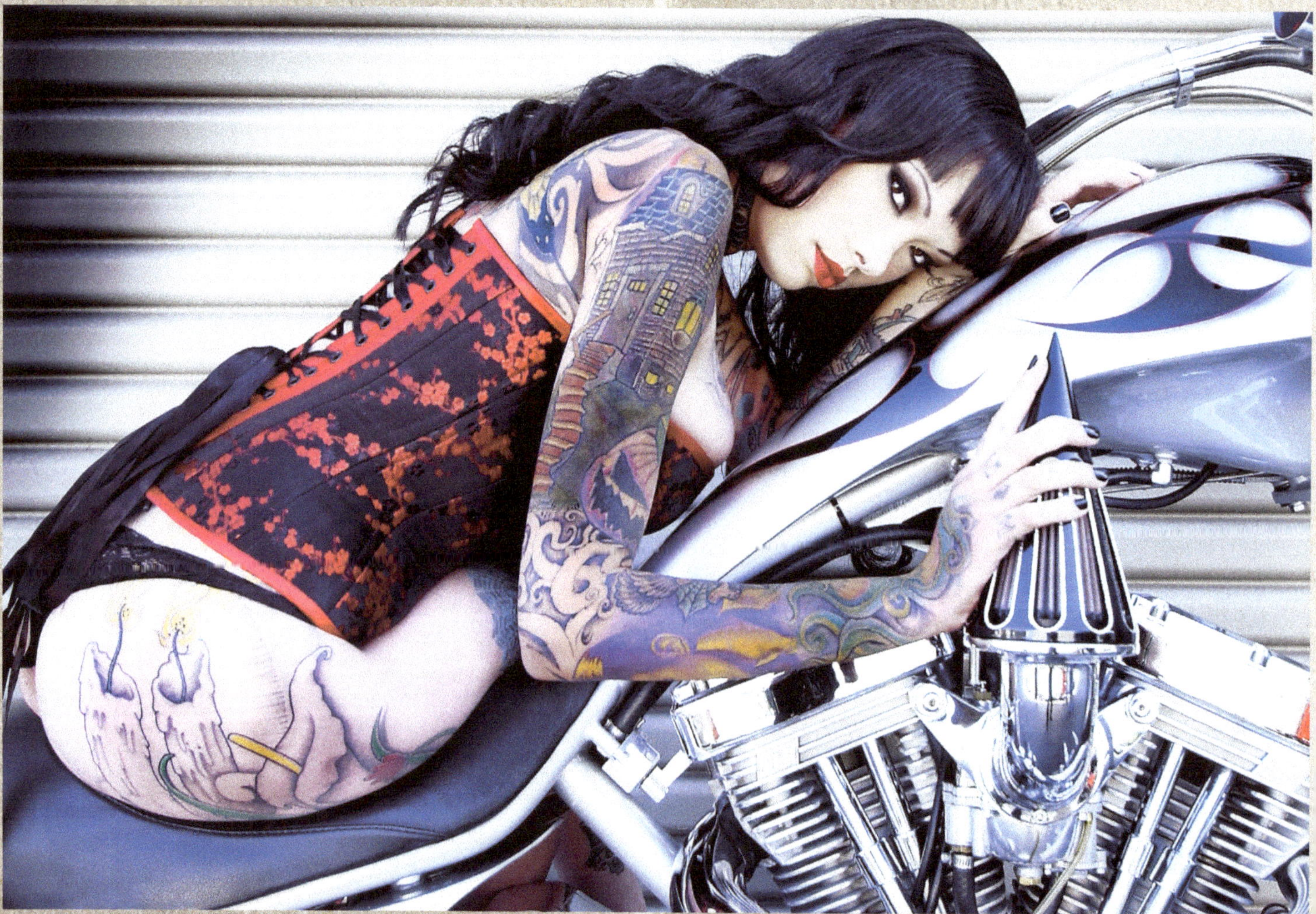

Dejah Garcia

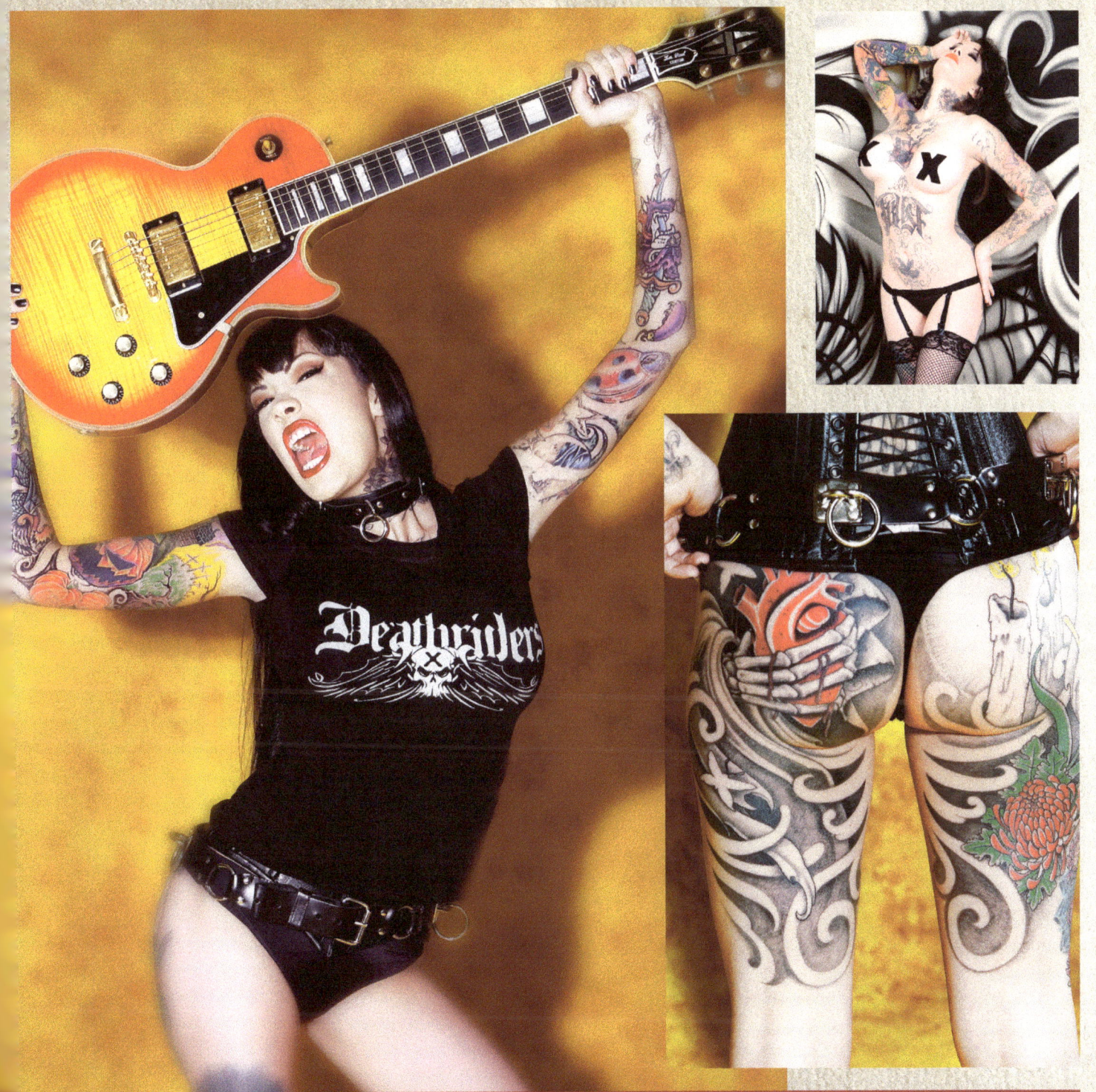

Dejah Garcia

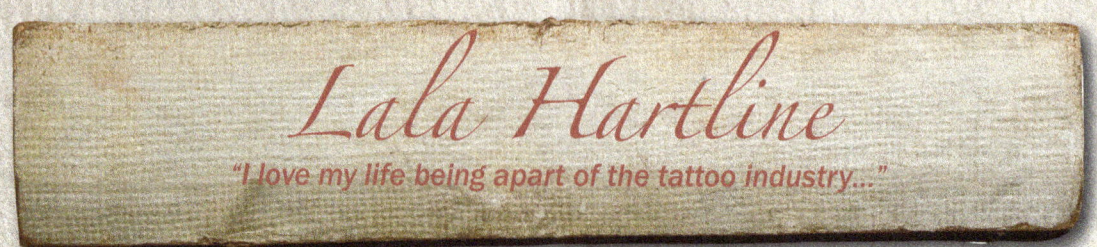

LaLa Hartline

"I love my life being apart of the tattoo industry..."

I am LaLa Hartline, a 30-year-old married mom, model, tattoo shop owner and body piercer.

What kind of modeling do you do? And what made you get into modeling?

I have done everything from runway and high fashion to adult entertainment. I started modeling at 18 after attending a local modeling open call with a friend. I had never even considered it until I was chosen number one out of over a 1000 girls. This is before I was heavily covered in tattoos.

Where have you modeled?

East Coast to West Coast USA; I even moved to California for a while.

What three words would best describe you?

Honest, responsible, and fun loving.

Please tell us little about your interests and about your favorite bands.

I love all that surrounds the tattoo industry; like hot rods, pin-ups and models. I have a 1959 Cadillac and 1930 Ford ratrod. I love playing the pin-up pretty when we travel to the tattoo conventions. When it comes to music I am a metal head at heart. My favorite bands are Lamb of God, Testament, Exodus and Black Sabbath.

A typical day in the life of LaLa Hartline would be?

I feel that I have a rather normal life. I wake up and get my daughter ready for school, pick up the house, go to work with my husband, deal with business stuff and then return home at night.

How did you come to tattoo?

I always had an interest in piercing. I pierced myself through my teen rebellion years, but then discovered that I could have a paying job doing piercings. I have always enjoyed drawing and once I settled into a shop environment everything just seemed to fall into place. I turned a teenage interest into a long-term career.

Which is your first one? And why did you choose it?

Like most people, my first tattoo has since been covered. I honestly don't care for any of my first few tattoos. It is very hard to make decisions at the age of 18 or 19 that you are going to be happy with for the rest of your life.

Among all your tattoos, which one do you prefer and why?

I love all of my black and grey pieces. Most represent my love of horror. My other favorite is my sewing machine, my second past time.

Please talk us through some of your tattoos and the reason behind them.

My husband, Shane Hartline, did my right arm, which is a smoky haze of horror themes depicted by Mark Ryden and Todd Schorr. My left arm is a graveyard collaborative done by Shane Oneill and Bob Tyrrell, I have a sewing machine by Russ Abbott and a hat box by Hannah Atchison on my hands. My rib piece says "Beautiful" with a smoky witch's brew (Halloween is my favorite time of year). That too was done by Shane Hartline, who also did the cats on my feet, the day-of-the-dead girl on my back and the caddy on my leg. Jerry Frost did the pin-up on my hip and Dave Sanchez did my girl and boy day-of-the-dead skulls on my ankles.

Have you got an idea for the next one?

I would like another rib piece by Carlos Torres. I love his work.

What do you think about the rise of tattoo, is it a fashion or a new breath for the body culture?

I though it was cool at first, but now I think it is a trend that will die hard. I think it was a good bit of education for all those who were unaware of the tattoo community, but it has also made us trendy and all trends must end sooner or later.

Do you regret any of your tattoos?

Like I said before, being young does not help in choosing a life-long tattoo.

www.evermoregalleries.com
www.facebook.com/lalahartline

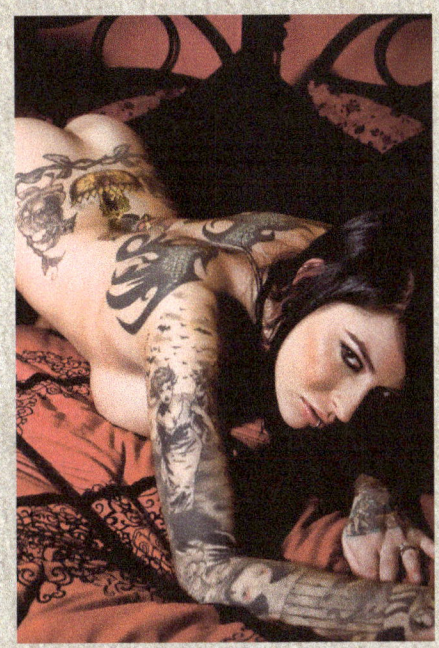
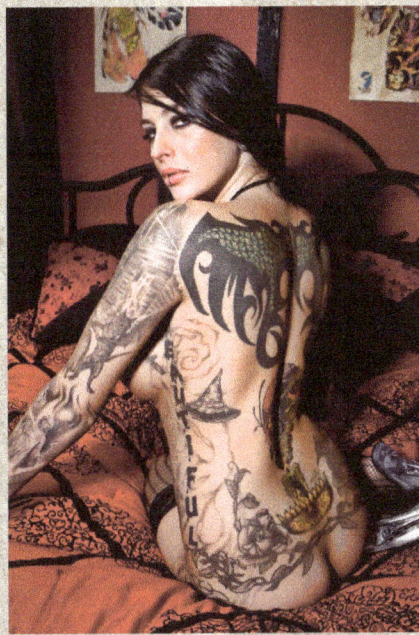
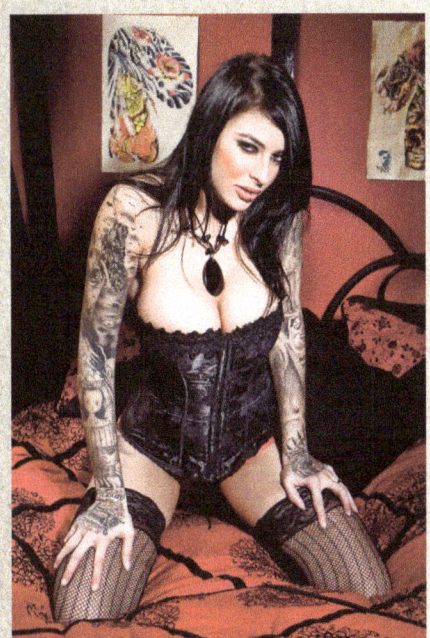

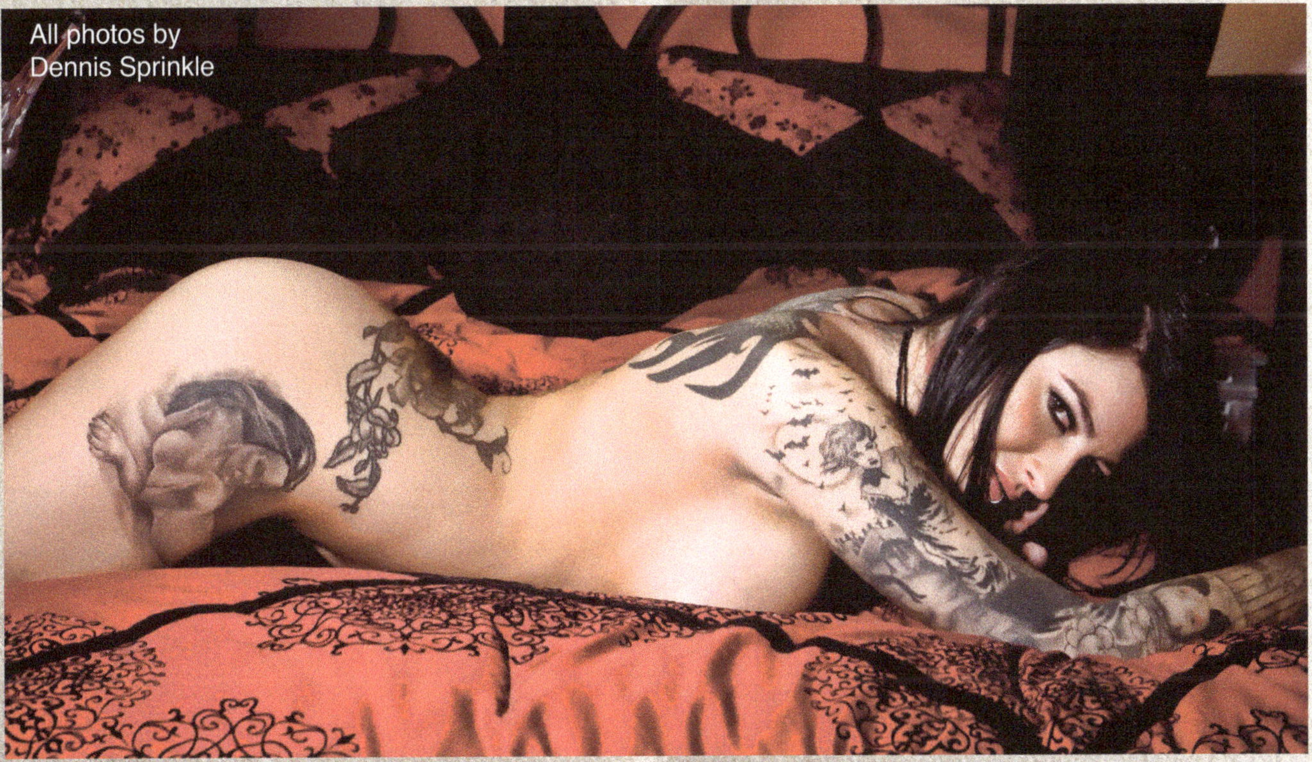

All photos by Dennis Sprinkle

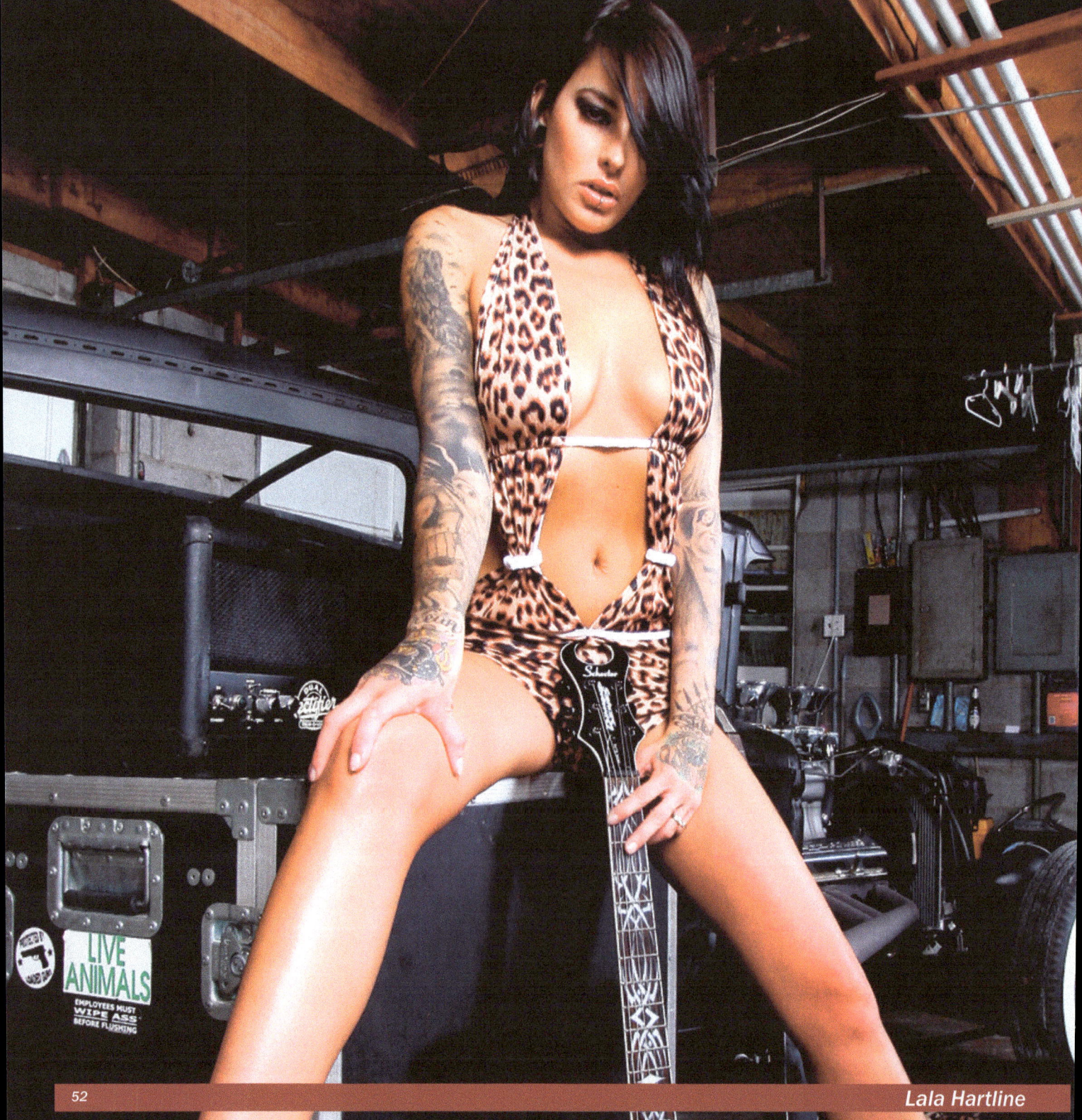

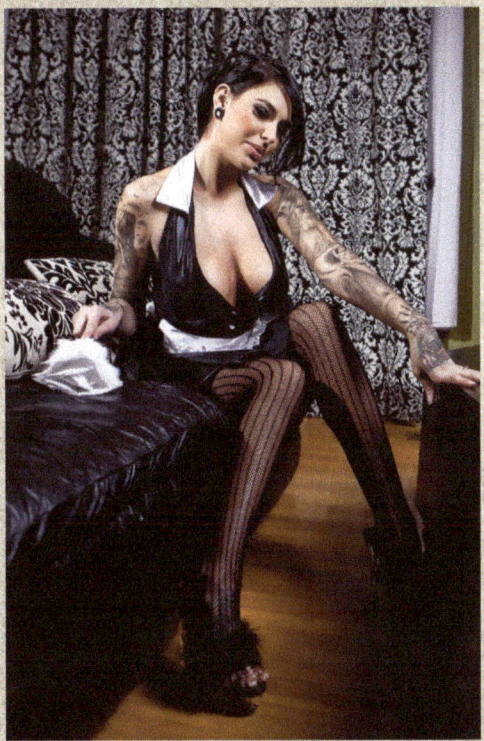
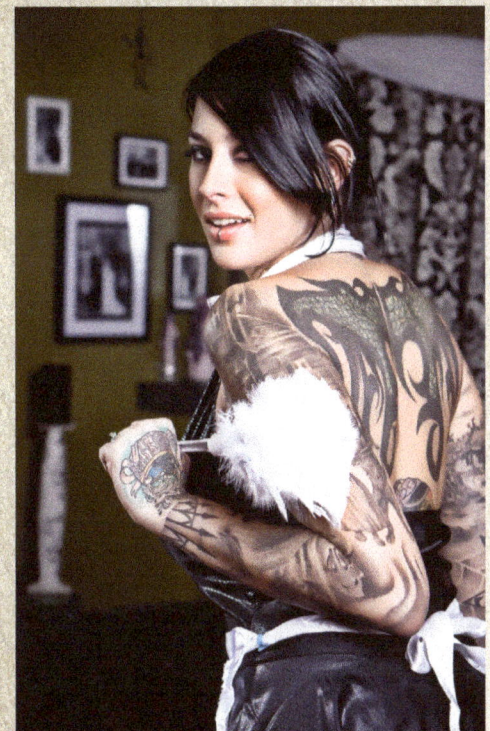
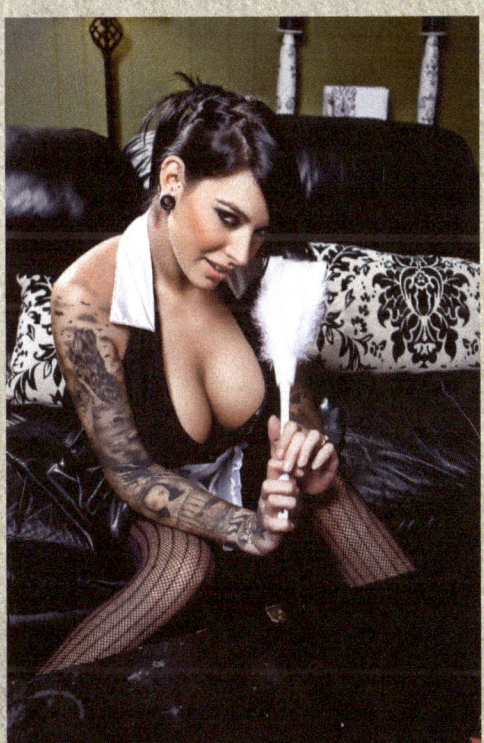
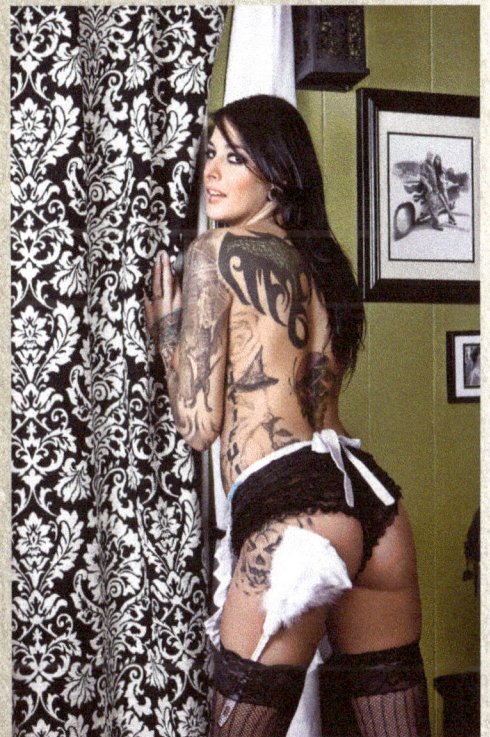

Lala Hartline

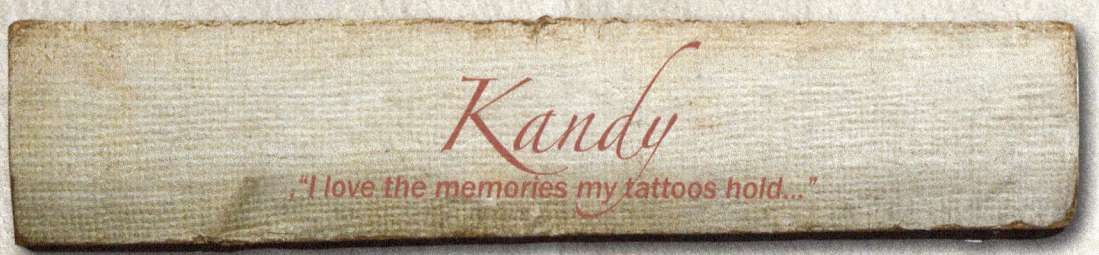

Kandy
"I love the memories my tattoos hold..."

I'm Kandy, a professional, published model and makeup artist imported from the United Kingdom, now settled in Phoenix, Arizona with my husband, son and our Boston Terriers. I'm a punk rock girl with a huge love for art, especially body art.

What kind of modeling do you do? And what made you get into modeling?

I mostly model for alternative clothing and accessory companies, Tattoo magazines and personal projects. I like to create images that linger in your mind and have some kind of twist to the concept. I love to work in a team of artistic minds and see what we come up with. I originally started modeling when I met a photographer at a fetish club, we got some great pictures and began shooting at his studio, I had a lot of fun and thought I'd carry on modeling and see where it took me. So far I've met many wonderful people and had great experiences so I plan to carry on.

How did you come to be tattooed?

I wanted my first tattoo when I went with a friend to get his first tattoo. I was only 15 and desperately wanted a little punk fairy on my stomach (to represent me and my love of punk). I mentioned it to my mother, who made it very clear I should wait till I was 18 or I wouldn't have a roof over my head! That was good advice, I waited and got the little fairy a couple of days past my birthday and still love it to this day! After that I had the tattoo bug and started on some more plans, I always knew I wanted a lot of coverage, I started with my right half sleeve and got a receptionist job at the same tattoo studio shortly after. Working in that environment was great and I got a lot of work done by the awesome artists there.

Among all your tattoo's, which ones do you prefer and why?

I honestly love them all and each has a story to tell, each tattoo represents a certain time in my life and I love the memories they hold. My back piece, by Jo Harrison, is especially close to my heart as it's a dedication to my mother who passed away from heart disease when I was 18, it has a negative heart, her favorite flowers and two colorful birds.

Please talk us through some of your tattoo's and the reason behind them.

Well, my right arm is my fun arm, it has a lot of Halloween pieces on it as it's my favorite holiday, I have my best friend's name and a cupcake on my hand, makes me feel hungry all the time! My knuckles say punk rock - by Steve Byrne, and I have a swallow with "fly away" on my other hand as I love to travel, by J Ranno. My left arm is made up of beautiful roses and a pirate girl which is based on a friend of mine who really affected my life. My chest is a locket with keys, by Dawnii at Painted Lady Tattoo Parlor, key to my heart, there's two keys as I believe love isn't always straight forward. On my stomach I have a pretty girl with "true romance" above it, my favorite movie, also by Dawnii. My neck has a rose with "Never Regret" for obvious reasons, by the fabulous Sean Herman, he also did a beautiful Lady with a cardinal in her hair on my thigh.

Do you enjoy the process of getting tattooed?

I don't like the pain, but I enjoy the excitement before and the rush you get afterwards. Being tattooed makes me feel great, I enjoy getting to know the artist and going back to friends for more work. It really does become an addiction, but I think it's a good investment, you'll take it to the grave!

Do you regret any of your tattoo's?

No, not at all.

www.kandyk.com
www.facebook.com/pages/KandyK/136360263108512

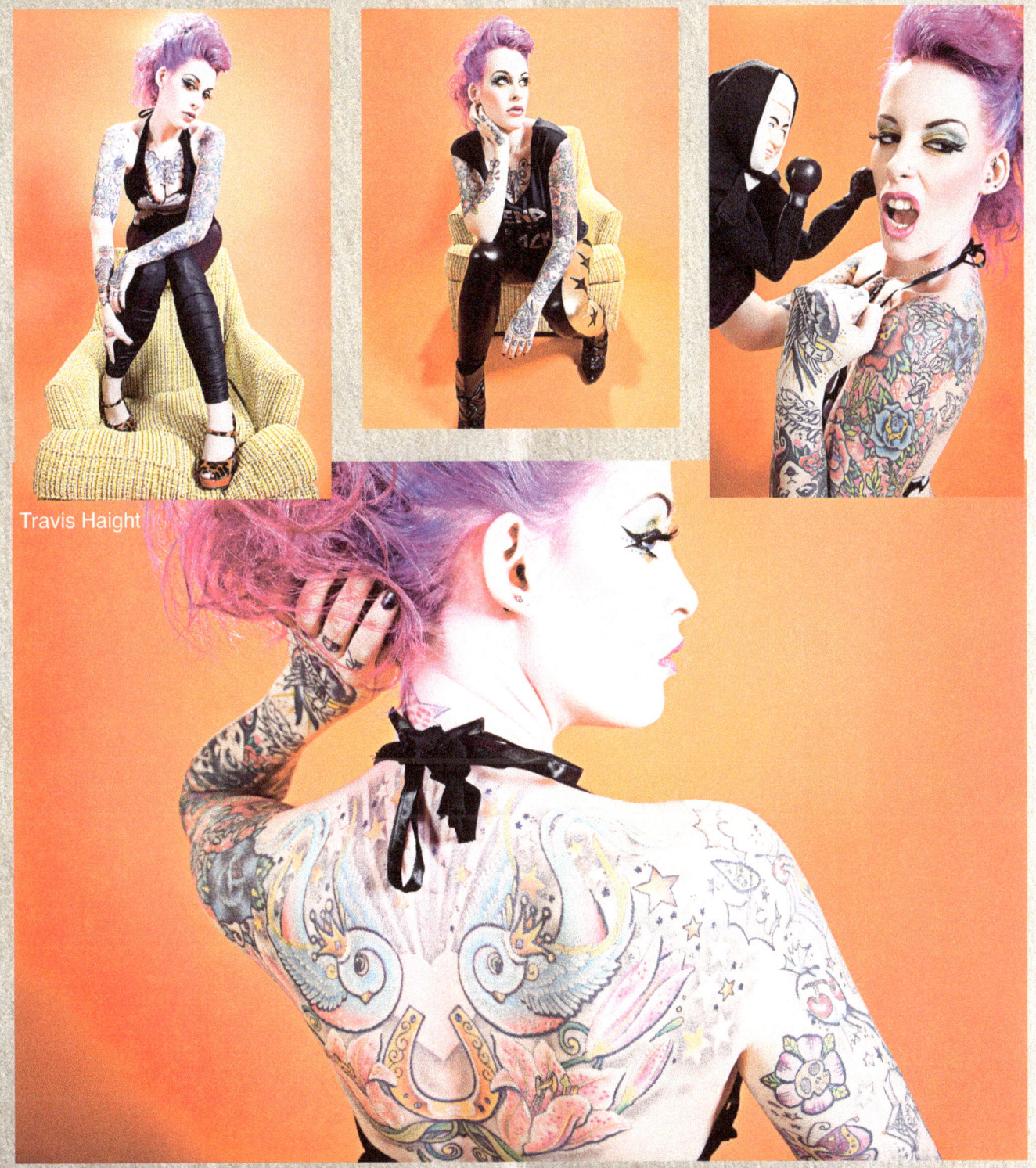

Travis Haight

Kandy

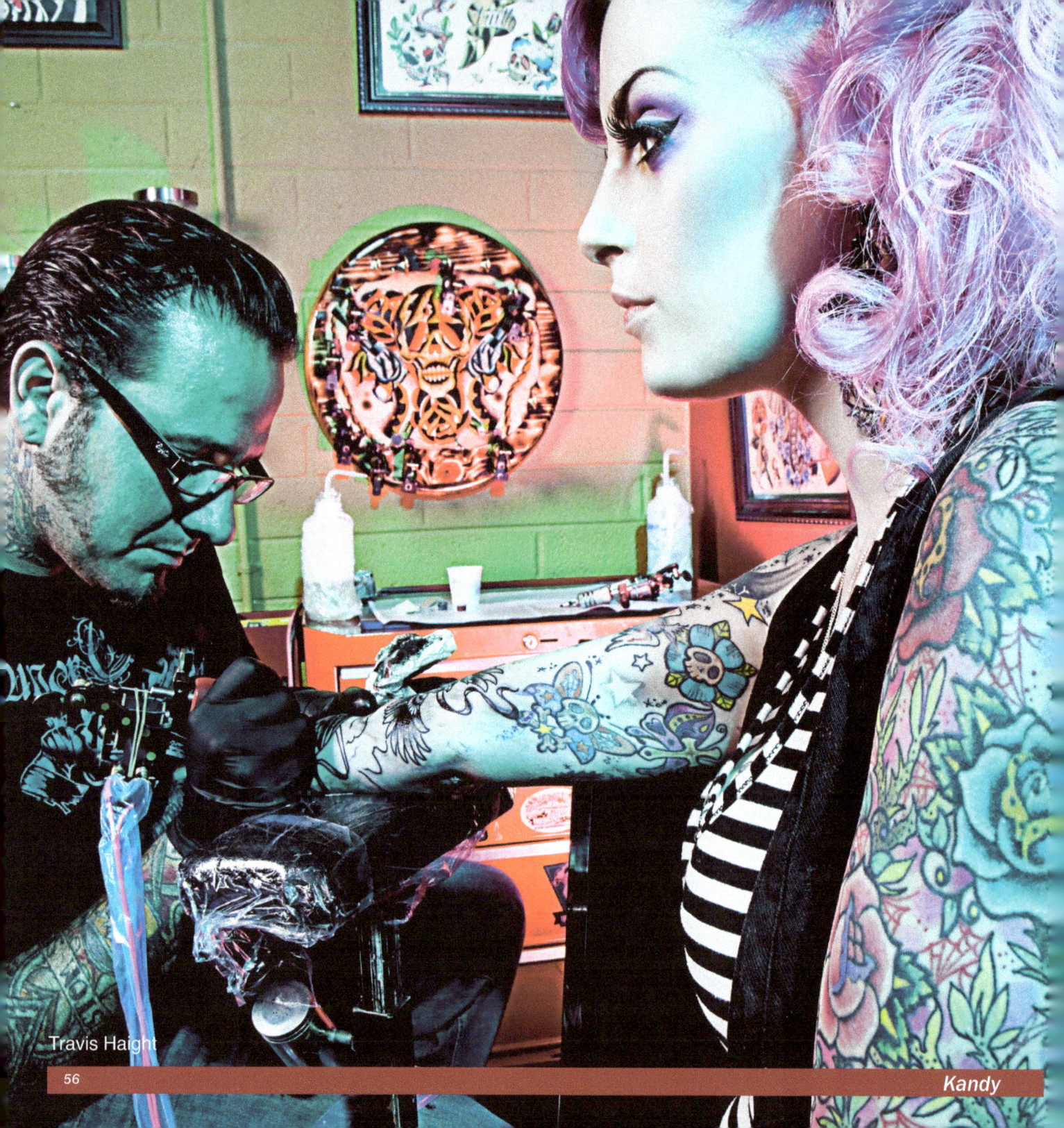

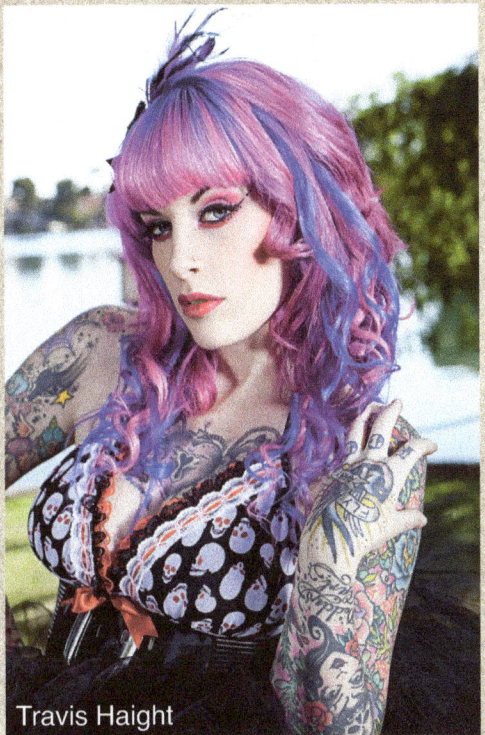
Travis Haight

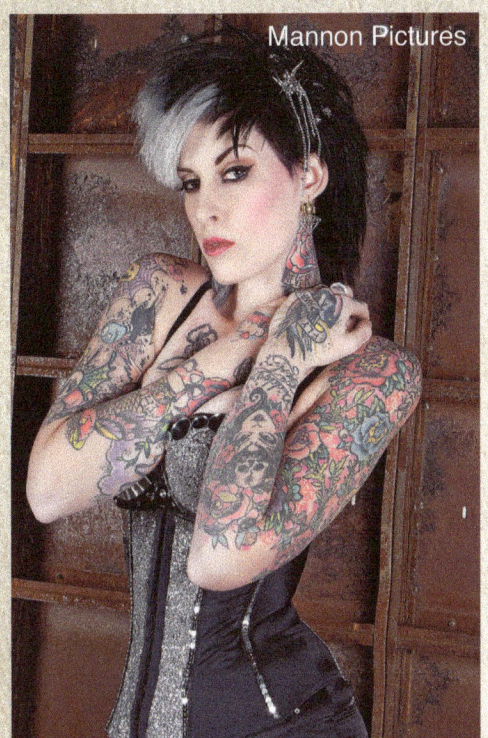
Mannon Pictures

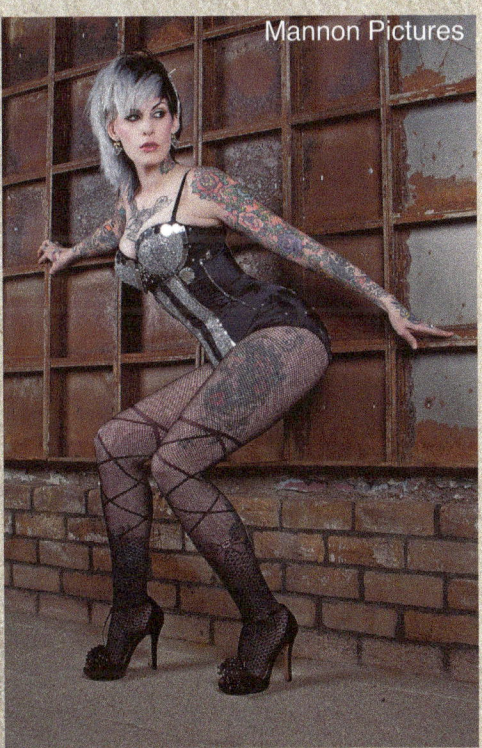
Mannon Pictures

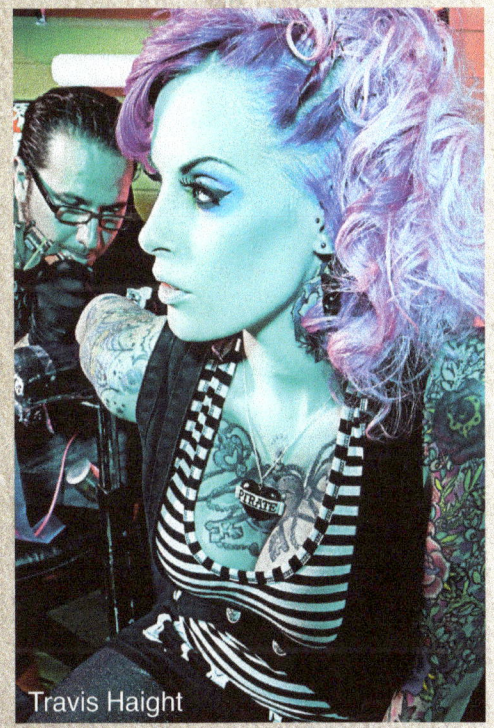
Travis Haight

Kandy

Demanda Lavette

"When I was younger every Christmas or birthday, all I wanted was a tattoo..."

I am Demanda Lavette and I live in Atlanta. In addition to modeling I work at the Graveyard Tavern in East Atlanta. I love good times with friends and a good cold PBR with a bucket of KFC. I get most of my tattoos at Liberty, by Shay Cannon; and some at Southern Star, by Chris Howell.

How long have you been a model, and what do you enjoy the most about it?

I've been in the industry for about two or three years now. I love to play dress up, and meet all the different photographers. Each one has something completely different in mind so it never gets boring.

What kind of modeling do you do? And what made you get into modeling?

I do all types of modeling. Anything from pin-up to fetish. As far as getting into modeling, I have always had people ask me about it so finally I just did it. I believe I was at a car show when I first decided to take it seriously.

Do you work with any special photographers on a regular basis?

Yeah, I actually work with Greg Truelove a good bit. I also work with Heather Dawn of Motorgrrrl Studios. I just love them both.

What is it about tattoos that appeals to you?

I just love to express myself. In a way I feel like it keeps me grounded. This is who I am and what I love.

Which is your first one? And why did you make it?

Stars on my wrists and my arms were the first tattoos. I got them because my friend and I were drawing on ourselves with sharpies one night a long time ago. I really liked the way they looked.

Among all your tattoos, which one do you prefer and why?

I prefer all of them. I don't have a favorite. Usually the most recent is my favorite at the time.

Please talk us through some of your tattoos and the reason behind them.

Wow, this might take a while. Let's see... my back was done a good while ago, it's actually my first big piece. I got it for my mommy. I got the two girls on my shoulders for me and for her. The sacred heart with Mom through it is for obvious reasons, the bottom half is the outline of a big butterfly. There are a few different things in the butterfly: The wings for freedom, the spider webs for entrapment, the roses for love, the diamond for wealth. Then I have a good bit of Sailor Jerry style pin-ups just because I love them so. Oh, and I have two little pigs on my leg with a banner that says "makin' bacon." I also have a dancing cowboy pork chop that says "put some pork on yer fork." I got both of those because they make me laugh.

Do you regret any of your tattoos?

Nope, not one. I love them all.

Do you think people treat you differently for being heavily tattooed?

No, not really. I think people either love them or hate them. But I don't think I have ever been treated differently because of the tattoos. I do live in downtown Atlanta though, so it's pretty common around here.

Of all the above-mentioned things that you've accomplished in your relatively short career what would you pick as the biggest achievements in your career?

Honestly, the fact that I have been able to make a name for myself in such a short time. I was super excited to be a part of Pinups for Pitbulls last year. That was a lot of fun and did a lot of good as well.

Is there anything else you would like to add?

"Put some Pork on yer Fork." Hahaha.

www.modelmayhem.com/DemandaLavette
www.myspace.com/demandalavette
www.facebook.com/profile.php?id=100000365552186
www.tumblr.com/tagged/demanda-lavette

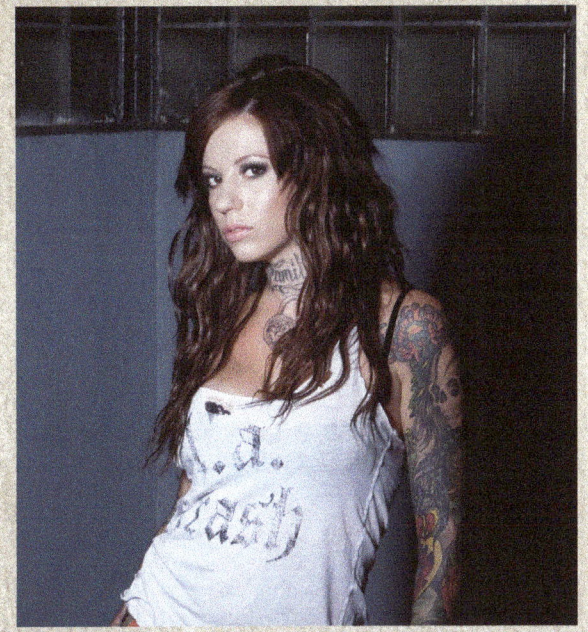
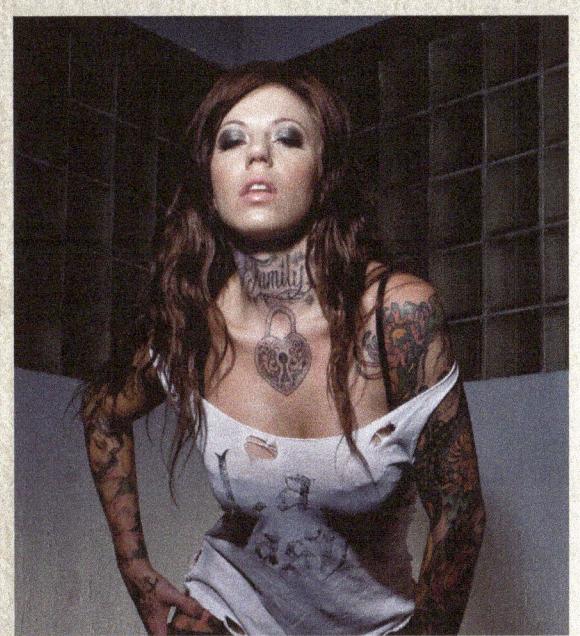

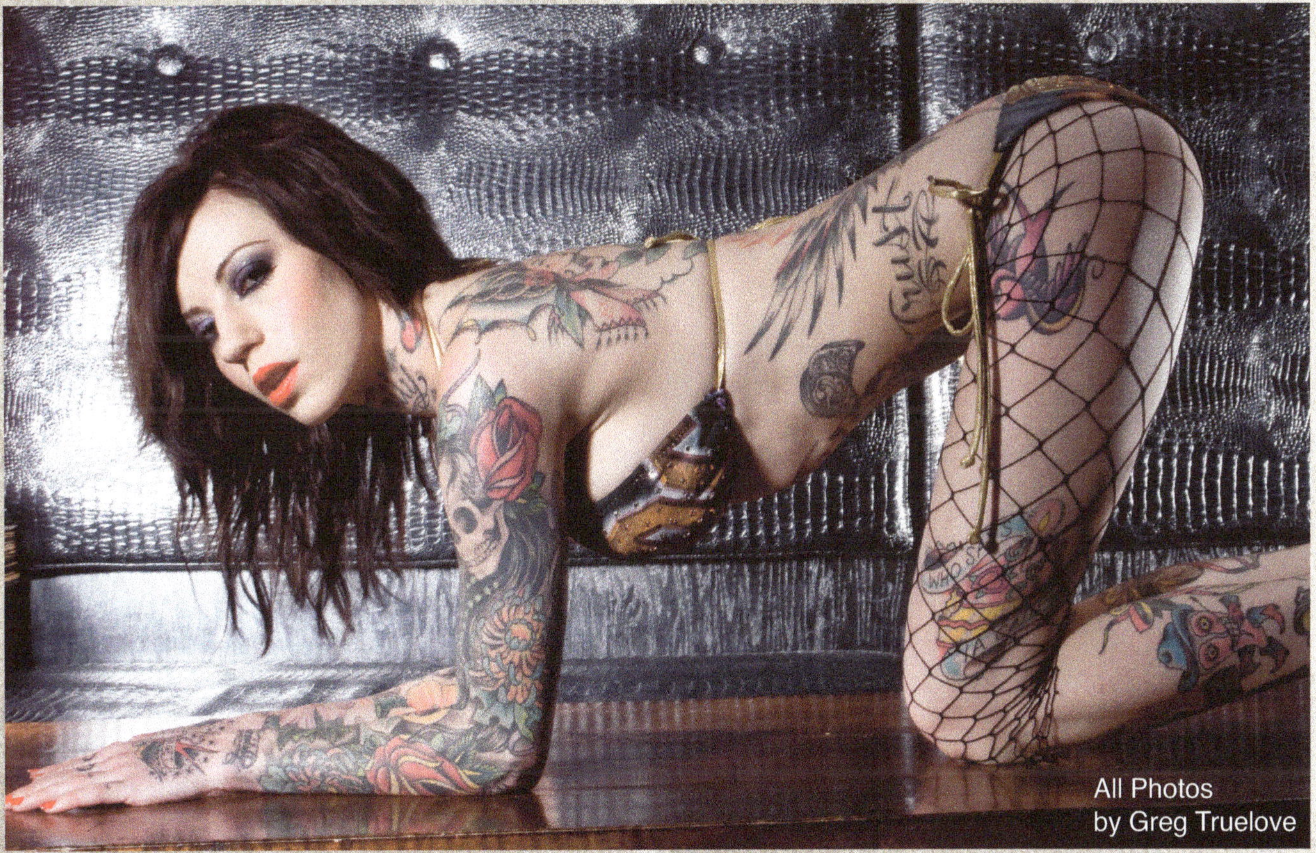

All Photos by Greg Truelove

Demanda Lavette

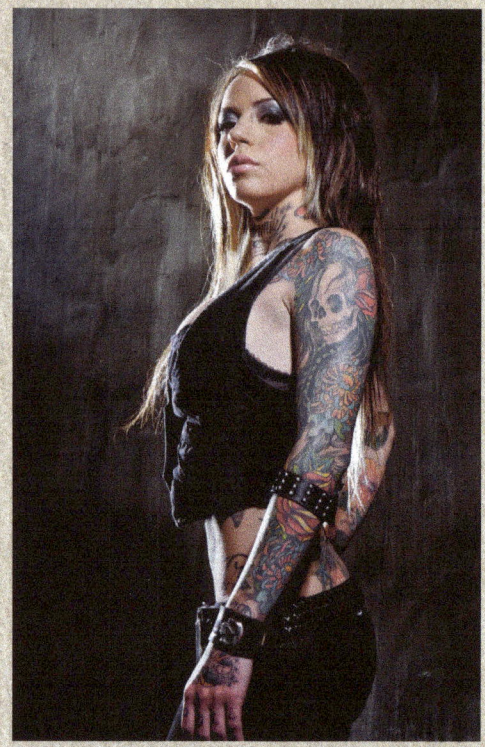
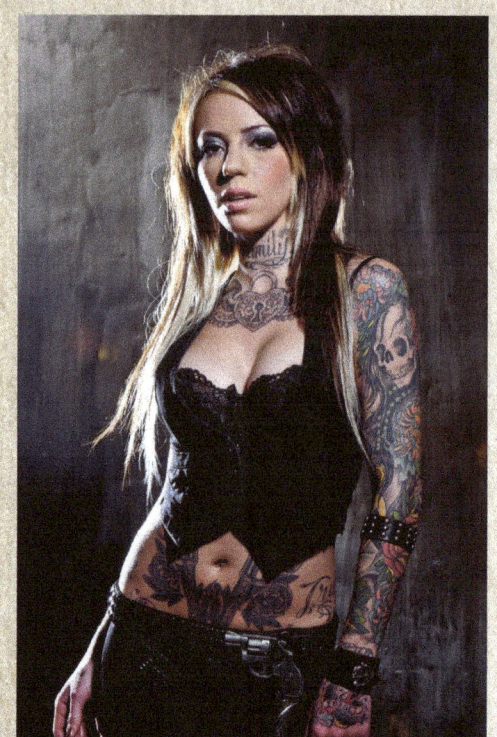
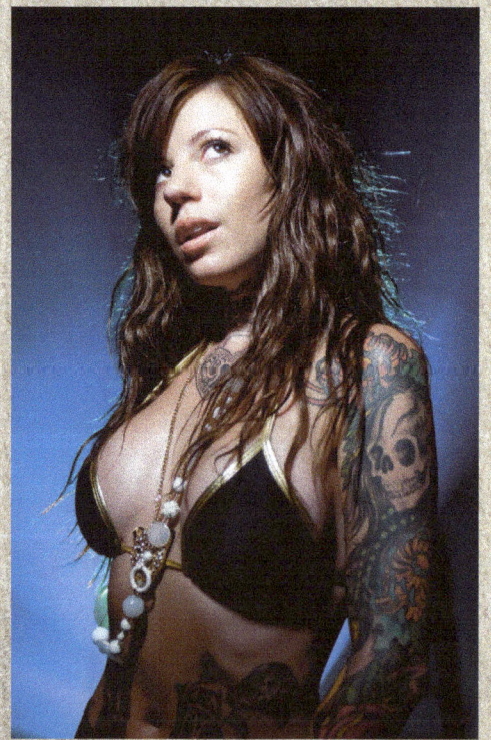
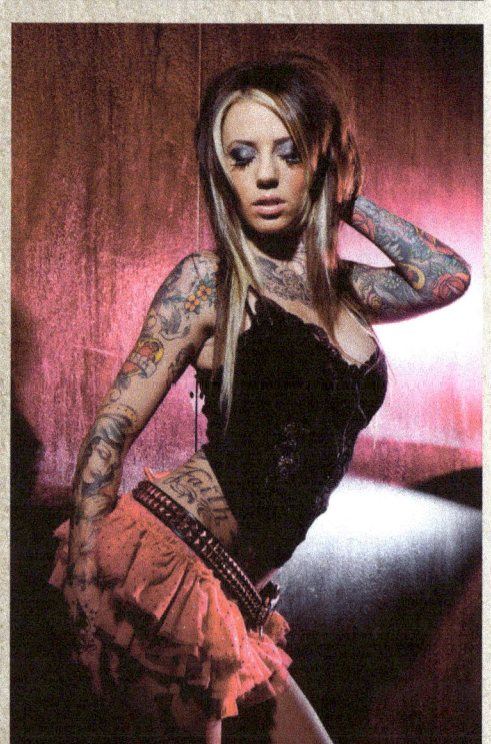

Demanda Lavette

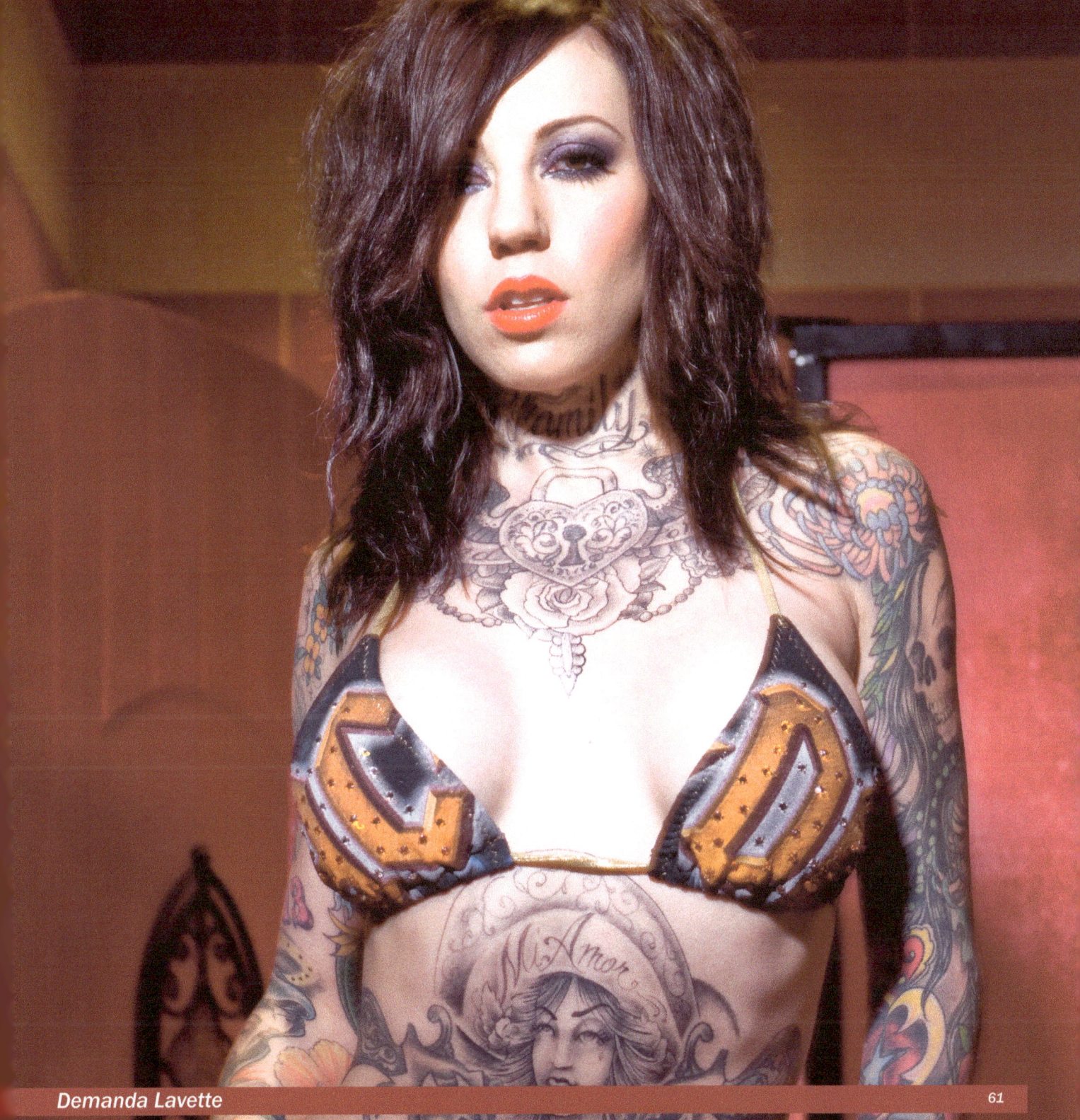
Demanda Lavette

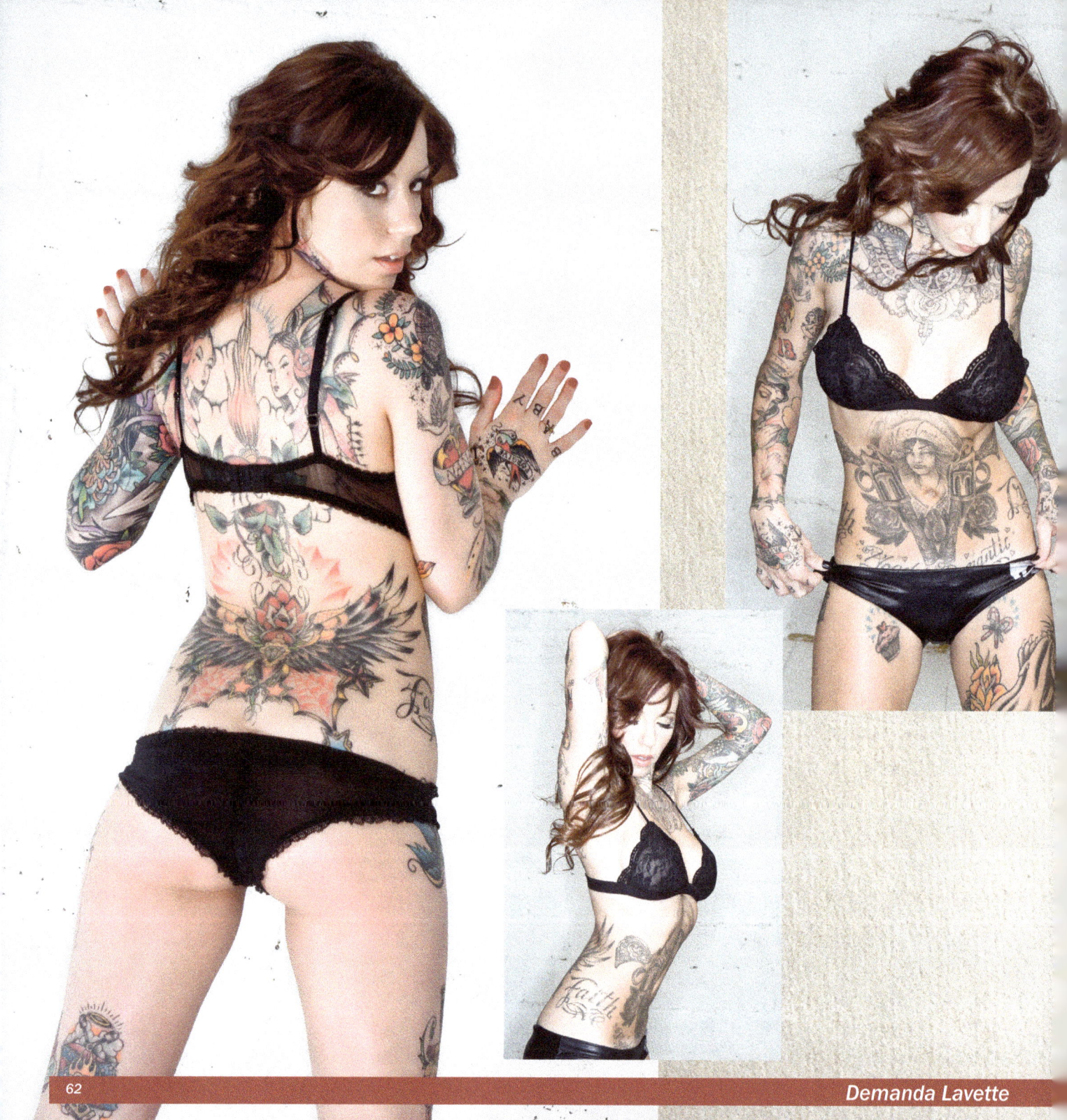

Demanda Lavette

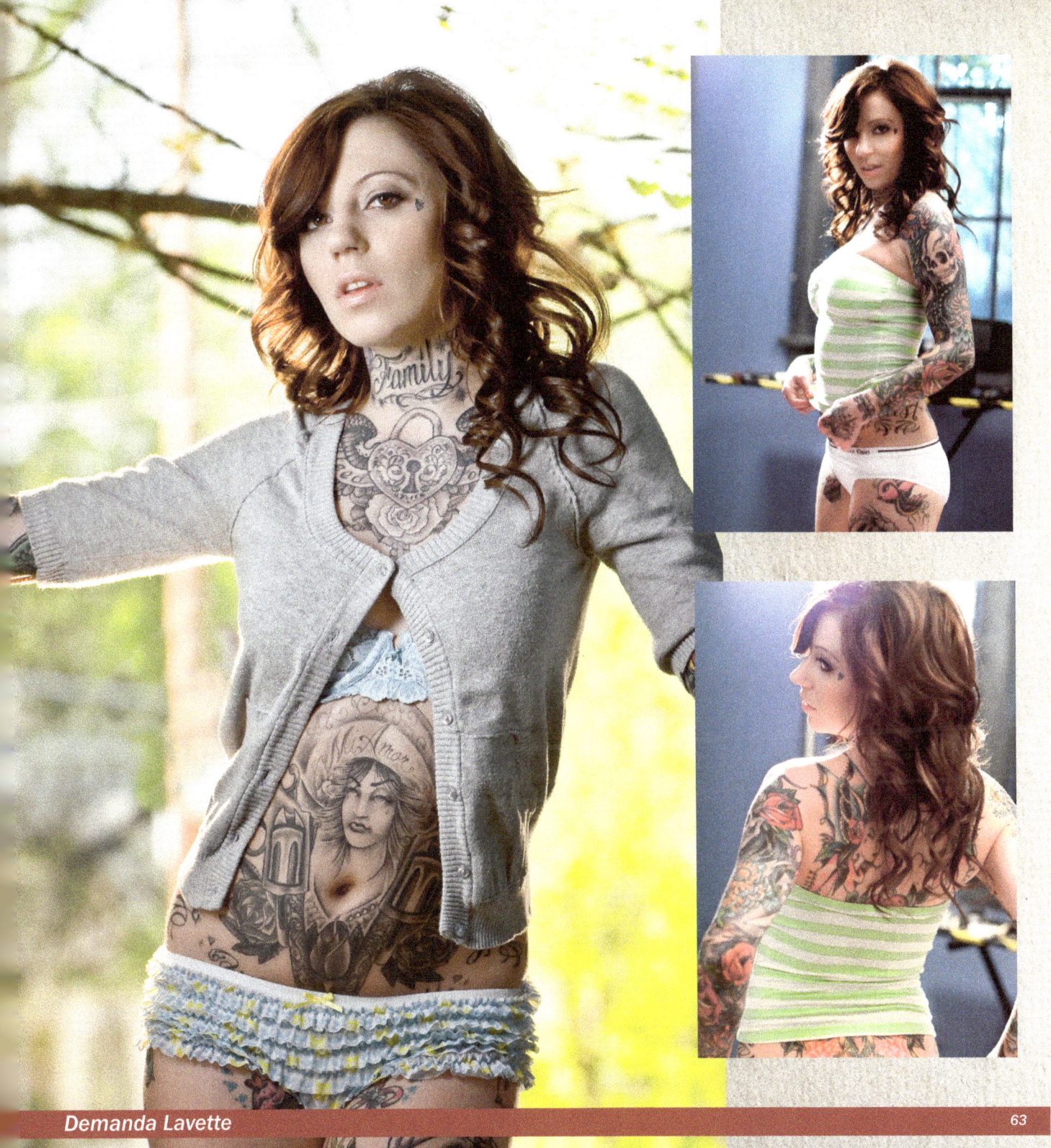

Demanda Lavette

Bernadette Macias

"My tattoos are an extension of who I am..."

My name is Bernadette Macias, I am the main host of SullenTV, a professional print model, and a national MC.

What is your definition of beauty?

Beauty is who you are inside. The presence you have and how you make others feel. I believe that beauty is strongest in those who love others, have compassion, smile a lot, and are themselves.

Have you always wanted to model? What made you say yes?

I never really thought about modeling. I wanted to be a journalist for ever and was randomly asked to model. It sort of went on a journey of it's own from there and I absolutely love it. On a side note, it's truly helped me build my self esteem and brought so many loving people into my life.

Tell us about your first photo shoot. Were you nervous?

Ohhhhh my goodness. I was so timid and nervous and wasn't sure I could do it 'cause I was so self conscious and had low self esteem. I didn't know how to pose or what to do. Thank goodness the photographer was a friend and helped me through with lots of constructive criticism.

How did your love for tattoos start?

I've always been very into art, grew up going to art galleries around the world and collecting art - which I posted all over my bedroom walls in a sort of collage. When I moved back to the States my first job dealt mainly with tattoo artists who all became my friends, since I knew no one else and had no family So here you have a girl in love with art, surrounded by tattoo artists. It was inevitable.

How old were you when you got your first tattoo?

I was 17. It's actually a funny story. I was sent to a boarding school in Thailand and hated it, so I snuck off and got tattooed thinking they'd kick me out since tattoos weren't allowed, but they didn't.

Please talk us through some of your tattoos and the reason behind them.

Hmmmm, I have my oldest daughter's name tattooed on my knuckles, which read "Anabella." I stole a Shakespeare quote, "Love all, trust few," which I put on the sides of each of my palms. I did this because this is a belief I live my life by. I have a pink ribbon tattoo to remind everyone of the fight against cancer.

What is your favorite tattoo so far, and why?

My left hand is a Nokia cell phone which reads "Dad" in the screen as if it's calling my Dad. Hey was a VP for Nokia my whole childhood and he's had to bail me out of trouble an uncountable number of times and so I put that on my hand with two roses.

How do you come up with the ideas for your pieces?

They are all views or opinions that I'm trying to get across or replicas of art pieces that I love. I have Salvador Dali and Marc Ryden tattoos.

What do your tattoos mean to you?

They are an extension of who I am.

Do you like to stick to one artist, or try a number of different ones?

Most of my tattoos are by Julius Vargas, owner of Paragon Tattoo in Moreno Valley, California. I've also been tattooed by Boog and a few others, but Julius Vargas has done all my big pieces.

Do you think people treat you differently for being heavily tattooed?

People assume that I fit the stereotypically mold of a tattooed female. People also either love my tattoos or hate them. I'm used to it though, comfortable and confident enough in who I am to not be bothered by the negative or judgmental.

bernadettemacias.com
www.facebook.com/MsBMacias
www.modelmayhem.com/msmurder
www.YouTube.com/SullenTV
itsmsmurder.tumblr.com/

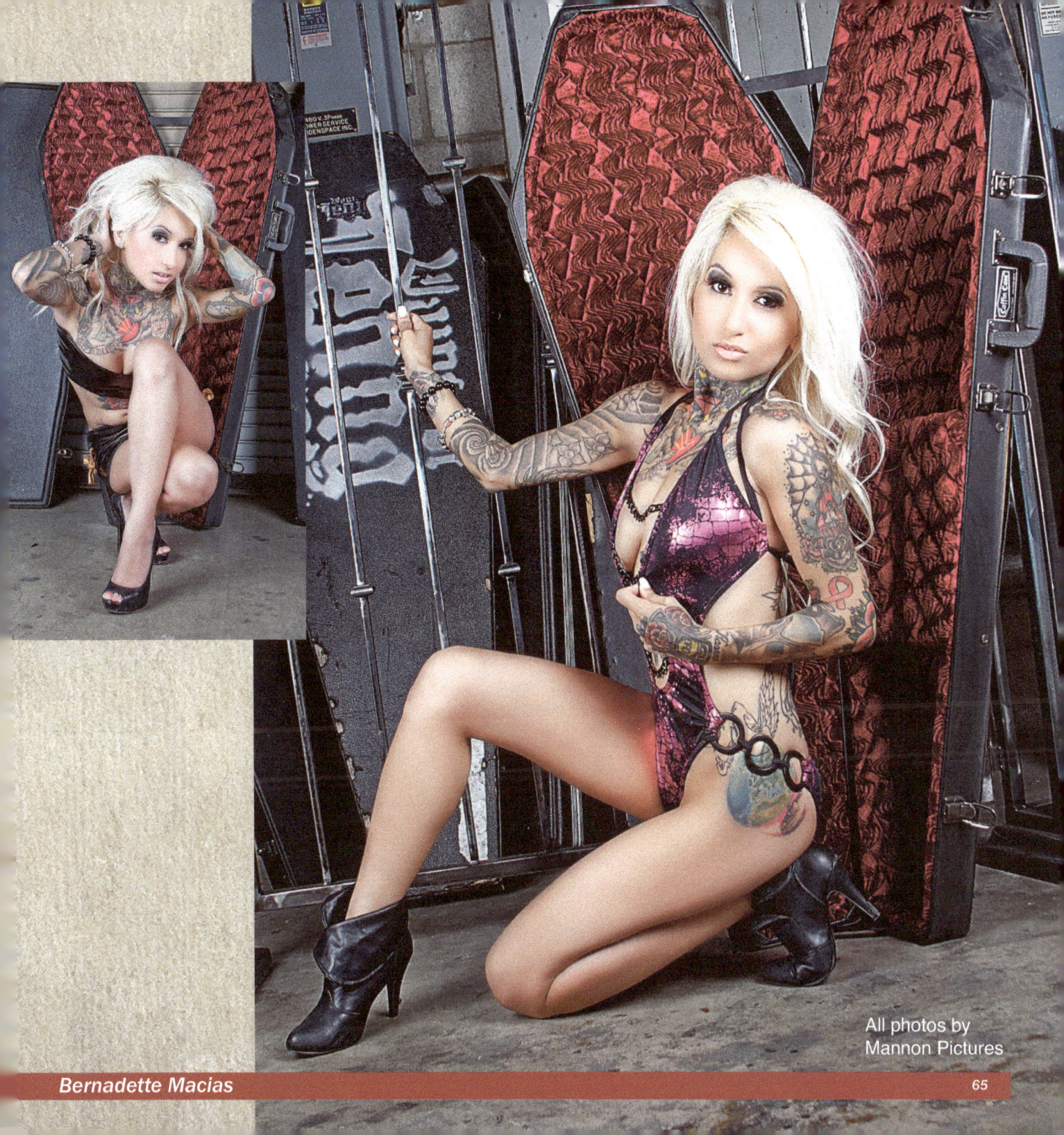

All photos by Mannon Pictures

Bernadette Macias

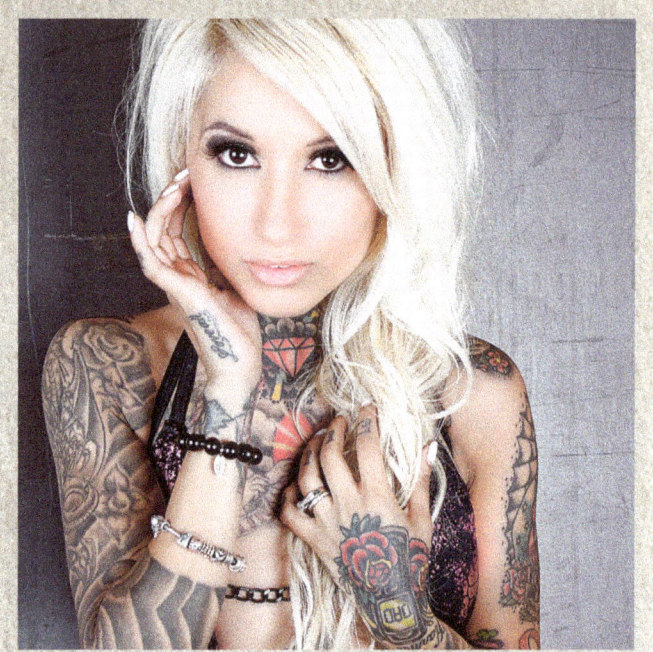
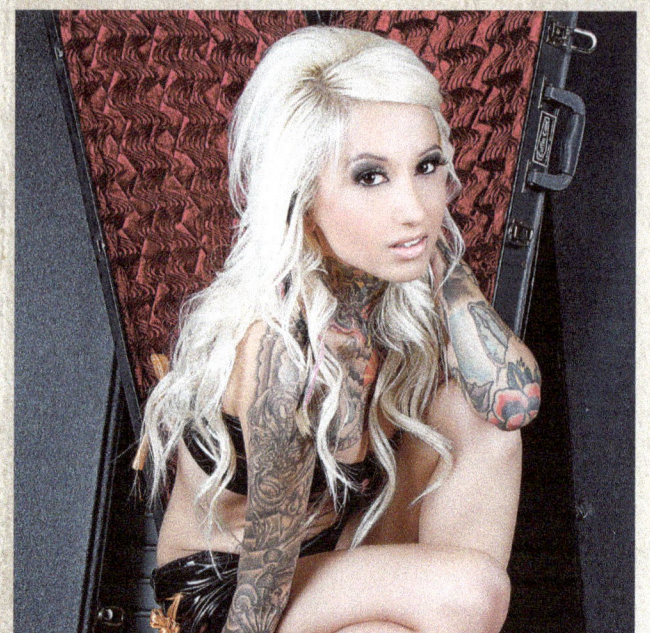

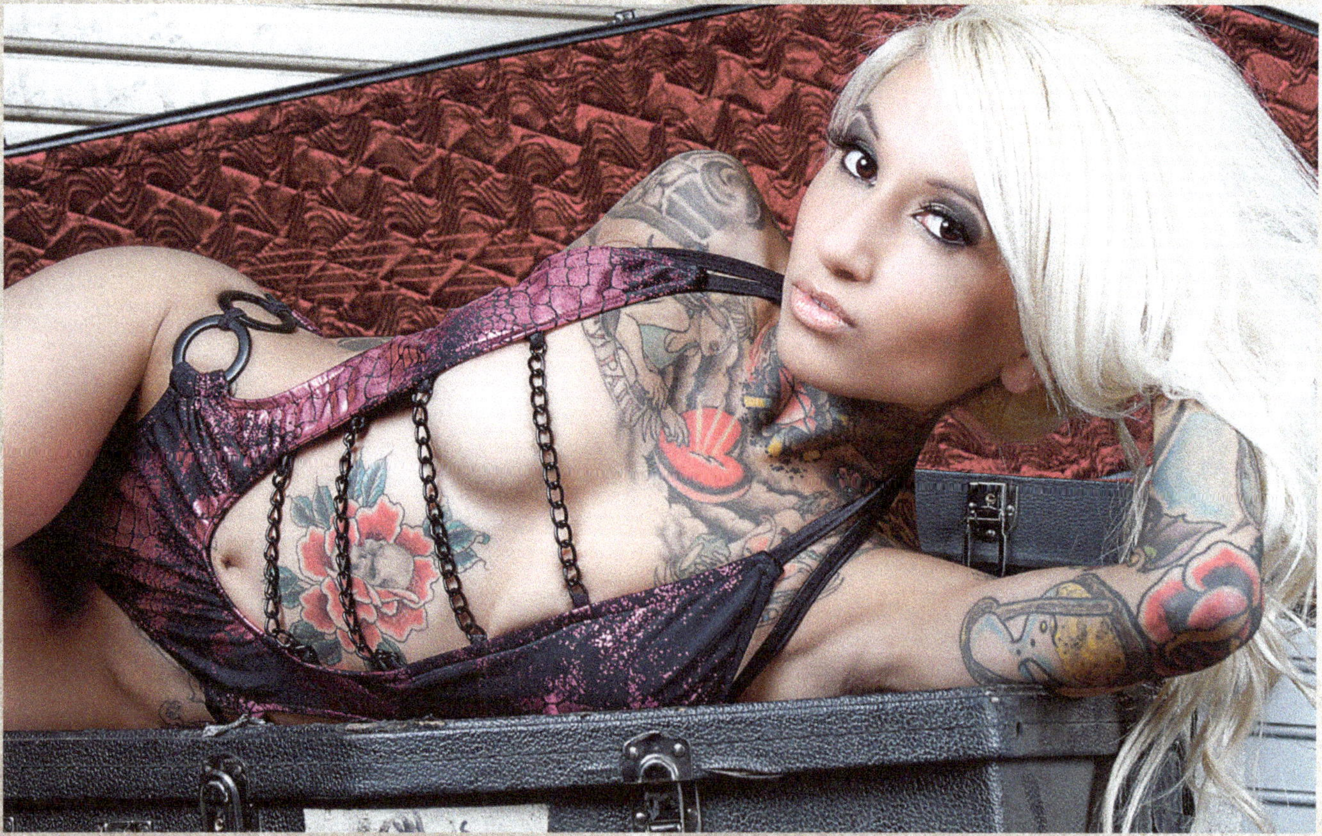

Bernadette Macias

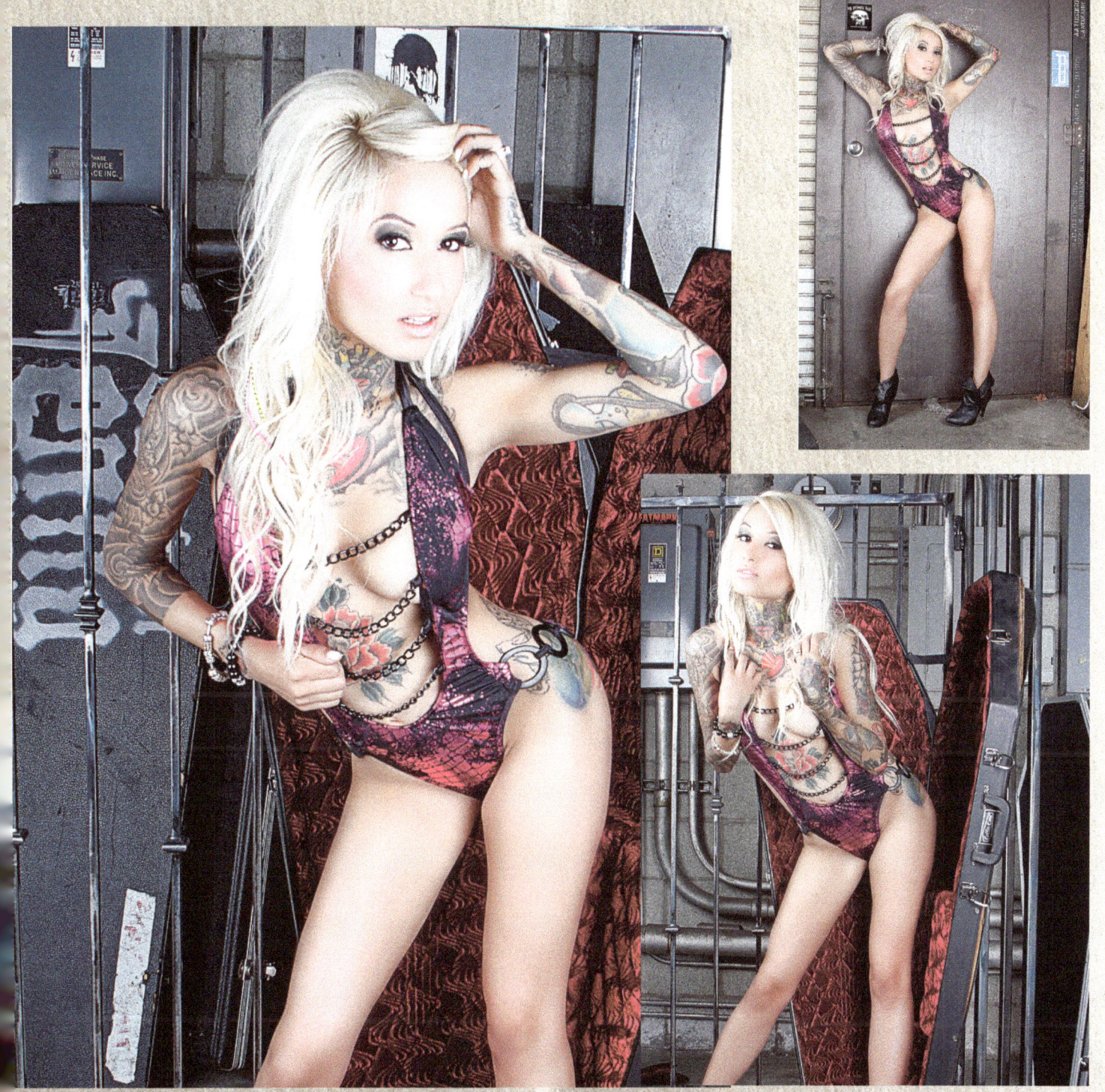

Bernadette Macias

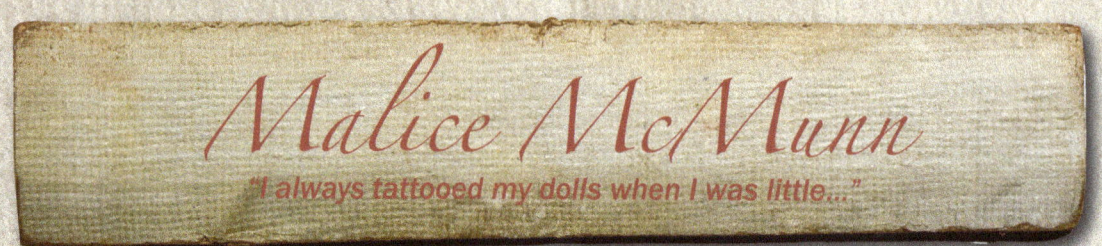

Malice McMunn
"I always tattooed my dolls when I was little..."

I am Malice McMunn, I dance, act, and model.

You have a great body, how do you stay healthy?

I was really not a healthy person until about 10 years ago. I was like a human dumpster; junk food, drugs/alcohol, I looked pretty bad and saw that I needed improvement so I stopped drinking/drugging and eating junk food or any meat.

What is your definition of beauty?

Beauty is an opinion thing, not everybody will agree. So when people say you are beautiful never let it get to your head because what may be beautiful to some is ugly or scary to others. I'm fine with not everybody liking me. If they did I'd be doing something wrong.

Have you always wanted to model? What made you say yes?

I started by allowing friends to photograph me for art projects and to help promote clubs where I worked, artists who worked on me, I just support art.

Any words of advice for a young lady who aspires to be a model?

My only advice to aspiring models is to check with other models before you work with anybody unknown and really double check with the ones that come from craigslist or Model Mayhem. There are a lot of scammers and perverts out there.

How did your love for tattoos start?

I always tattooed all my dolls when I was little. I didn't plan anything, you should see the walls in my room, there's barely a plain spot wherever there's room for a piece of art. My van is covered in graffiti and stickers, I just love to decorate everything.

How old were you when you got your first tattoo?

I never had friends who were into tattoos or had money to get any till my late 20s. I had a few stick and poke tattoos when I was 16 but no real ones till I was 21.

Which tattoo style do you like best? And how would you describe the style of your tattoos?

I love black and grey work and cholo, portrait, or prison style tattoos. I try to get those because they are bad ass. Almost all my tattoos deal with death, religion, music, and some of them are just funny.

What is your favorite tattoo so far, and why?

I can't pick a favorite tattoo, but I can pick my favorite artist, it's my sister Christy Fish. She and another artist, Pedro Dorsey at her shop Optic Nerve Arts in Portland, Oregon, have taken up the most space and done some of the favorite tattoos on my body.

How do you come up with the ideas for your pieces?

The ideas just come from my interests and life experience. I was force fed religion, lived on the streets for many years, I've died a few times and went to prison (another reason to stop doing drugs), I watch a lot of horror films I listen to punk and metal; and love animals and dark art.

Do you like to stick to one artist, or try a number of different ones?

I have had many different artists work on me because I like so many different artists' take on the styles. Each artist has their own interpretation, some artists are also better at certain things.

Do you think people treat you differently for being heavily tattooed?

I do have a hard time finding jobs with my tattoos. It might have more to do with the content of the tattoos, mine are not pretty flowers and butterflies. They are upside down crosses, chopped up nuns, Jesus wearing black metal face paint, spiders, skulls, demons, naked ladies covered in blood. I can't work just anywhere with tattoos like that.

www.palaceofmalice.com
http://twitter.com/#!/Malice666Mcmunn
www.facebook.com/pages/Malicexpdx/105763076143610
www.modelmayhem.com/2015099
www.tumblr.com/tagged/malice-mcmunn

Alice McMunn

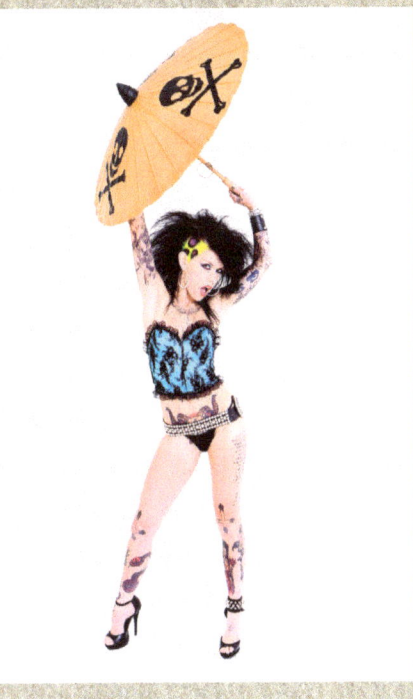
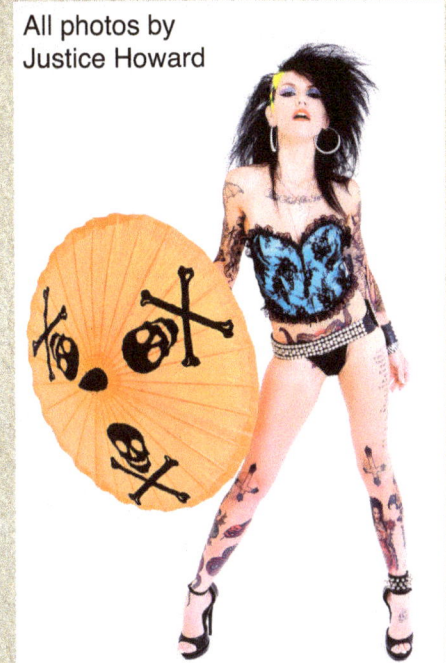
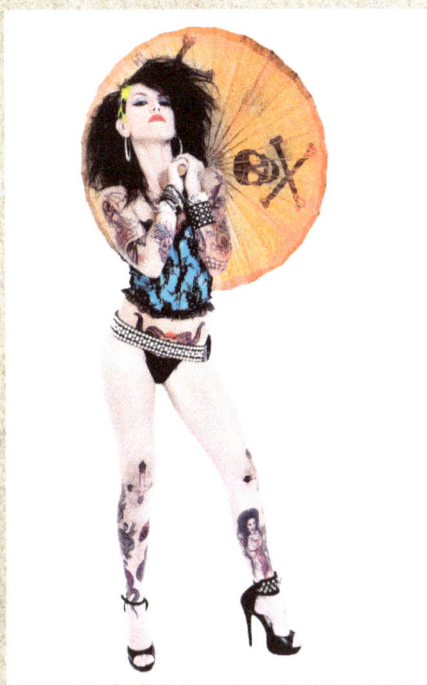
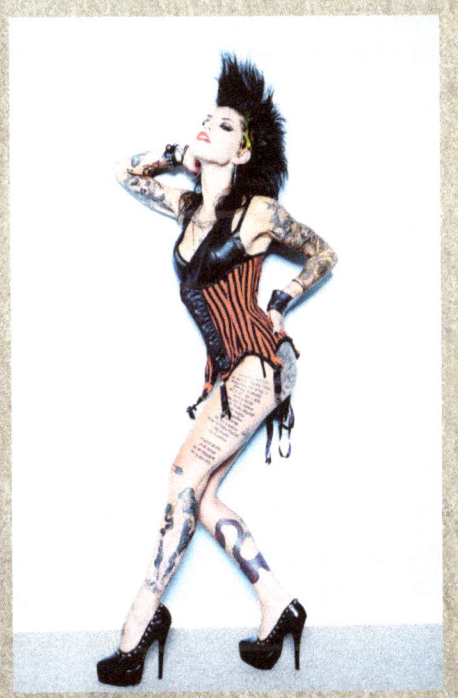
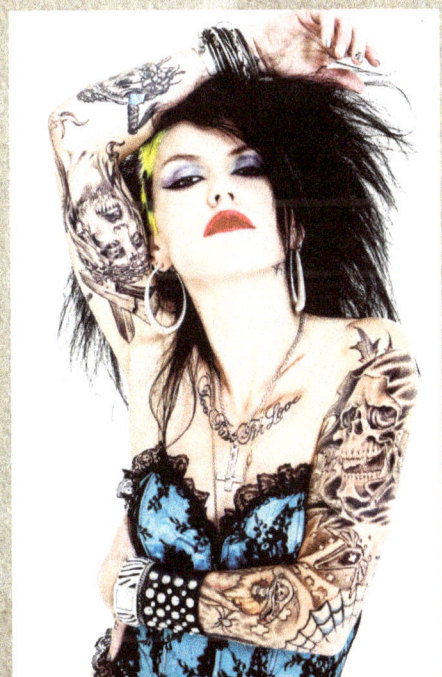
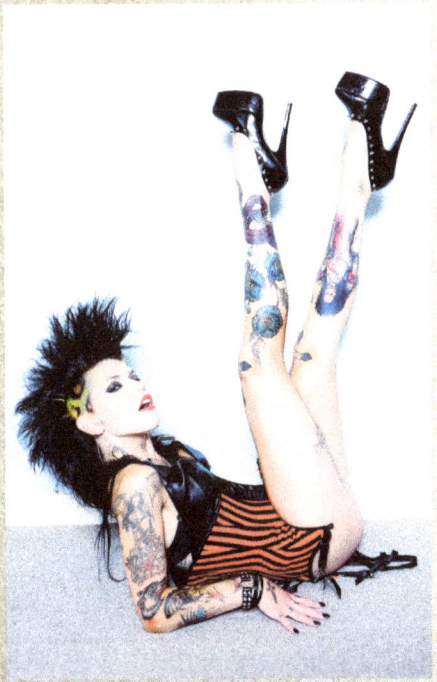

All photos by Justice Howard

Alice McMunn

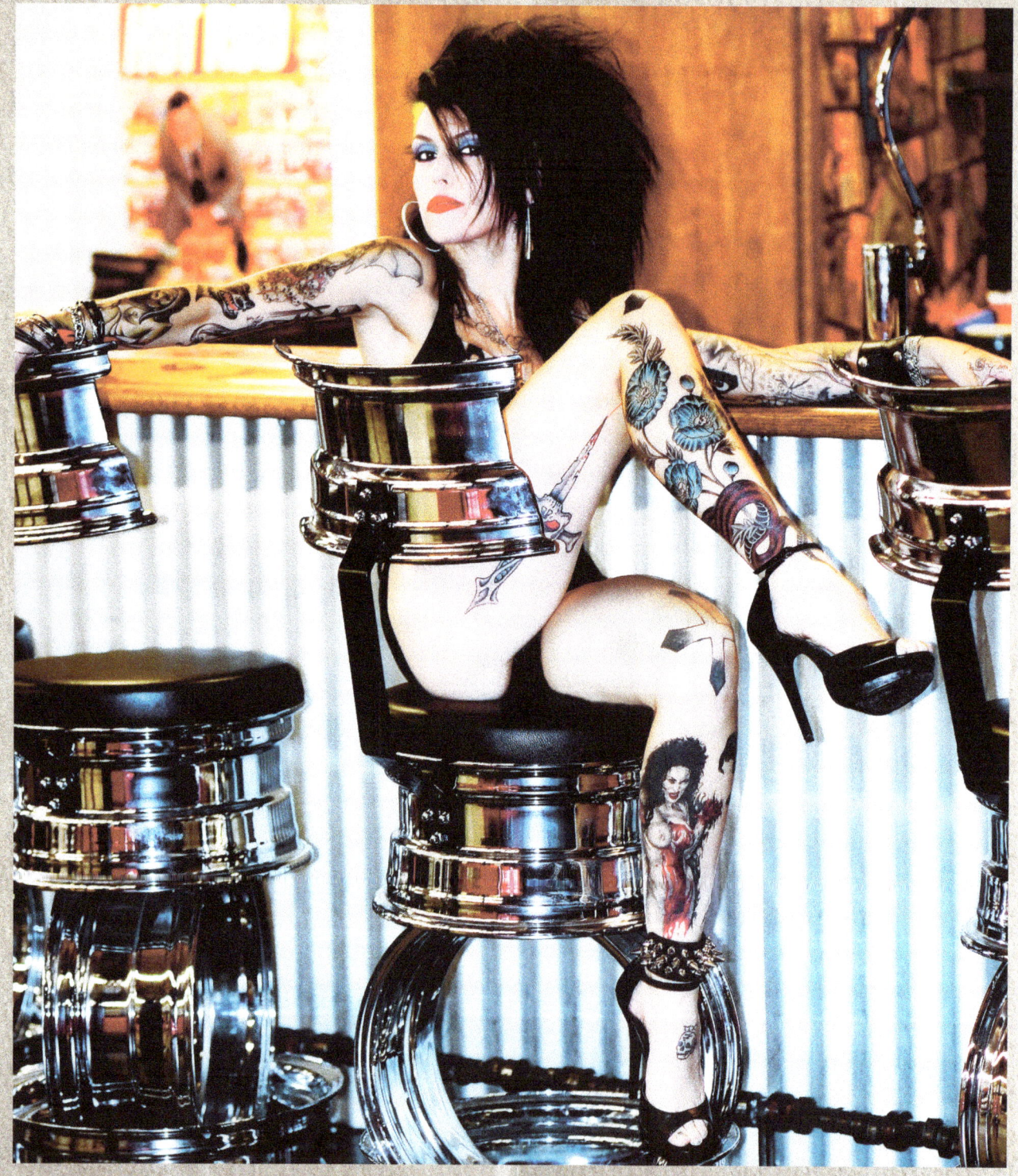

Alice McMunn

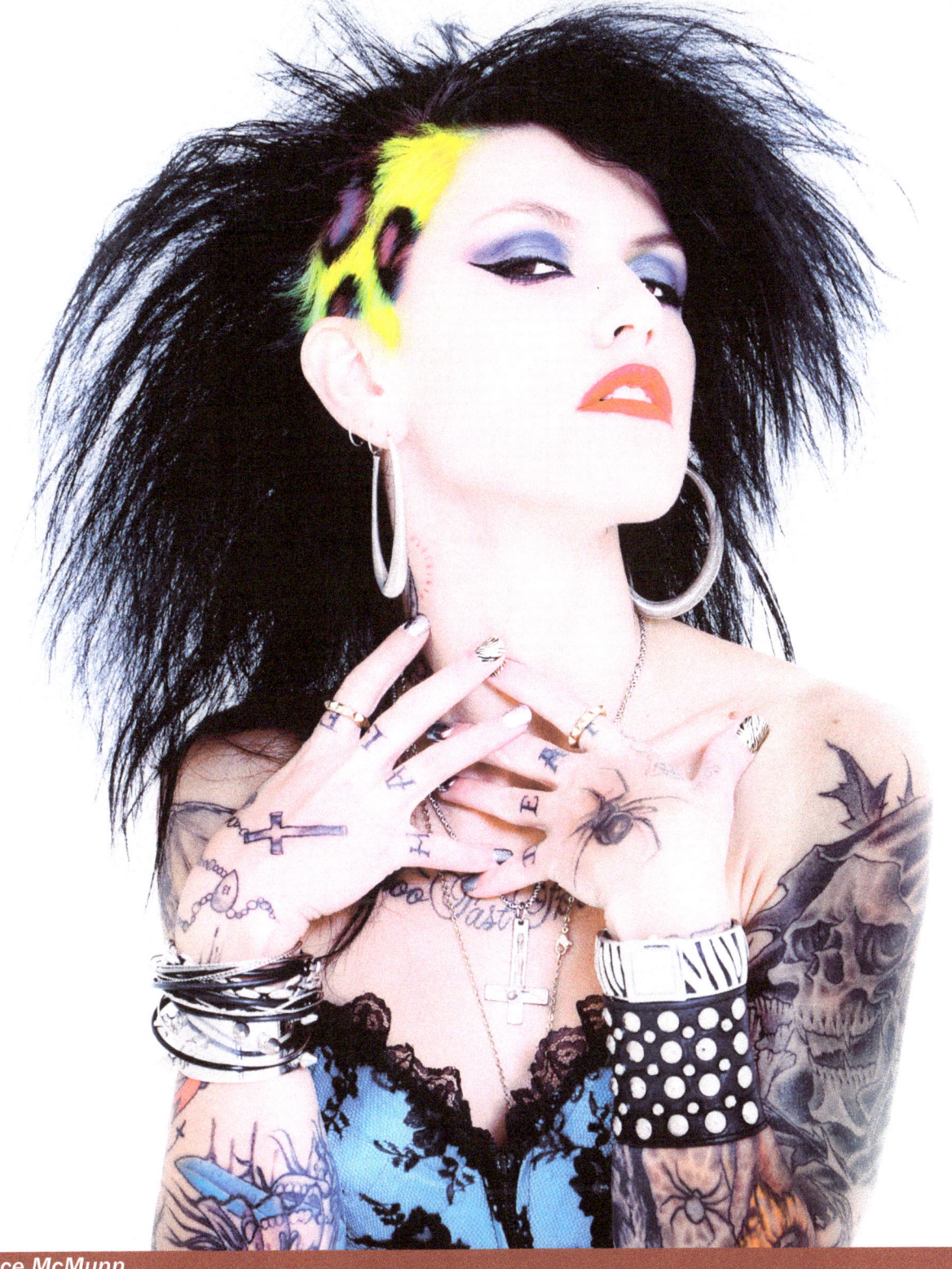

Alice McMunn

Heather Moss

"I have had only one tattoo artist: my husband Bobby Moss..."

I am Heather Moss, wife to a wonderful man, Bobby Moss. I have a beautiful step-daughter, and my husband and I have a two year old son of our own. Together we own a tattoo shop called Timeless Art. I go to school full time to pursue my other dream of cosmetology.

Have you always wanted to be a model? What made you get into modeling?

I honestly never even thought about modeling until recently. I began modeling in January of 2011. I own a tattoo shop with my husband so I am constantly surrounded by tattoo models and women in the industry. One day I thought, "I can do that." So I made a lot of mistakes and learned a lot of lessons, but I was lucky to find some amazing people in the industry and began working with the best of the best. My great friend and mentor Amber Viktoria and Levi Mannon of Mannon Pictures, along with my husband Bobby Moss, have been such an amazing support system for me.

You have your own tattoo studio called Timeless Art Tattoo and you're a tattoo artist too. Could you tell us about your shop and your art, please?

I am not a tattoo artist, which gets confusing to a lot of people, I am a piercer but that has kind of taken a back seat to modeling and school. I pierce mostly at tattoo conventions across the US. Our shop and crew do about 10 conventions a year. Our shop is an all-custom shop, Bobby and I have been in business for almost five years. We have a very solid crew: Boomer, Johnny Scillieri, Adam Harris and Troy Jones have been such an amazing team to work with. We have such a great following and reputation, it has really been a blessing for us. We are branching out into a clothing line and merchandise. Hopefully that will begin soon.

When did your interest in tattoos begin? And how long was it from then until you got your first one?

I always wanted a tattoo for as long as I can remember. I got my first one when I was 18 by a different artist, but when I met my husband a couple years later he completely redid it and made it an absolutely unforgettable piece. It was stars going up my ribs. He changed it all to black and grey, added the swirls, background shading and then we added 10 dermal anchors to finish the piece. It is the one piece I have that gets the most attention.

Talk us through some of your tattoos and the reason behind them.

My right sleeve is all about my marriage and my family. It says Timeless Love for our shop and for our relationship. There is a clock with numbers falling off of it that has our wedding date hidden in the numbers. My son's name is on the inside of my arm and my daughter's name on the lower outside. On the inside of my forearm is a cracked hour glass. It symbolizes the idea that it doesn't matter what you do with your time, its going to keep spilling out, so cherish each moment. My left sleeve says "'til death," its a sleeve that I love and is inspired by an artist by the name of Johnny Quintana. I also have a full back piece that I have used to collaborate a lot of designs that my husband and I came up and as a tie-in with my sleeves.

Which areas have been the most painful to tattoo? And where would you never get a tattoo?

My back! It hurts a lot which is weird because I thought it would hurt the least. I will never get a tattoo on my face. And I am really debating on my legs too. I love my legs so I am probably not going to do those either. Which means I am almost out of room.

www.heathermossmodeling.com
www.facebook.com/HeatherMoss313
www.glendaletattooshops.com
www.h2oceanmodels.com/
<http://www.h2oceanmodels.com/> heather/

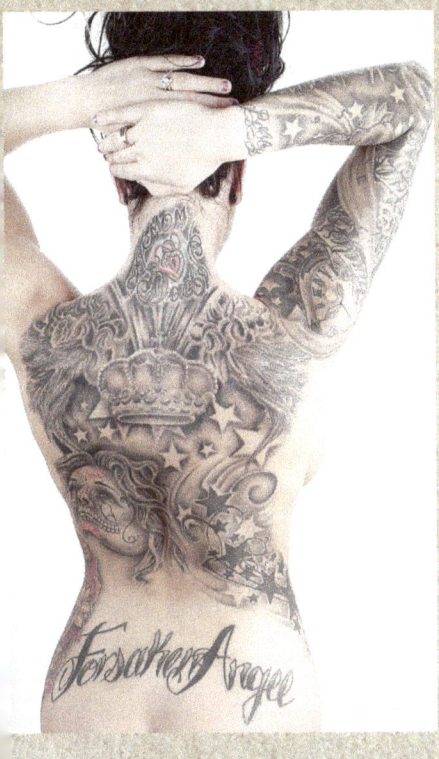
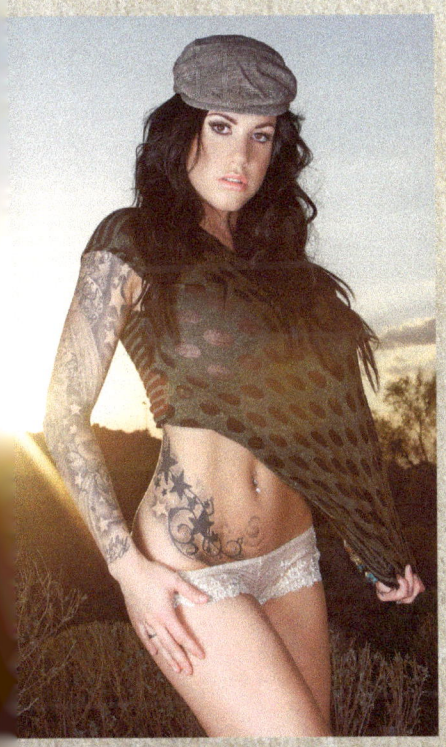

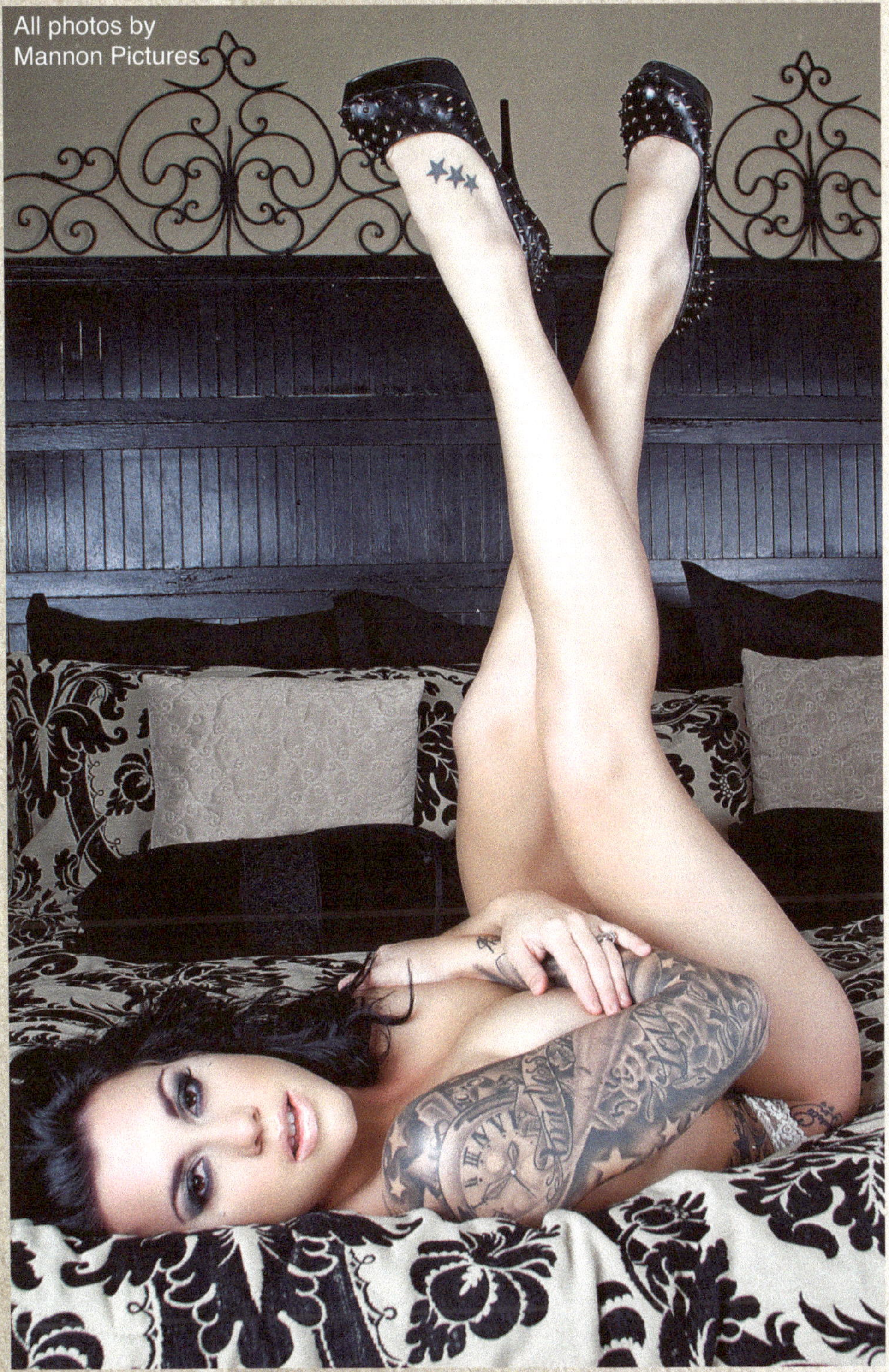

All photos by Mannon Pictures

Heather Moss

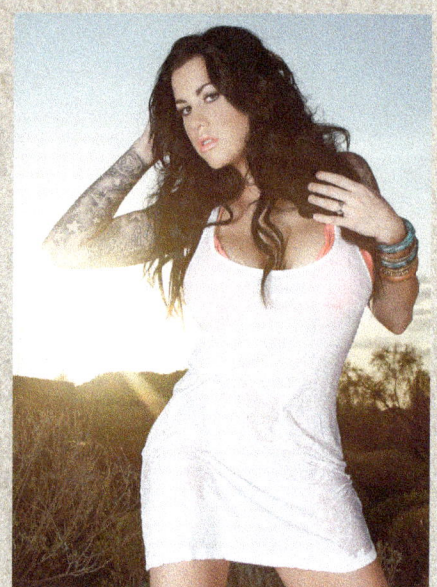
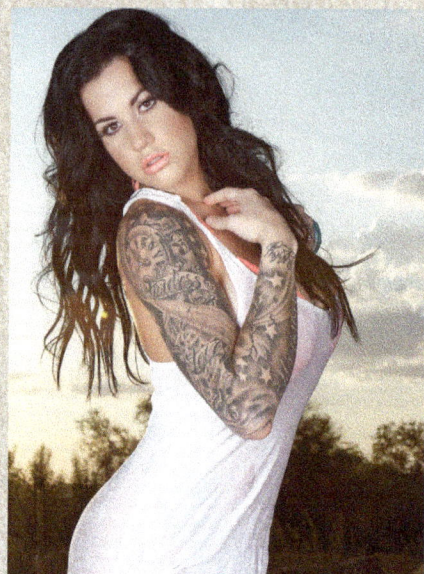
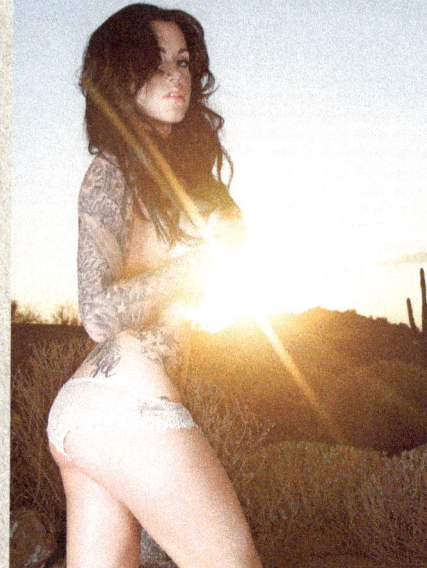

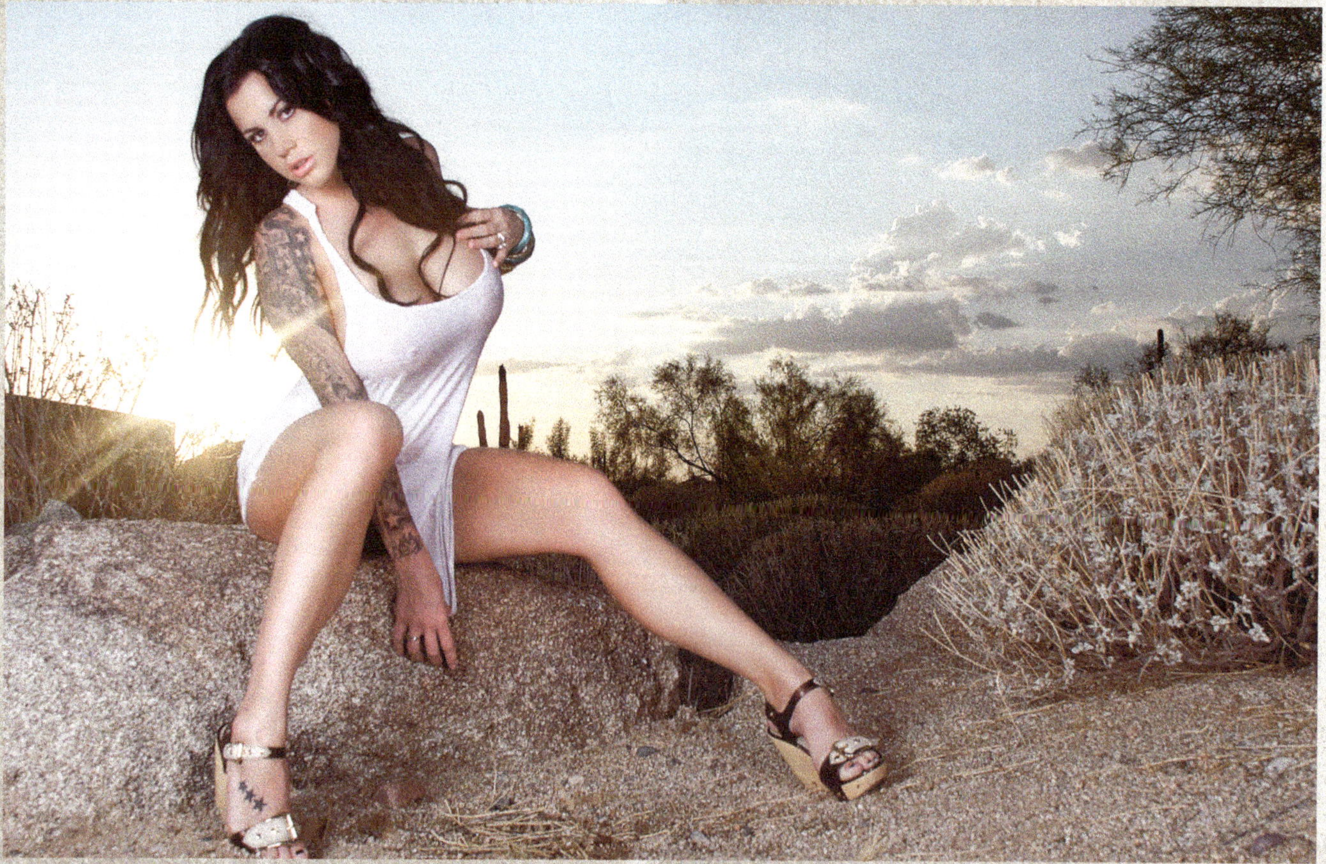

Heather Moss

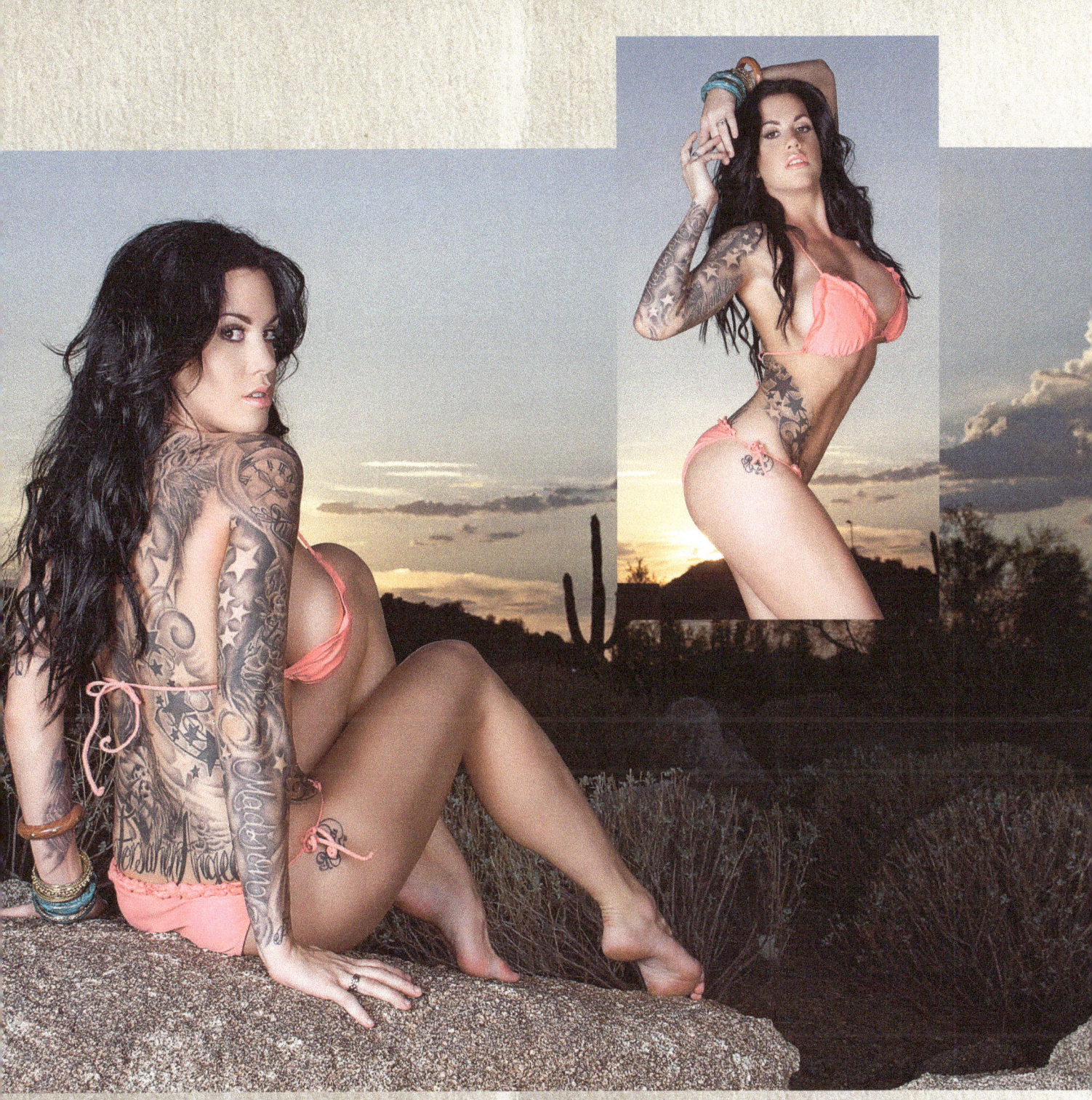

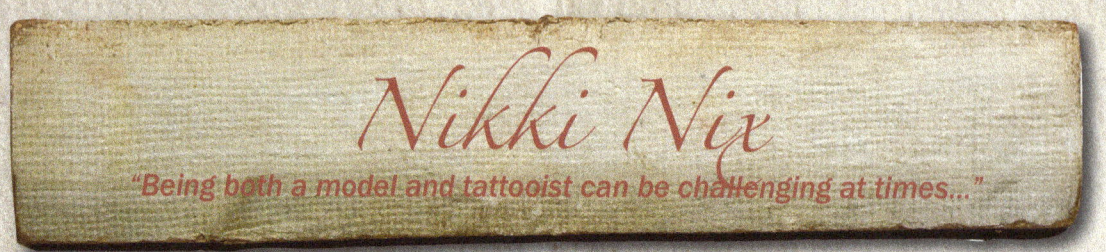

Nikki Nix
"Being both a model and tattooist can be challenging at times..."

I am Niki Nix, full time tattoo artist, part-time model and burlesque dancer. I have lived in Canada all my life, mostly in Calgary were I grew up, went to school and worked as a dental assistant (Yawn!). I had no clue really what I wanted to do for the rest of my life, but sticking my fingers in someone else's mouth was not part of it, and like a zombie I mindlessly did it for over eight years, until a tattooer friend of mine saw my drawings and convinced me that was the direction I should follow.

How did you get your start in modeling?

It started as another creative outlet. I did it for fun at first, I like to play dress-up, feel sexy, be girly and feel glamorous. I think I just fell into it and ended up being good at it. I still love modeling to this day.

How long have you been a pin-up model, and what do you enjoy the most about it?

I have been modeling for quite some time, but alt/pin-up modeling for the past seven years, I used to do mostly commercial modeling until my collection of tattoos and piercing got too big. It's so great also because having curves (breasts and hips) is so celebrated, and you can look however you want. I love lingerie, corsets and latex, that's really sexy!

When did your interest in tattoos begin? And how long was it from then until you got your first one?

Hmmm... probably when I was about 13 and I realized that drawing on myself with a marker was too much work. My parents are real hard asses, and would not allow me to get a tattoo, so on the day of my 18th birthday I got a friend to secretly drive me to a tattoo studio, Smilin Buddha Tattoo here in Calgary, to get one. I hid it for months, haha.

What do your tattoos mean to you? Are they symbolic or do you just dig the art?

At first I just wanted whatever. Now I am much more into planning and putting meaning into each one. They represent periods in my life that I want to bookmark, and are representative of what I am into and want others to see. But of course having rad art on my body is always cool.

My butterfly-tiger-face- "tramp stamp," I drew it up, thought it was original, but it's no secret it's been done before, so I found out later. Haha.

Among all your tattoos, which one do you prefer and why?

Another difficult one to choose from... they are all my favorites, probably cause they are all so well done and awesome. But I will base the answer to this question by the "Niki Nix Pain Rictor Scale." My stomach, which I just had done, hurt like a son-of-a-gun. It was done by tattooist Trevor Varem of Enso Tattoo.

You're a tattoo artist too. What made you want to become a tattoo artist?

I was sick and tired of working a 9-5 job, I felt very unfulfilled. I wanted to do something I would enjoy for the rest of my life. Like I said, a friend suggested I pursue tattooing since I have always had a talent in art so I did. It was really difficult getting my foot in the door, but I worked hard to show I was serious. Now I get to do what I love and that is draw and be with people.

Which tattoo style do you like best?

Neo traditional is awesome, I love the bold blending of colors and being able to mix different ideas or concepts to make a rad, punchy looking tattoo that stands out. I also really enjoy pin-ups.

http://nikinix.com/
www.facebook.com/#!/the.Niki.Nix.Army
www.modelmayhem.com/330354

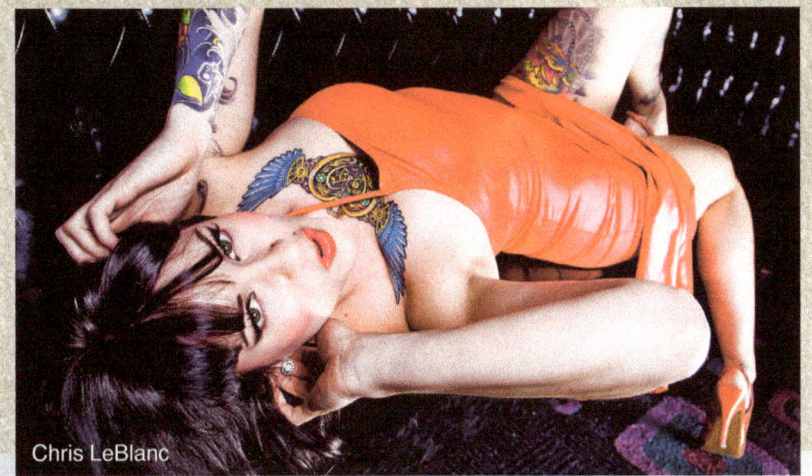
Chris LeBlanc

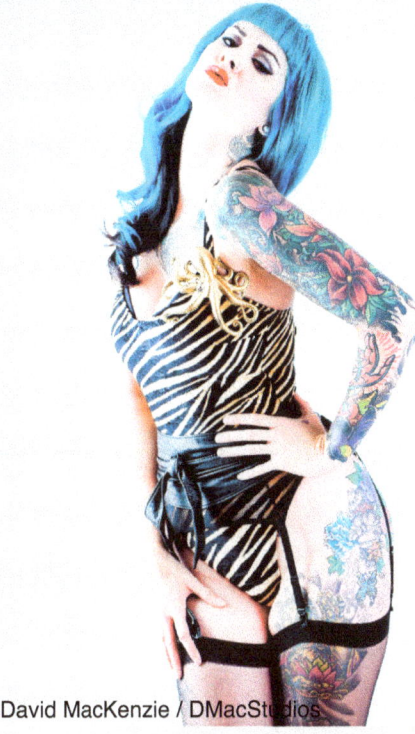
David MacKenzie / DMacStudios

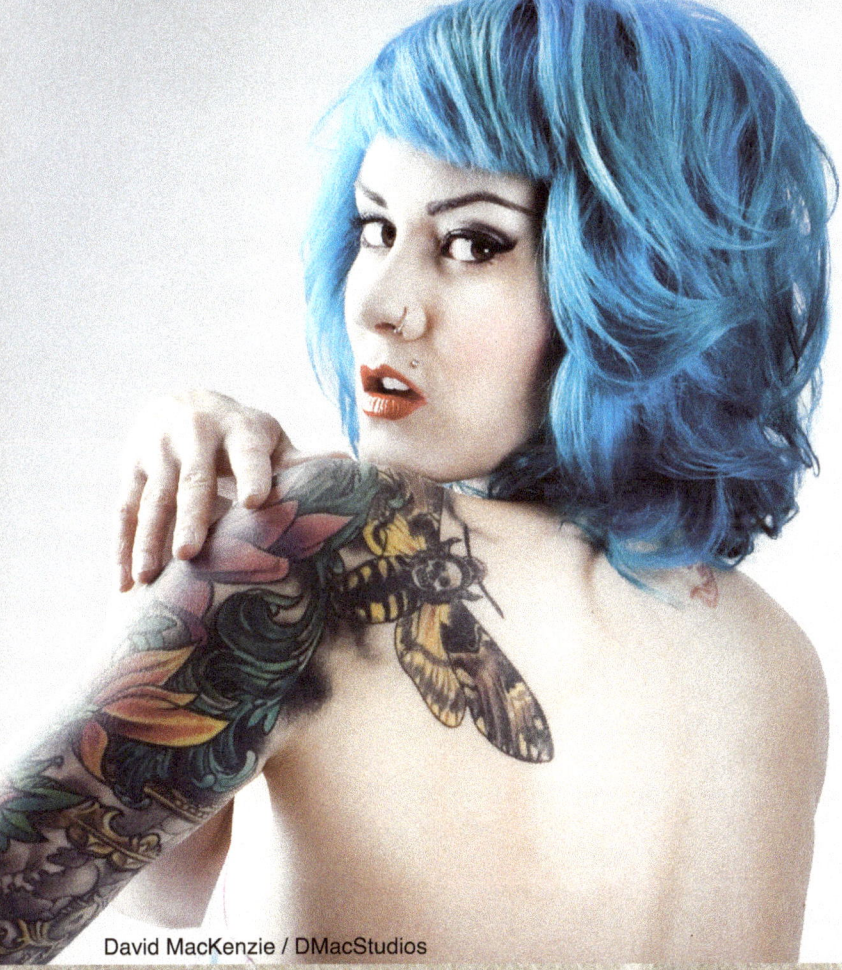
David MacKenzie / DMacStudios

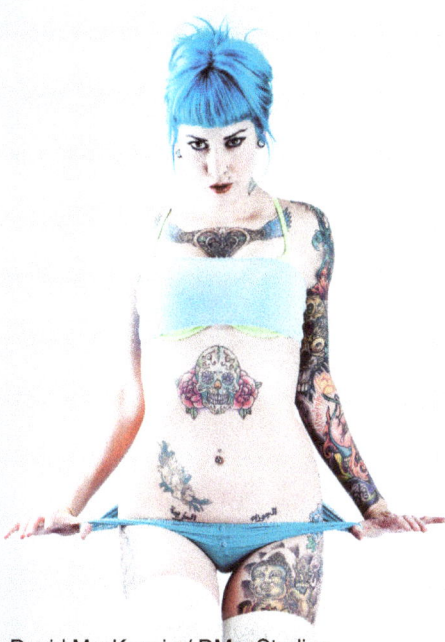
David MacKenzie / DMacStudios

Nikki Nix

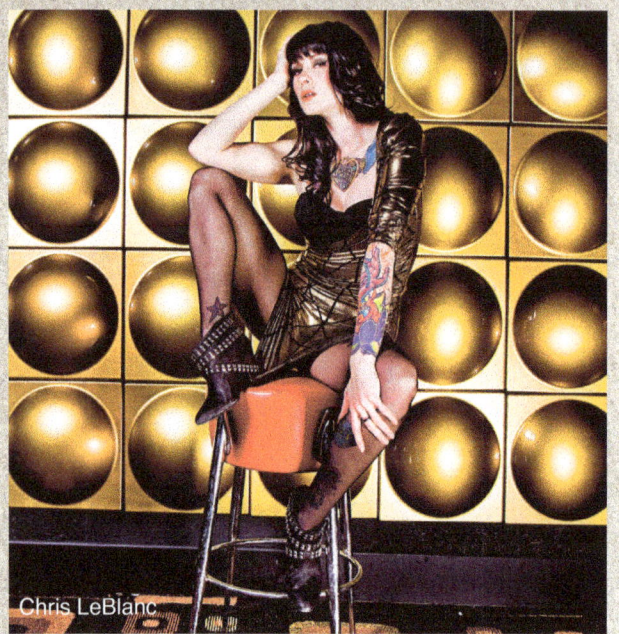
Chris LeBlanc

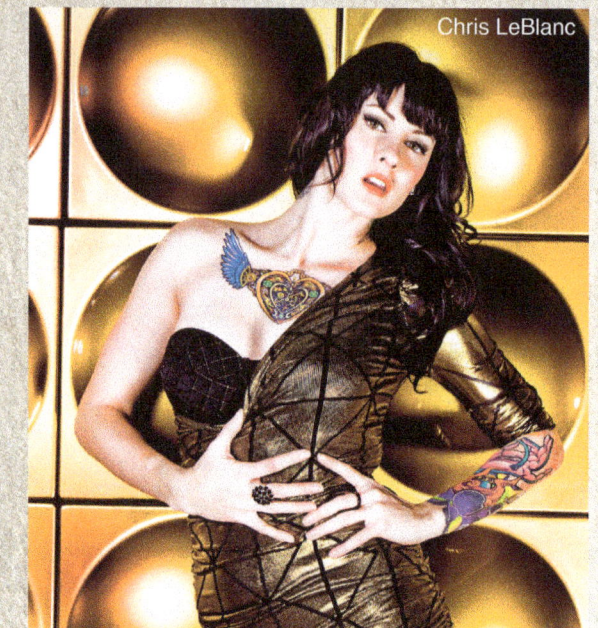
Chris LeBlanc

Dale Hannaford / Pictor

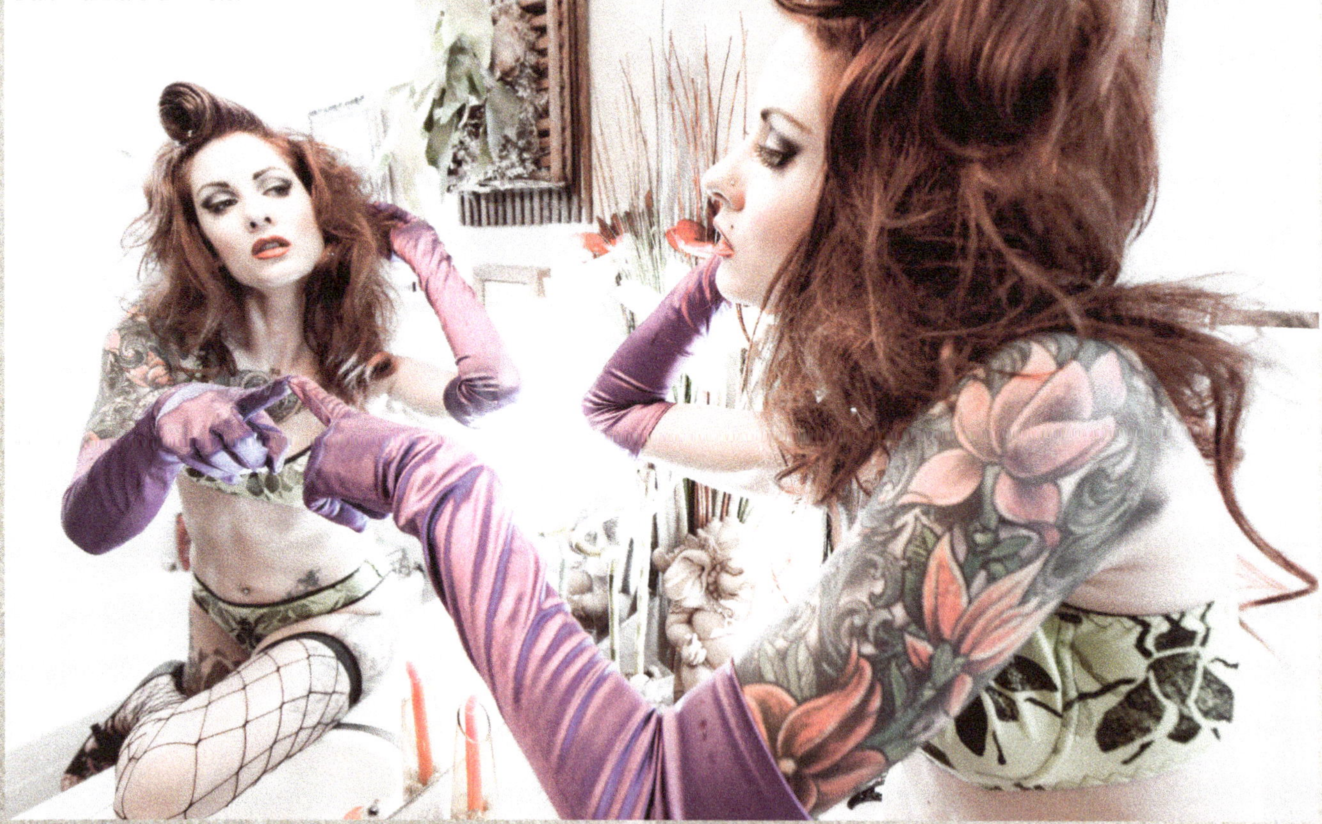

Nikki Nix

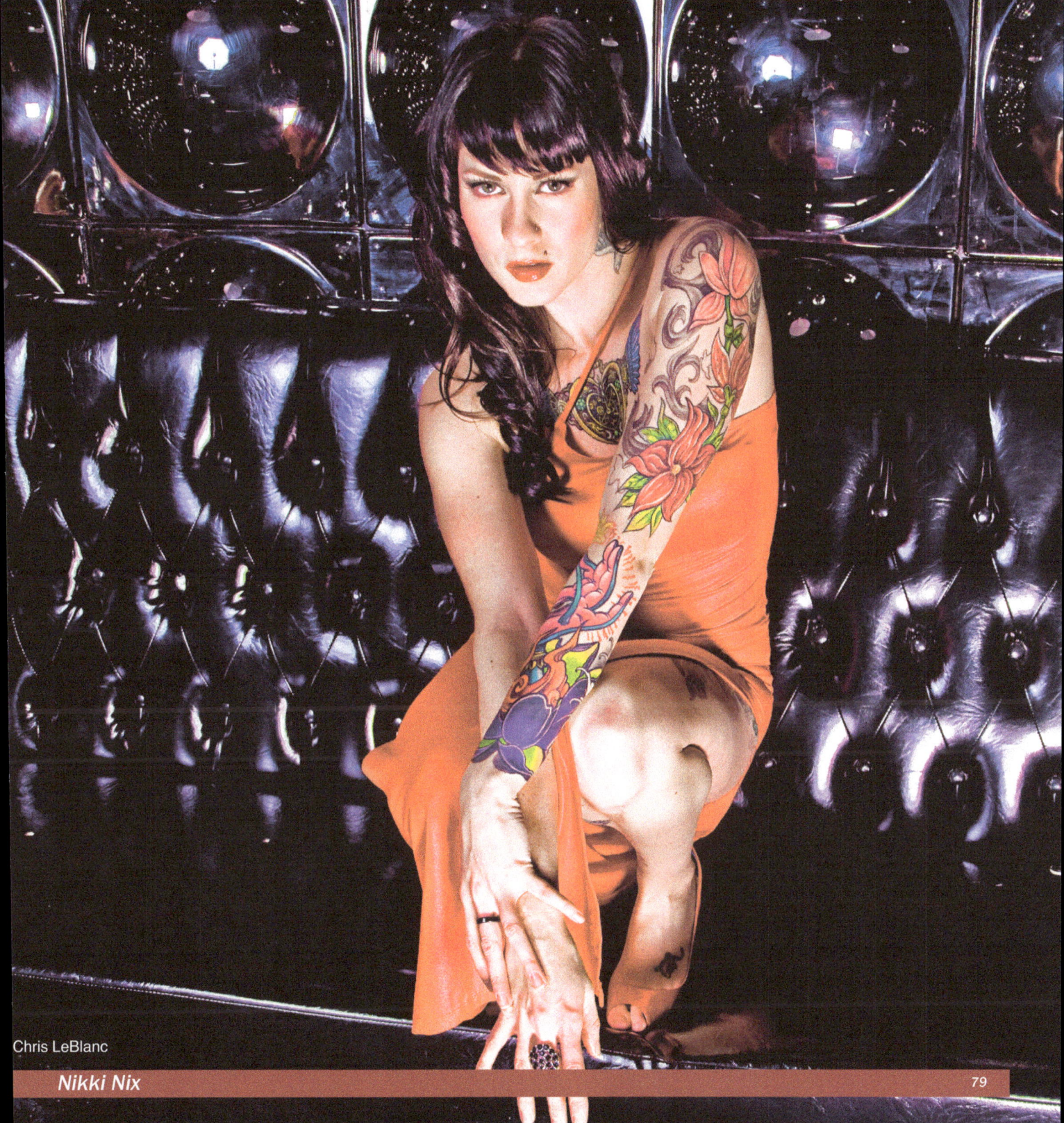

Chris LeBlanc

Nikki Nix

Katie Omand

"Tattoos are a huge part of me, each one symbolizes a part of my life..."

I am Katie Omand, business owner, mother, and model. For me, modeling is a great way to express myself without having to say a word.

How long have you been a model, and what do you enjoy the most about it?

I started modeling when I was 18. A modeling agency saw me while I was shopping in San Francisco. Guess that's how I got my "big break." I continued modeling off and on 'till now. I took a few years off and spent those raising my daughter. I love being in front of the camera and just feeling sexy and beautiful both inside and out.

How did you get your start in modeling?

An agent found me when I was 18, I always had an interest though, my mother was a model when she was young. She was a huge inspiration!

Could you tell us about your friendship with photographer Keith Selle?

Keith is an amazing photographer. First time I met him I knew he was awesome. He made me feel right at home and super comfortable. He's quick and takes amazing shots.

When did your interest in tattoos begin? And how long was it from then until you got your first one?

I've always loved tattoos, they were quite popular in Santa Cruz where I grew up, to say the least, haha. I got my first tattoo when I was 20 and haven't stopped since. I plan on getting my mother's portrait on my forearm. She passed away two years ago. Just recently I started my half sleeve. I got a portrait of Marilyn Monroe, she is another idol of mine. She believed in herself and did as she wanted and never cared what anyone thought.

Which is your first one? And why did you make it?

It was a butterfly on my foot, it represented me being a free spirit.

What do your tattoos mean to you? Are they symbolic or do you just dig the art?

Actually it's both, they are all symbolic and art as well.

Among all your tattoos, which one do you prefer and why?

I would have to say "Beauty of My Heart," down the side of my ribcage. It was for my mother. All my life she would tell me that. A great friend of mine who is a tattoo artist did he work, so it means that much more to me.

Please talk us through some of your tattoos and the reason behind them.

I have a huge back piece with two koi swimming up my back with water and beautiful cherry blossoms surrounding them, which represents my daughter and me swimming upstream in life, and having to overcome all our obstacles to reach the top together. I have "Perfectly Flawed" on my other ribcage which is pretty self explanatory, none of us are perfect and I am proud of all my flaws. It's what makes me the woman I am - you gotta love yourself from within.

What do you think about the rise of tattoo art, is it a fashion or a new breath for the body culture?

I think tattoos have always been popular. It's a way to show and express yourself through body art. Tattoo art has been around for hundreds and hundreds of years.

Of all above-mentioned things that you've accomplished in your relatively short career, what would you pick as your biggest achievements in your career?

My biggest achievement would have to be raising my daughter and opening my own business – West Coast Tanning. I am very proud of myself and can't wait to see my company grow.

What's the next step for Katie Omand?

I would have to say just raising my daughter and watching her grow into the beautiful young lady she is becoming. Maybe one day finding love.

www.modelmayhem.com/PinkyStar
www.westcoasttanningco.com
www.facebook.com/pages/Katie-Pinky-Omand/104239182967597

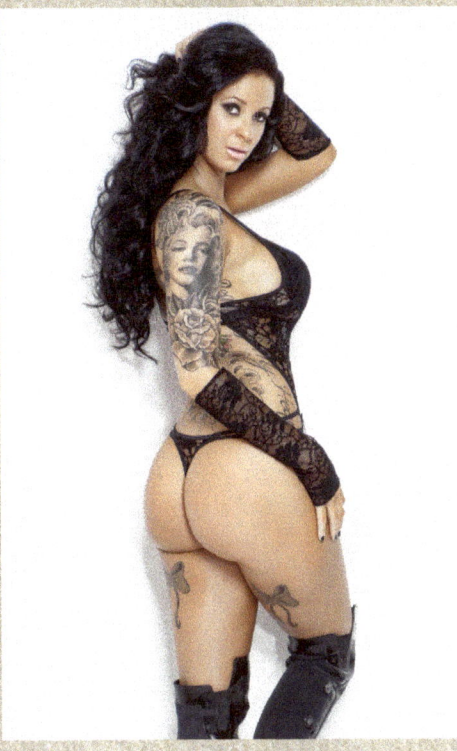
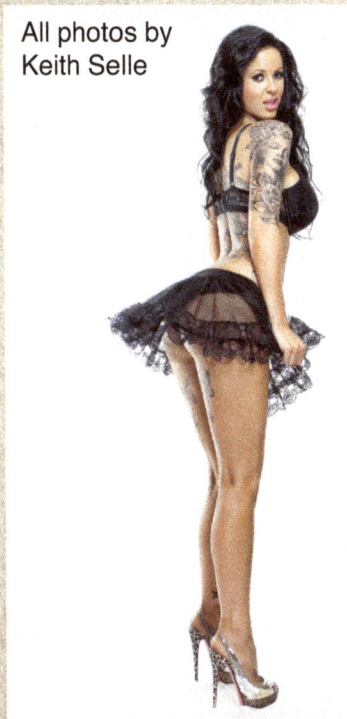

All photos by Keith Selle

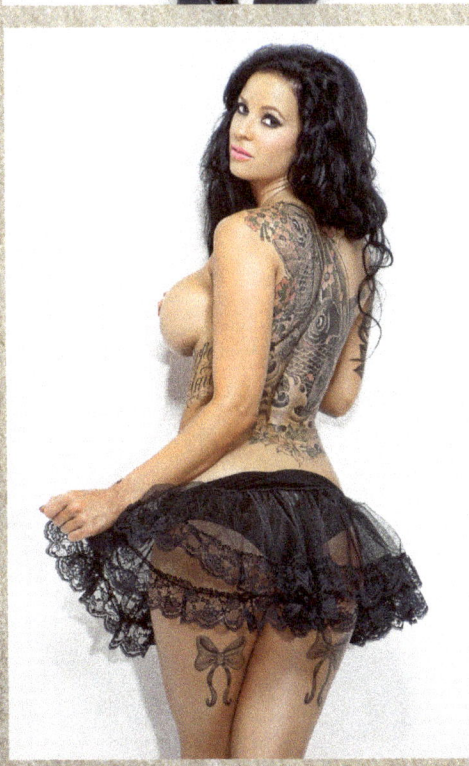
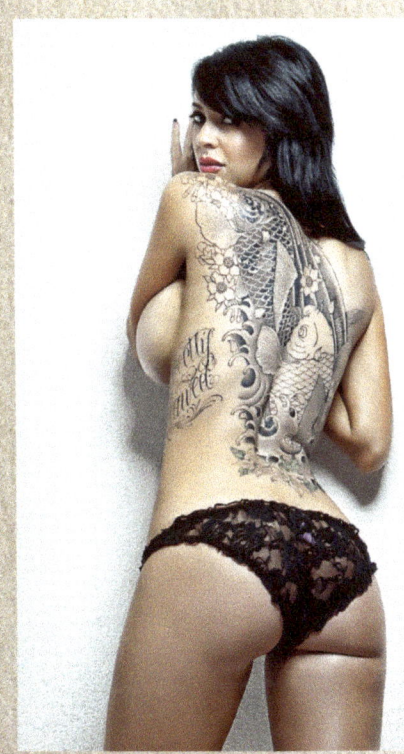

Katie Omand

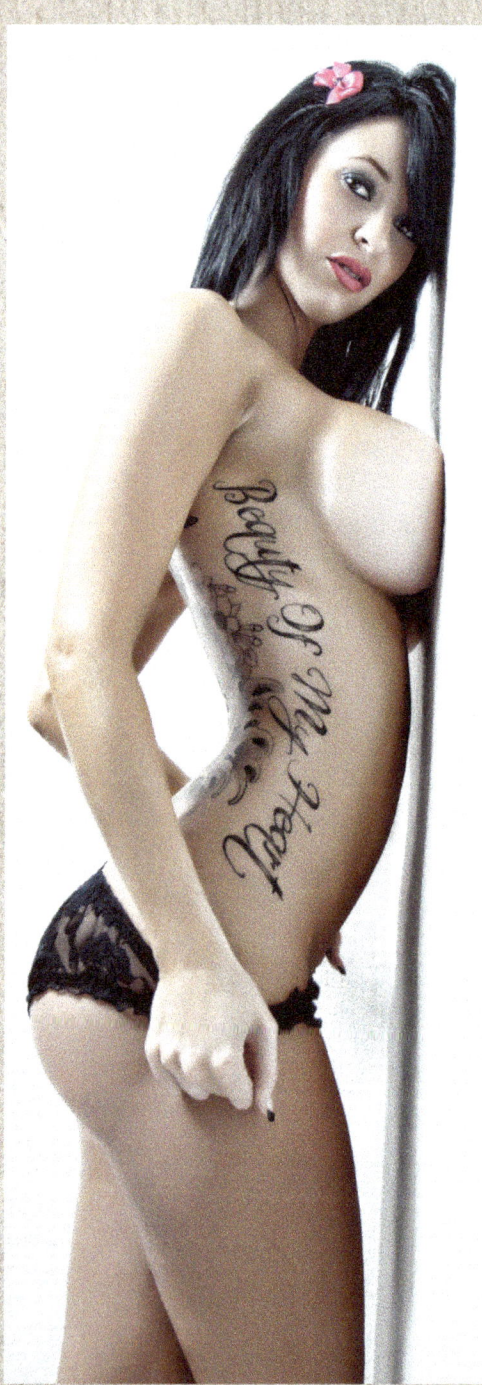

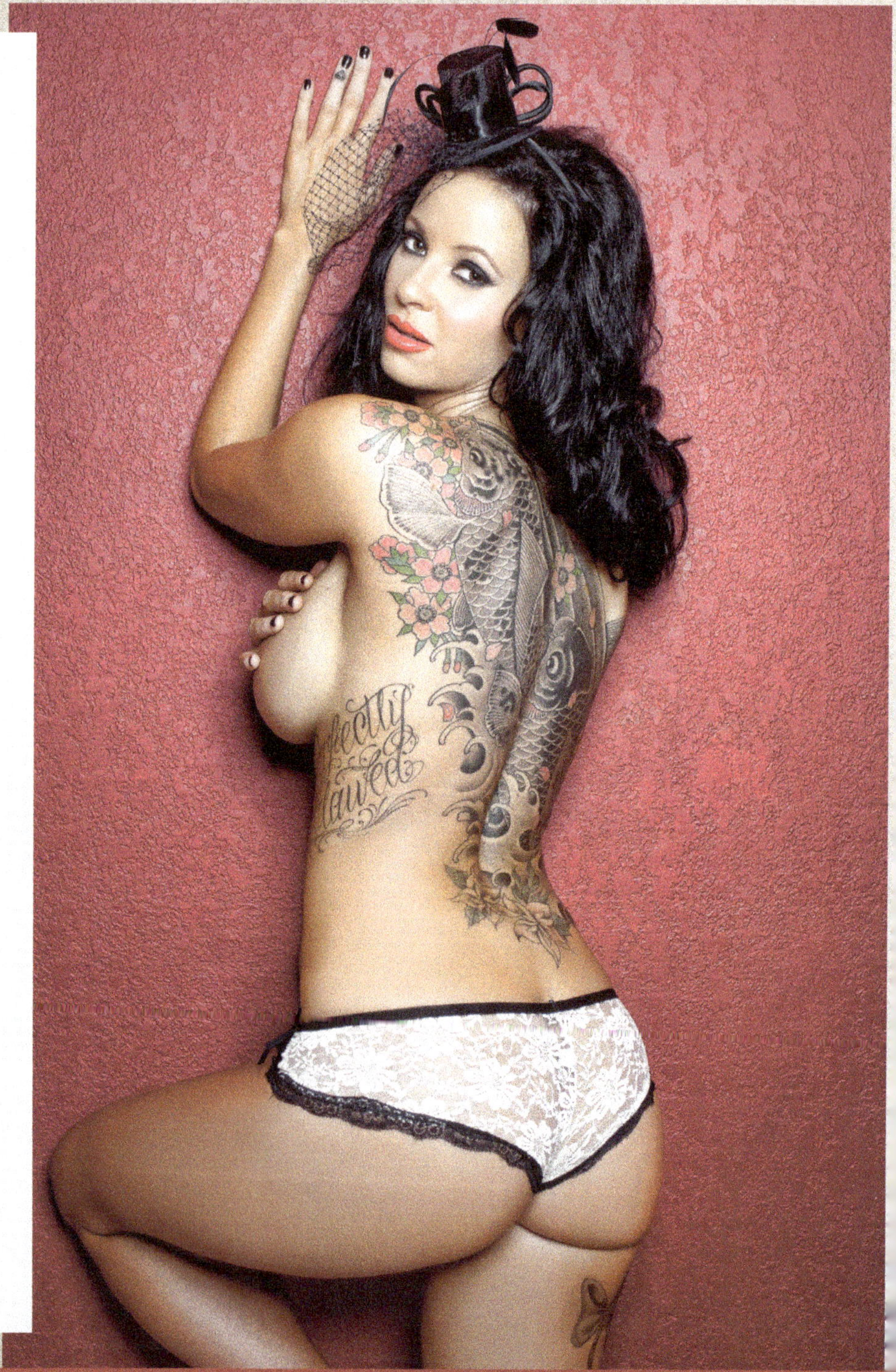

Katie Omand

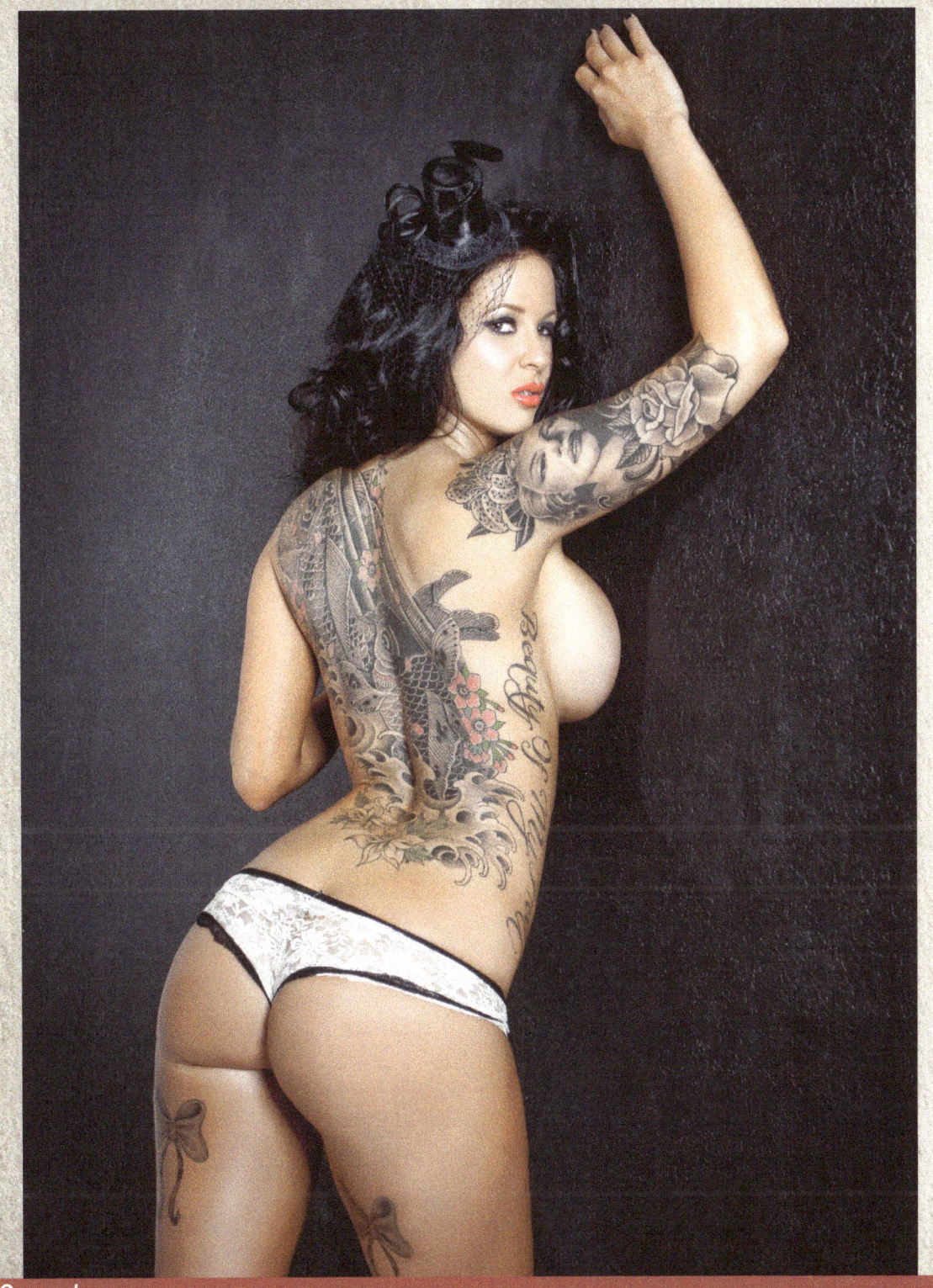

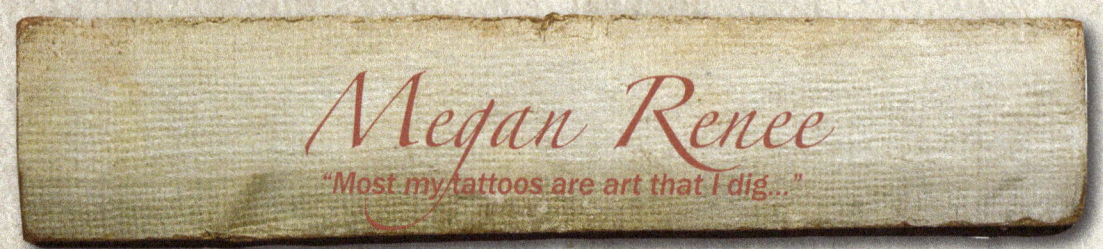

Megan Renee
"Most my tattoos are art that I dig..."

I am Megan Renee, I am a full time model living in southern California.

What do you enjoy the most about modeling?
I enjoy the challenge most of all. I have so much to learn, so much to grow from, I will never get bored, I will never back down.

How was the shooting for you with Keith Selle?
Ah, shooting with Amelia and Keith was SO rad. They are the two nicest people I have ever met. Amelia and I have been good friends for some time now, I have a blast shooting with her. This was my first time actually working with Keith and he had me laughing the whole time! He is so funny and an amazing photographer, it was an honor to work with both.

When did your interest in tattoos begin? And how long was it from then until you got your first one?
I have been interested in tattoos ever since I can remember seeing them on my parents, I got my first tattoo as soon as I could. On my 18th birthday I made an appointment to get my first tattoo and two days later I was inked. And I haven't stopped yet, probably won't.

Which is your first one? And why did you make it?
My first tattoo was a hibiscus flower with my mother's name in the center. I made that my first one because my mom and I are very close. I wanted to have that so I would always have her with me.

What is it about tattoos that appeals to you?
I like that it's a way of expressing yourself. I like the freedom.

What do your tattoos mean to you? Are they symbolic or do you just dig the art?
Most of my tattoos are art that I dig. I'm really into the tattooing art, so I keep getting more. I do have a few though that I got for a certain reason.

Among all your tattoos, which one do you prefer and why?
I really do like all my tattoos. Each and every one is special to me, and I do not regret any of them, but if I had to choose a favorite tattoo it would probably be my latest one, the phoenix on my thigh. I love all the detail and color. It was a lot of work and a lot of pain, but so worth it.

Yes, I always have ideas for new tattoos I have in mind or that I want to get, right now I'm itching to get an owl tattooed on me, maybe I should start a back piece.

Of all the above-mentioned things that you've accomplished in your relatively short career what would you pick as your biggest achievements in your career?
Some of my biggest achievements would have to be landing a cover girl spot on some big magazines like Skin Art, Deadbeat, Tattoo, and Bella Morte. It was also a huge achievement for me to be one of 13 billboards in the OC/LA area for a local tattoo expo!

Do you often receive fan mails from different men?
Yes, I receive a bunch of fan mail, they usually say something along the lines of, "you're beautiful, I'd love to get to know you and be friends..." There have however been weird messages. One man wanted me to smoke a cigarette topless. He offered me $500, and no, I did not take him up on that.

Is there anything else you would like to add?
I would like to add that all of my amazing tattoos were done by Jason "Jdogg" Kirkpatrick in Orange, CA, at Lefty's Tattoo.

www.modelmayhem.com/MeganReneeL
Meganreneel.tumblr.com
twitter- @Megan__Renee
megan-renee.deviantart.com/

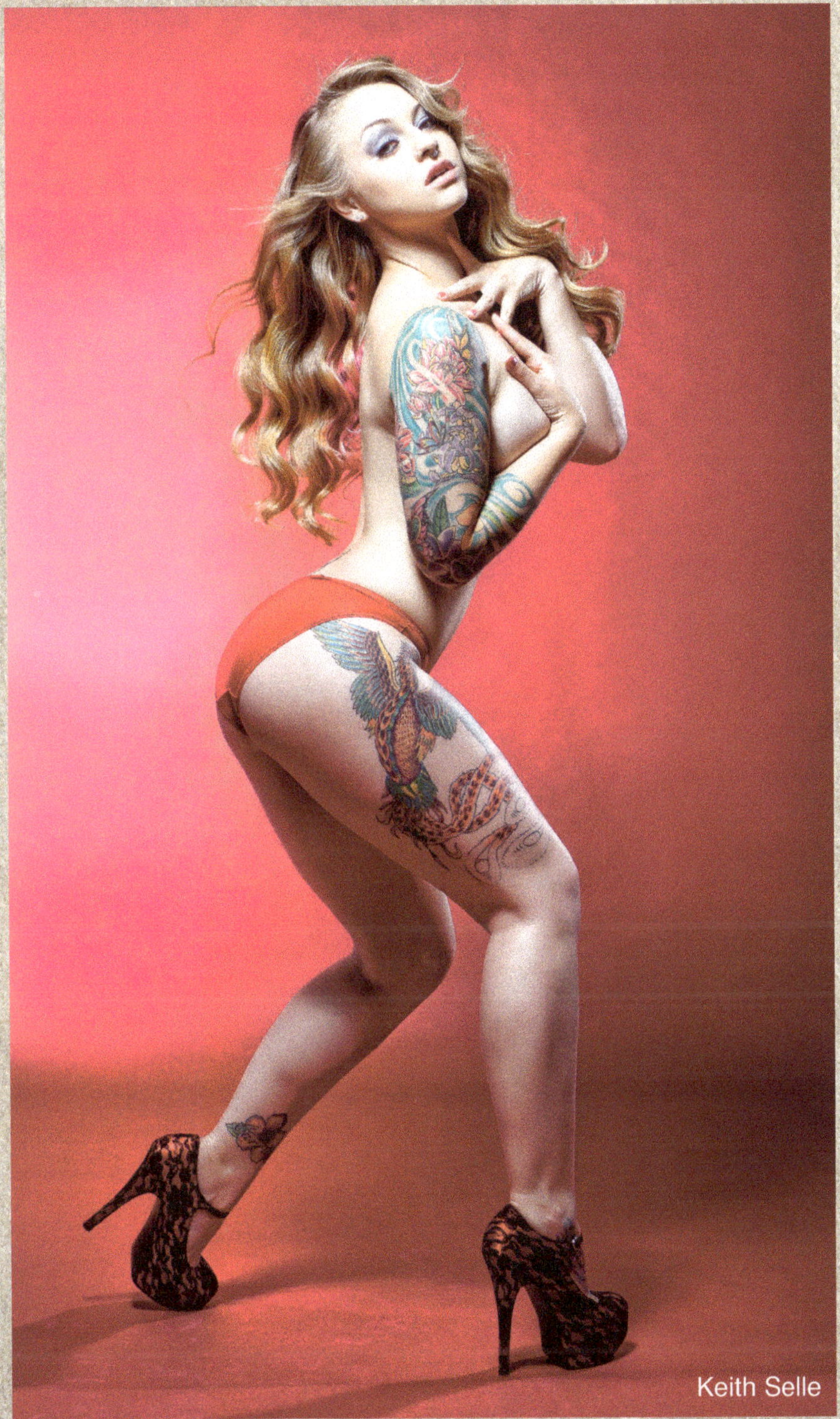

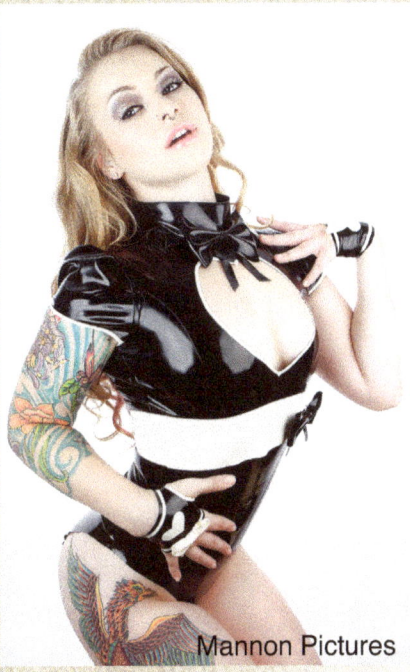

Mannon Pictures

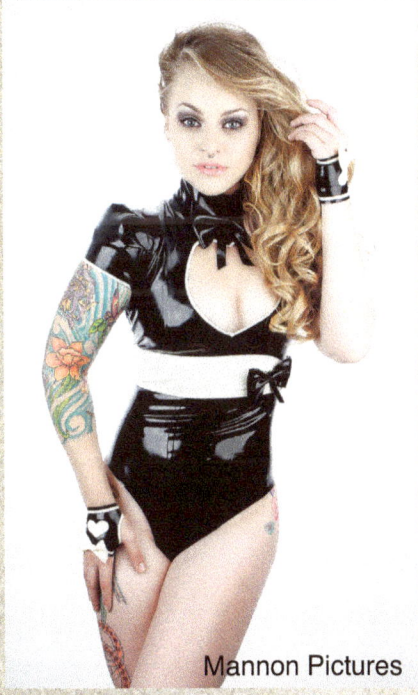

Mannon Pictures

Keith Selle

Megan Renee

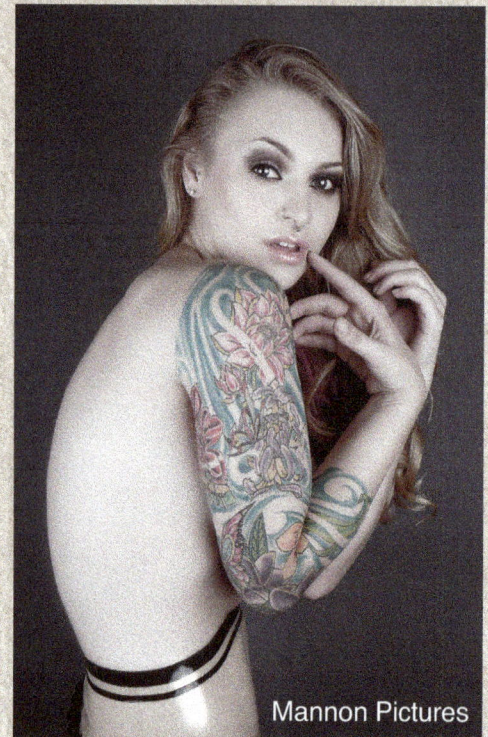

Mannon Pictures

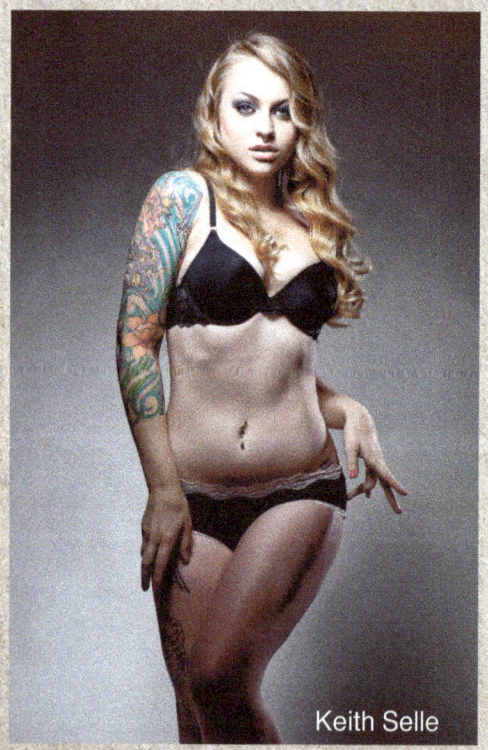

Keith Selle

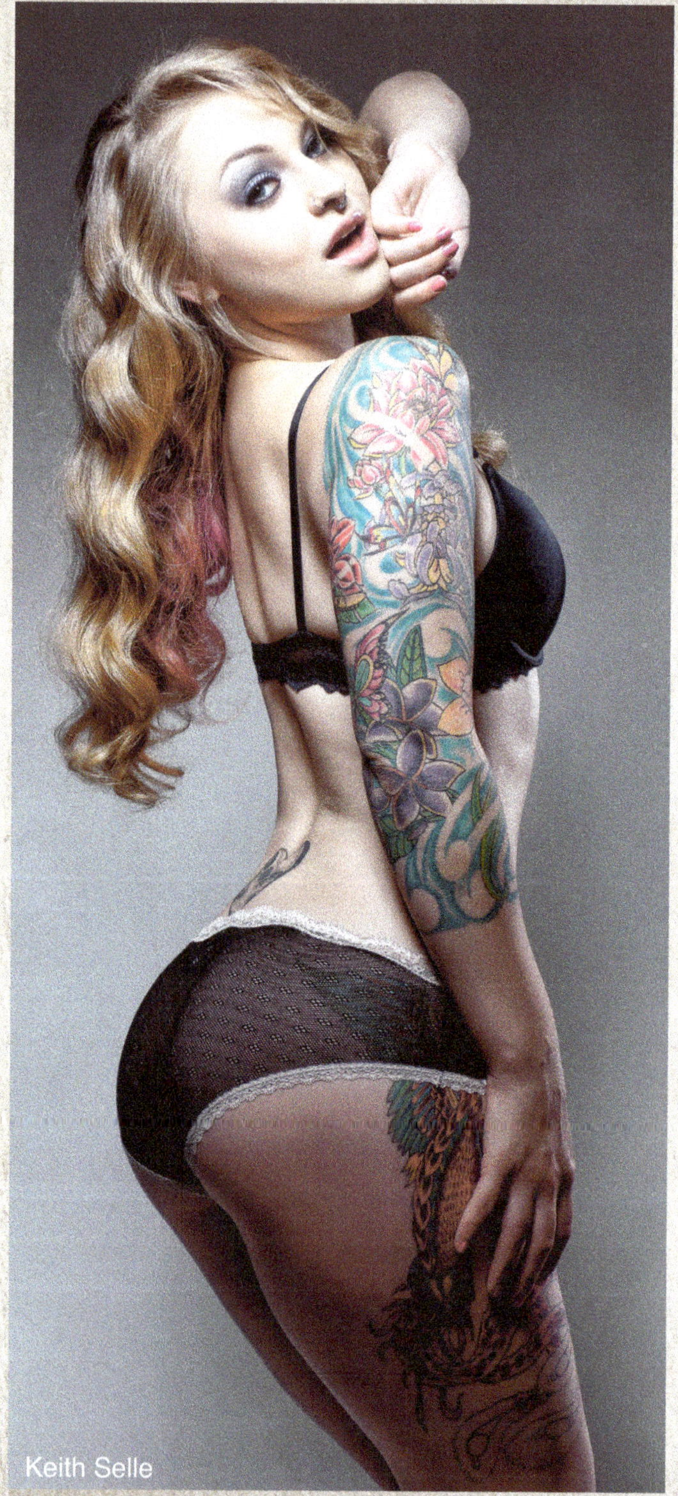

Keith Selle

Megan Renee

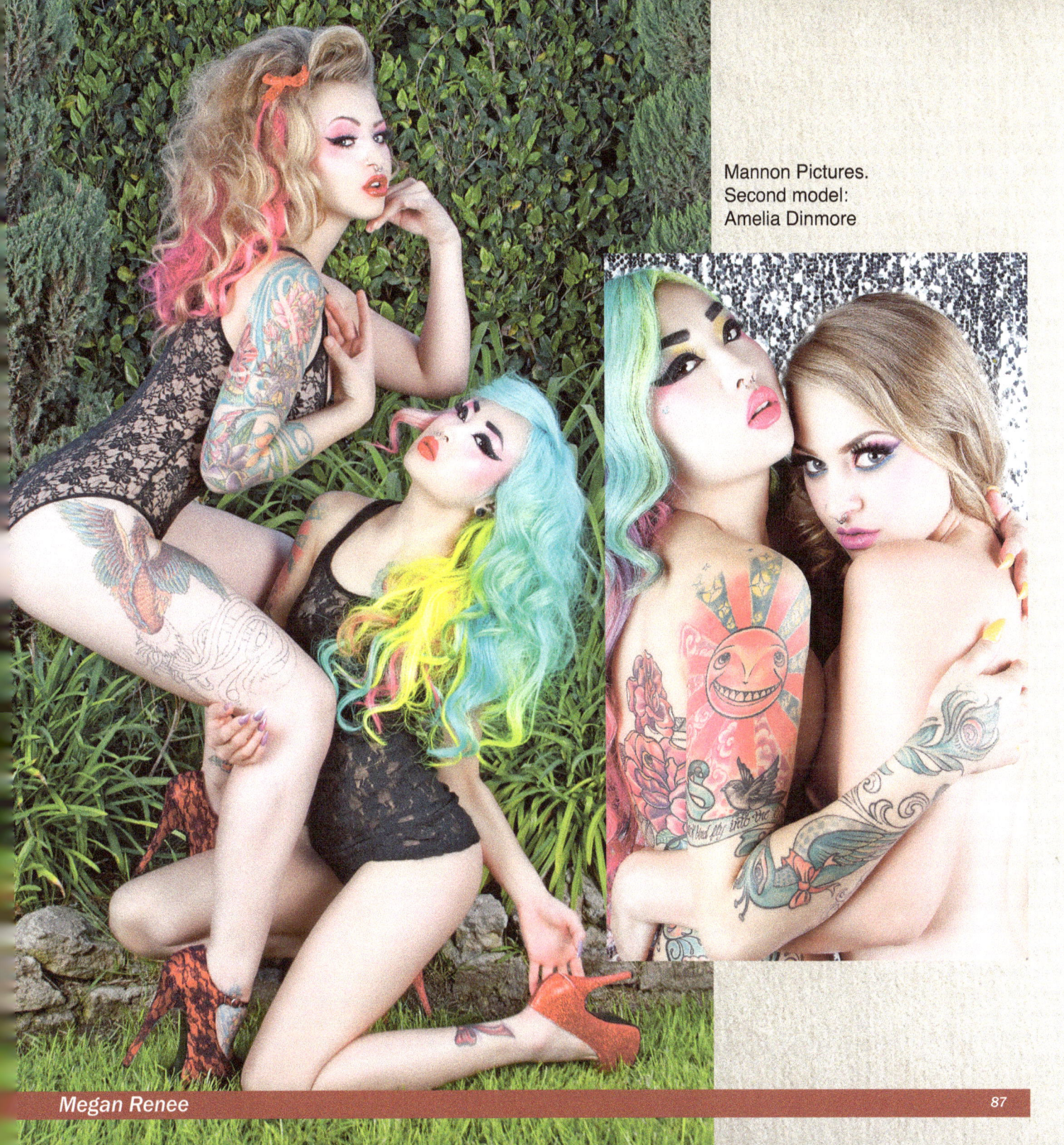

Mannon Pictures.
Second model:
Amelia Dinmore

Megan Renee

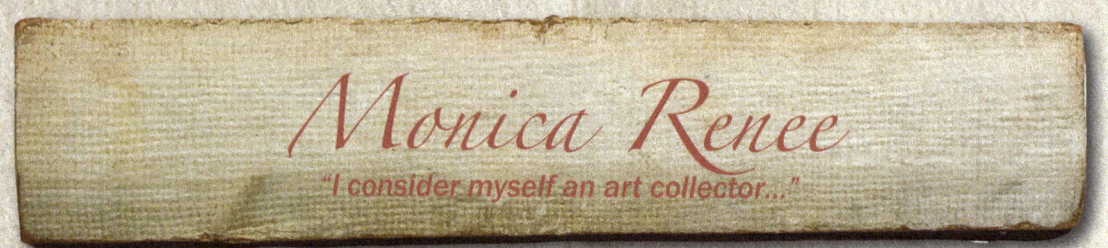

Monica Renee
"I consider myself an art collector..."

I am Monica Renee, a full time model and part time host from Southern California.

What kind of modeling do you do? And what made you get into modeling?

I wanted to model ever since I was a little girl, but didn't get the chance until I was 18. Once I got a taste, I was hooked and knew that I wanted to do it professionally. I started out trying to sign with major L.A. agencies and getting into high fashion, but was turned away because I was too curvy and just a little too short. So I decided to look for new venues of modeling that would accept a girl like me. I found my way into the rockabilly/vintage/pin-up scene and found that it was a perfect fit. I was able to have tattoos and piercings and womanly curves and still be able to be a successful model! It was terrific! From there, I have branched out into more mainstream modeling. I now work with big name companies as their token "tattooed model" and am fortunate to grace the pages and covers of multiple magazines worldwide. It is a dream come true.

How did you started to collecting your tattoos?

I have always been fascinated with tattoos. I always knew I was going to get one, but did the right thing and waited 'til I turned 18. After that, I was hooked! I slowly started working on my back-piece, which now covers half my back, then moved on to my hips and, eventually, started on my arms. Now my right arm is sleeved and I have a large piece on my left upper arm. I am not planning on stopping anytime soon though. I have plenty of skin left!

Please talk us through some of your tattoos and the reason behind them.

My tattoos are simply pieces of art. I consider myself an art collector and put things on my body that I find beautiful and expressive. My right sleeve is all Halloween themed because I am obsessed with that day. Champ at 454 Tattoo helped me piece it together after I had to leave my first shop because they treated my with extreme disrespect. He did the dagger with the "wicked" banner, wrapping it around on the underside of my upper arm. He also did the black cat, the haunted house and coffin on my forearm. He did a terrific job! All my other pieces were done by the disrespectful shop.

What do you think about the rise of tattoo, is it a fashion or a new breath for the body culture?

I like that tattoos are becoming more accepted in society. I think it is making society realize that not all tattooed people are criminals or low lifes or thugs. We are unique individuals who happen to love to express ourselves through body art. I think this movement of acceptance by society is a huge stepping stone for the tattooed community. We will never be fully understood by society, or fully accepted, but that's okay. Isn't that why we got tattooed in the first place?

Do you regret any of your tattoos?

I definitely regretted getting the pieces done on my wrists. They were done by an apprentice tattoo artist with little experience. I asked for sparrows surrounded by wind bars. What I got was birds that looked like fish! They were awful. I ended up getting laser tattoo removal and have since had them covered up with black roses.

What's the next step for Monica Renee?

Well. Since the launch of my website www.MonicaRenee.com I have been busy traveling all over the United States doing various photo shoots for companies and magazines. I am also working on my hosting career. I'd love to one day have my own show where I get to go around interviewing bands and hosting events. I have been putting a lot of time and effort into this career change and it is all starting to pay off... so keep an eye out for me!

www.monicarenee.com
www.facebook.com/TheRealMonicaRenee
www.modelmayhem.com/275734
www.tumblr.com/tagged/monica-renee

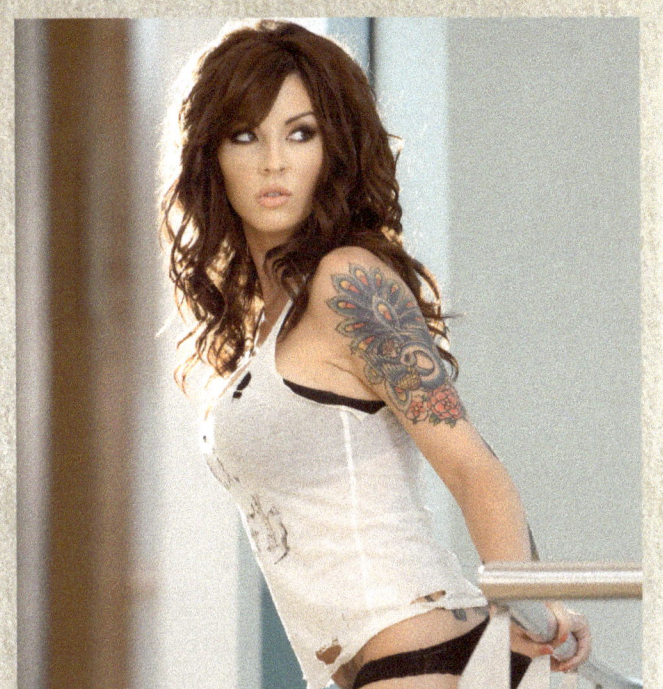
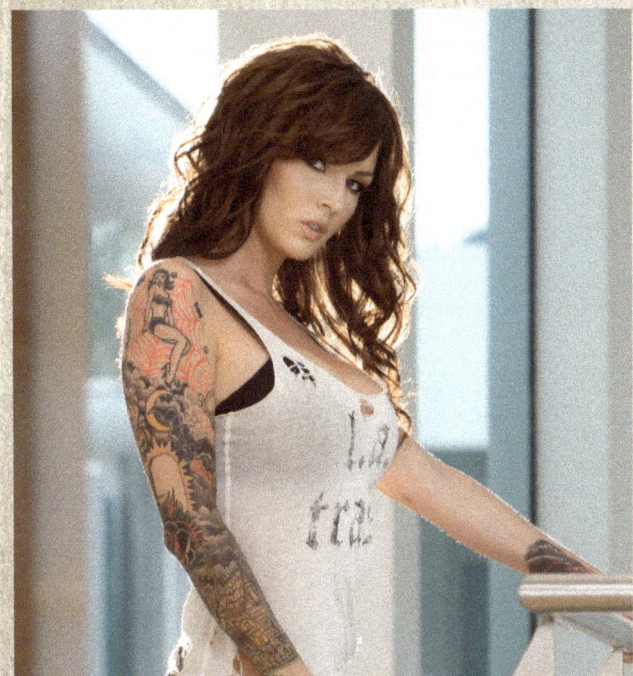

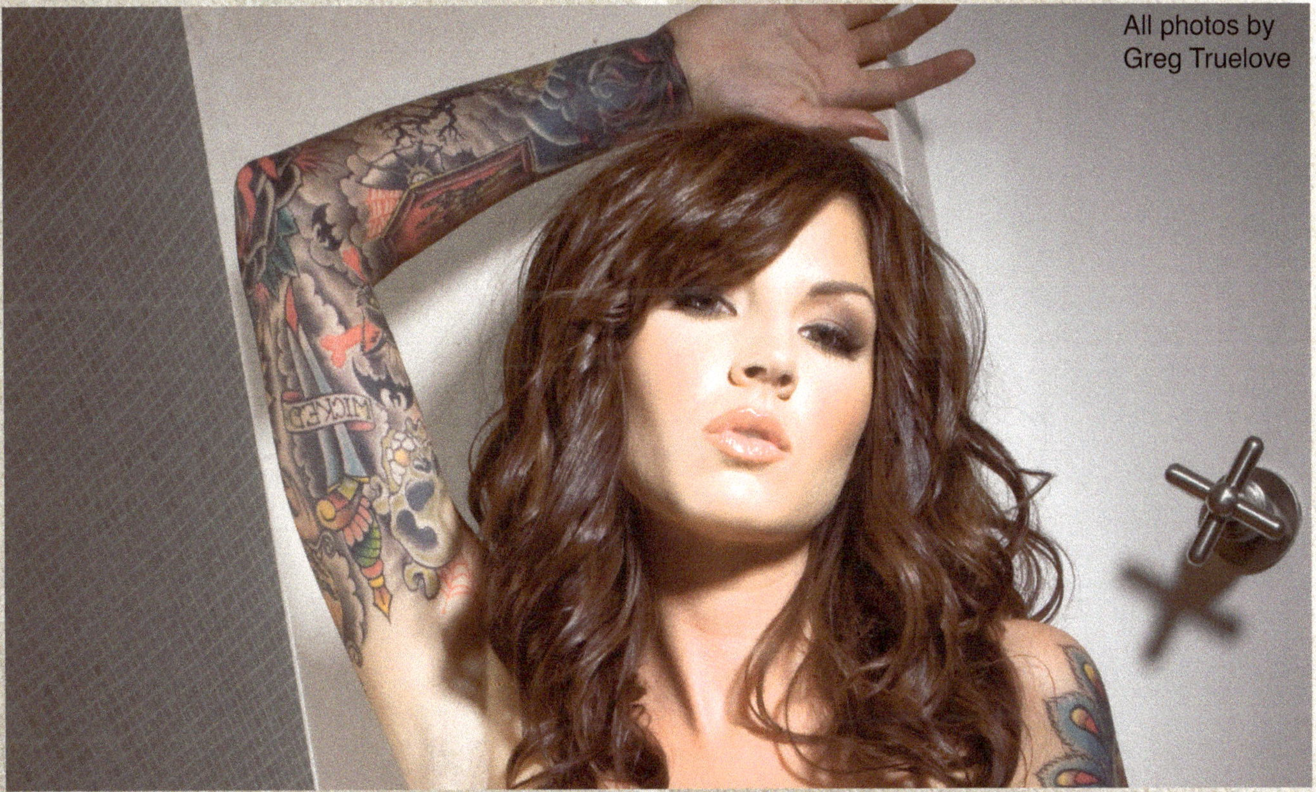

All photos by Greg Truelove

Monica Renee

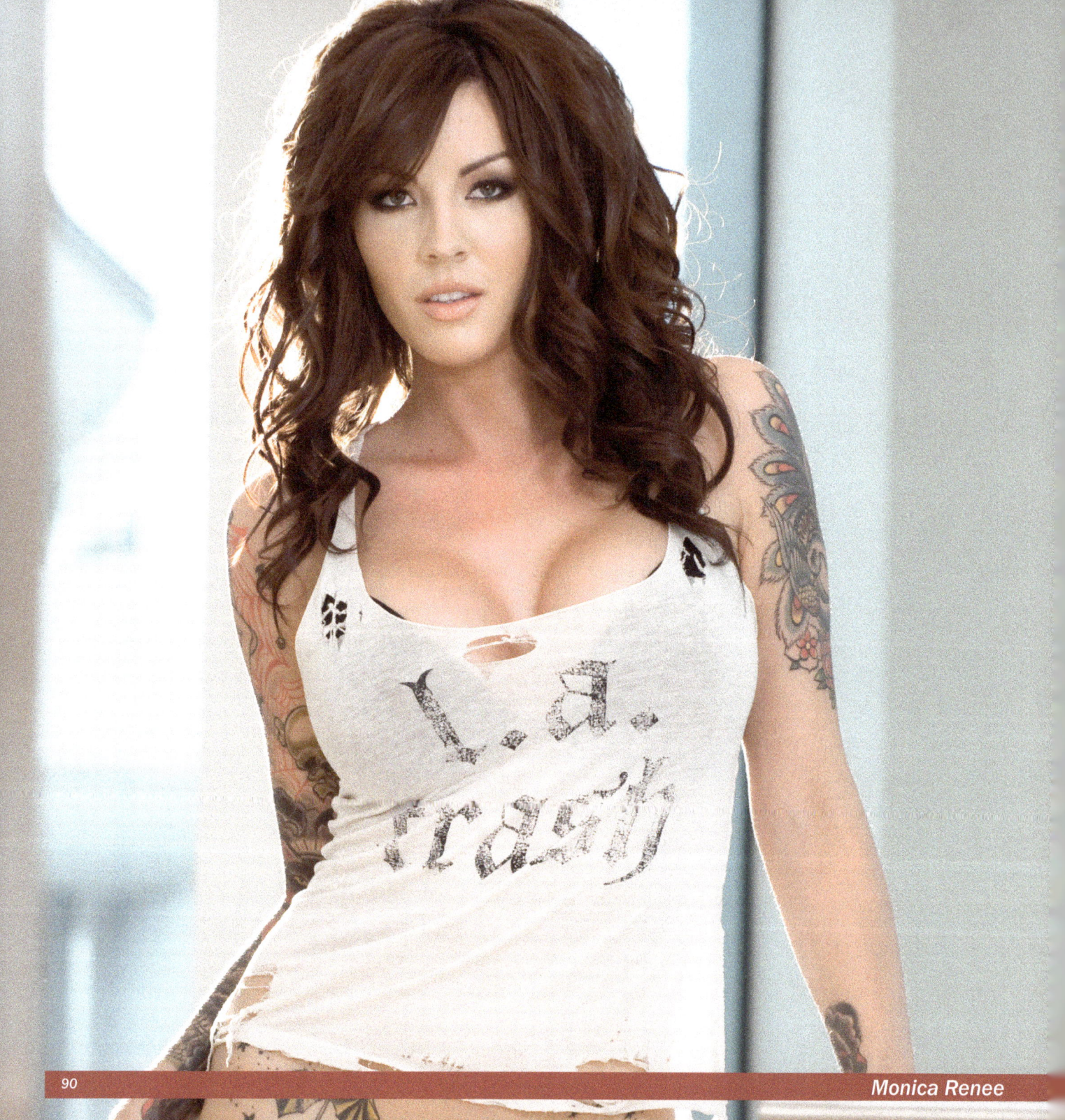

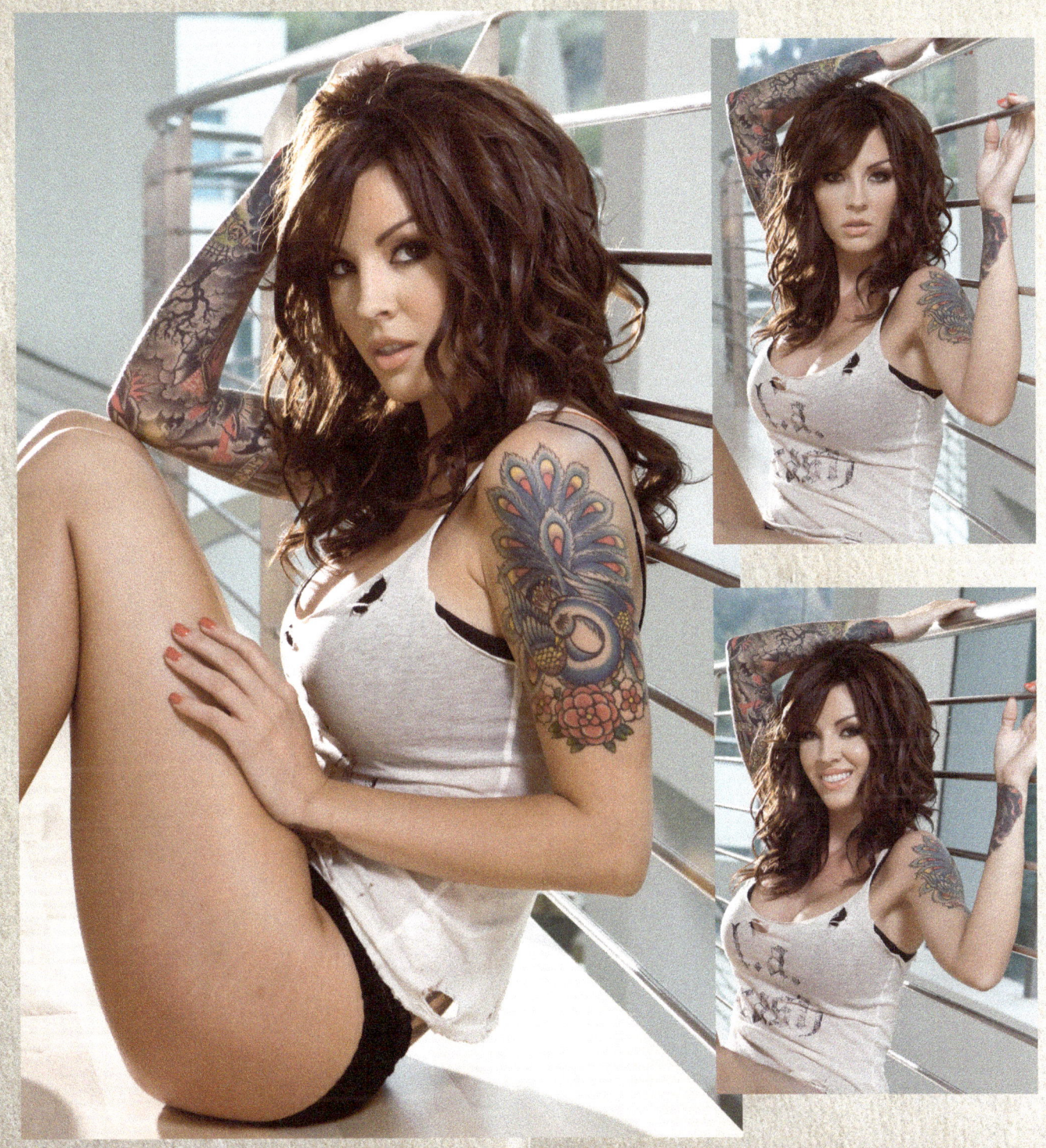

Monica Renee

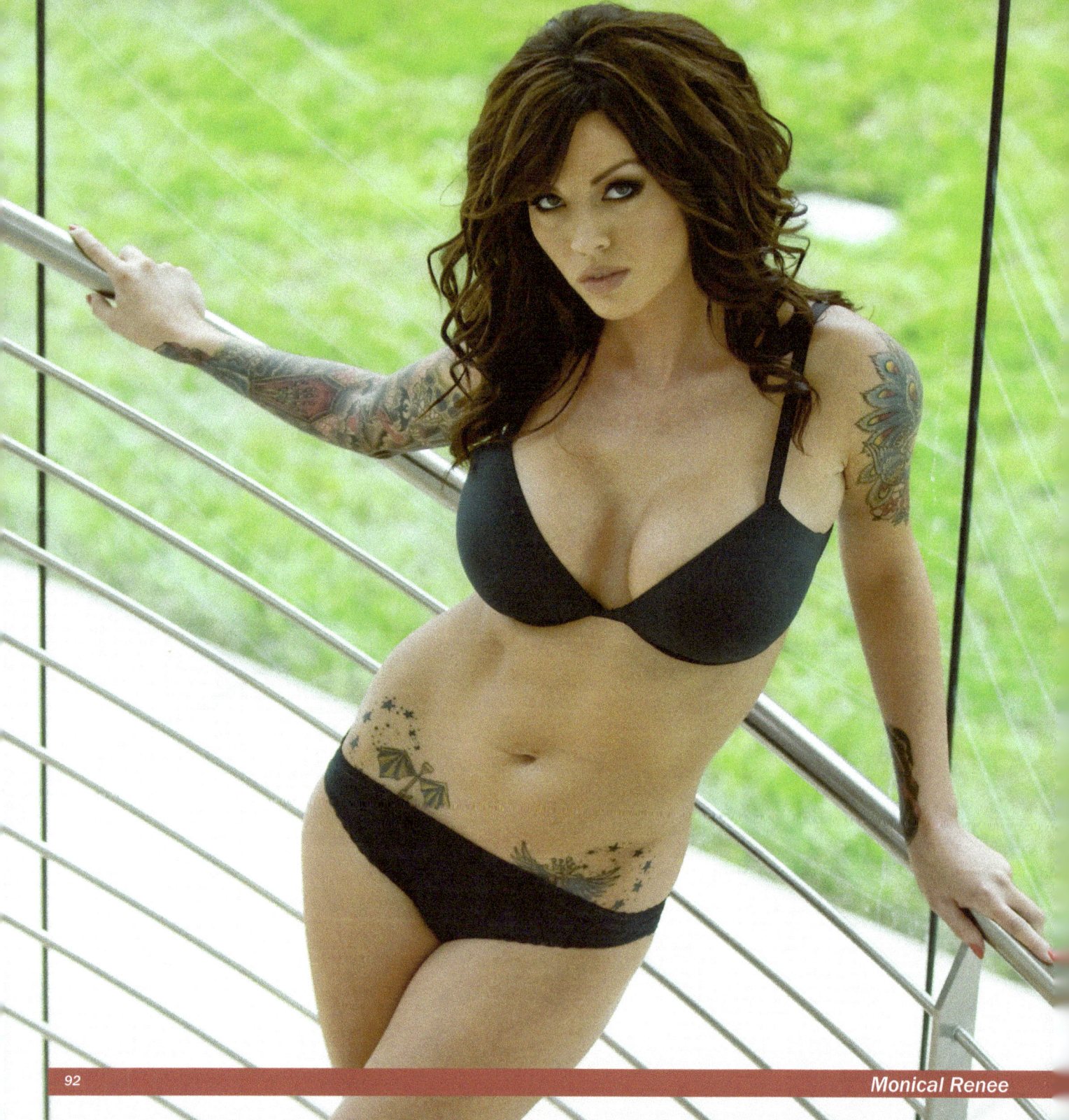
Monical Renee

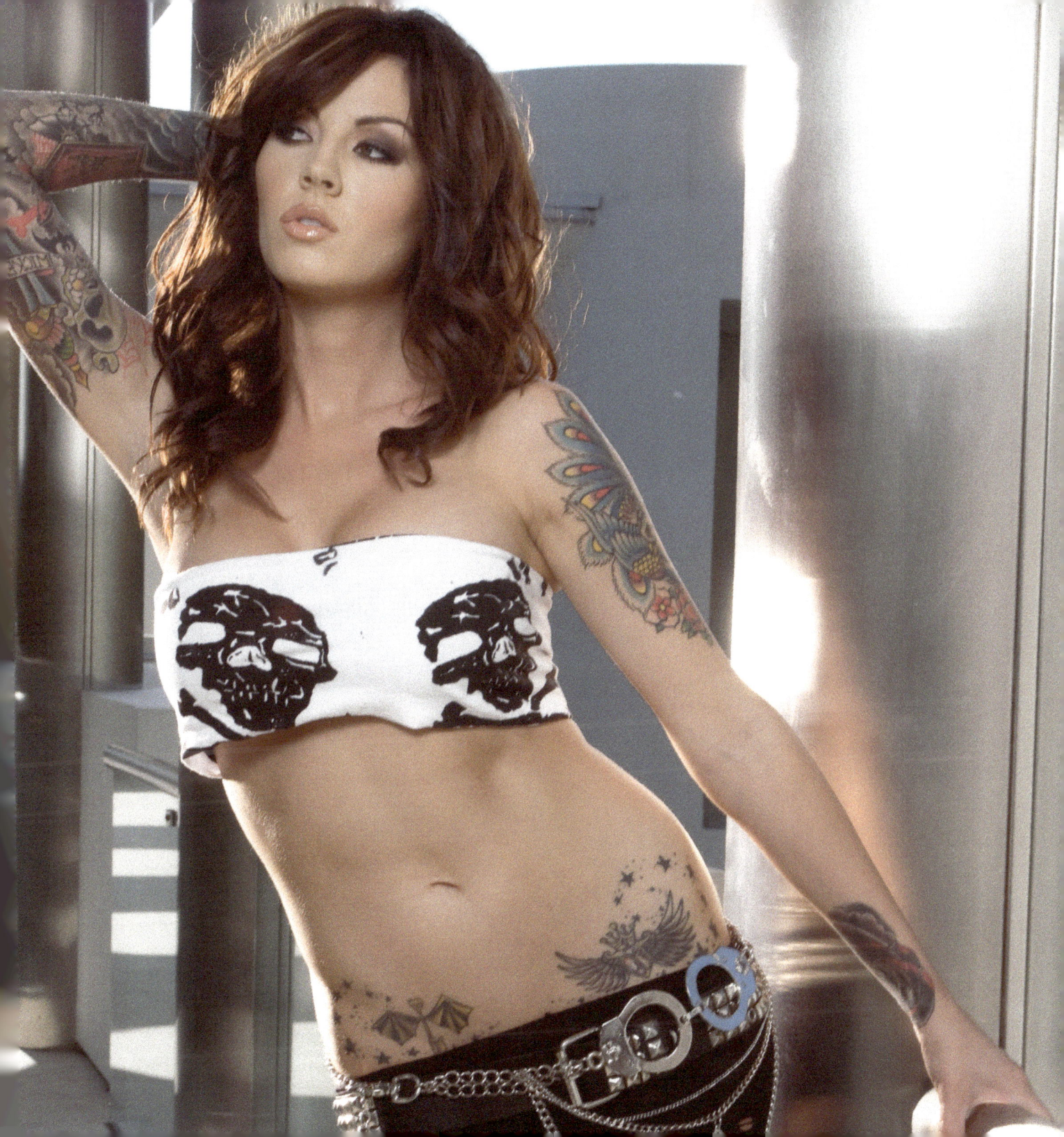

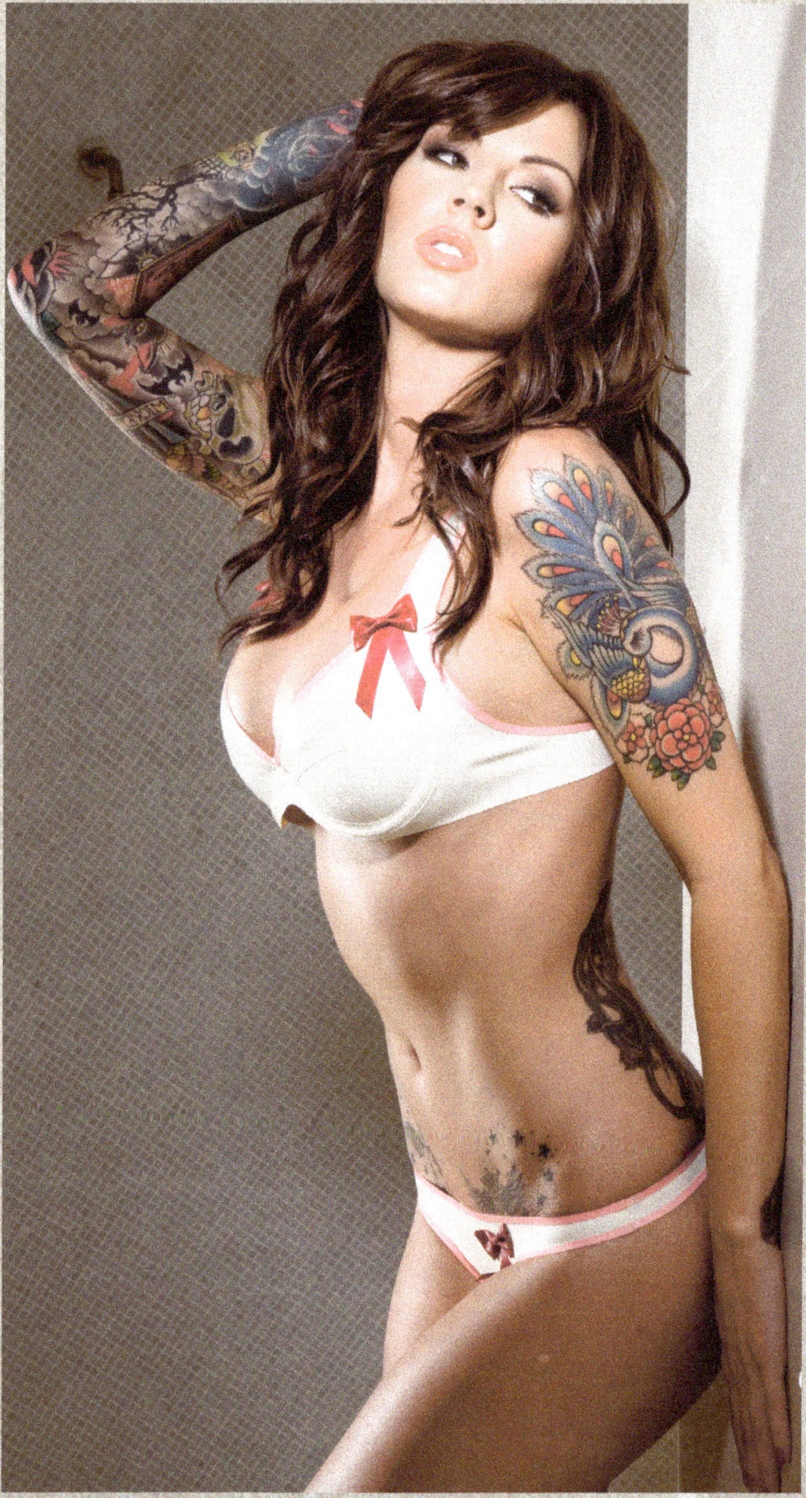

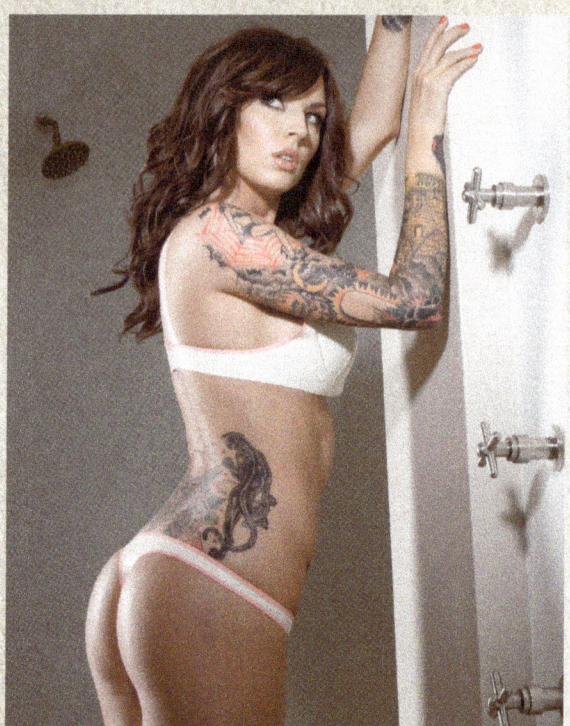
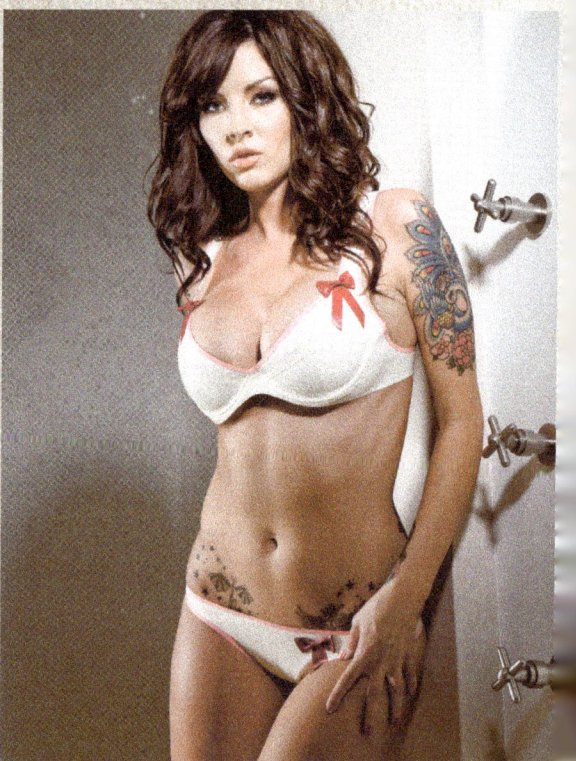

Monical Renee

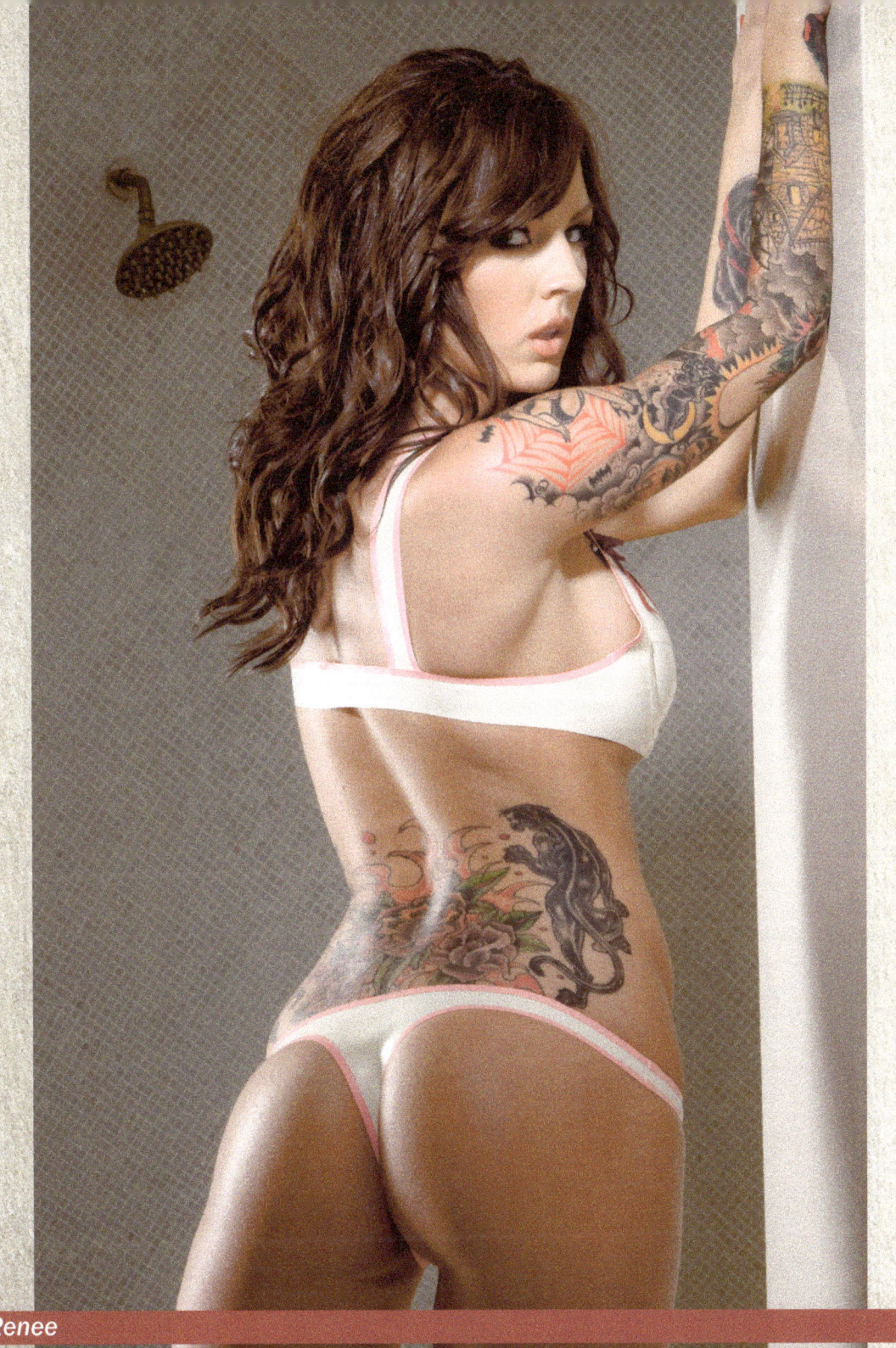

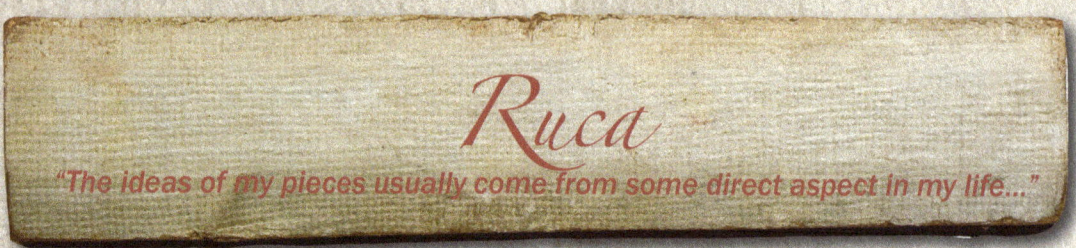

Ruca

"The ideas of my pieces usually come from some direct aspect in my life..."

My name is Ruca and I live in Dallas, Texas. I'm tiny, crafty and tattooed.

What do you do for a living?
I currently work at a law firm and am pursuing my Nursing degree.

Where do you draw your influences? Who are your role models?
My mother and my late grandmother. Both women are the definition of love and creativity. I draw from them in all aspects of my life.

When modeling, when are you having the most fun?
I simply like to create art, so when I get to work with photographers and artists that are open minded and creative, I'm in heaven.

What's it like having a following of adoring fans?
It's pretty rad. I don't think I can ever express how appreciative I am of all the support and encouraging words.

Do you have any fears?
Failure. I feel I can always do better! And on the lighter end of it, spiders. And roaches.

What got you interested in tattoos? And how old were you when you got your first tattoo?
I was always drawn to tattoos, all the bands I listened to when I was younger had them. I got my first tattoo when I was 16 - and NO I do not recommend it - at a shop that didn't card me.

How do you come up with the ideas for your pieces?
The ideas usually come from some direct aspect in my life, a thought, goal or random funny idea. They are all personal and describe me at some point in my life.

Do you like to stick to one artist, or try a number of different ones?
I have a solid group of artists who I continually seek out for more work. They are all Texas artists out of, Dallas, Houston, Austin, Corpus, etc. I've got to represent and keep it Southern!

It's a difficult question, but do you have a favorite tattoo artist?
That really is a tough question. I love all my artists for different reasons, for their unique styles, for the experiences I've had with them. That's why I continue to go back to each and every one of them. They are a huge part of the reason why I get tattooed.

What is your favorite tattoo so far, and why?
Another tough question. I love all of them obviously, but currently my recently finished stomach piece by Lil Chris and my left arm by Clint Leifeste are the ones I schmooze over.

Do you think you will miss getting tattooed when you consider yourself as finished, if that time ever comes?
I think so, but I still have a long ways to go before I reach that point. I will be having quite a bit of laser removal in order to add new pieces and will always be able to "freshen up" my work. So, technically, I'll never be done.

Which areas have been the most painful to tattoo?
Honestly as silly as it sounds, my toes. They were AWFUL!

On which part of your skin would you never get a tattoo?
I would tattoo it all, but I promised my mother that I'd never tattoo my hands, face or neck.

Do you regret any of your tattoos?
I don't regret any of them because they are all a part of my life, but the tattoos I got when I was 16 and 17 weren't the best decisions and are either covered up or are being lasered off.

Do you have any funny/weird stories about a tattoo experience?
I have been tattooed by highly inebriated artists at 5 A.M. That's about as funny as it gets.

www.facebook.com/RucaModel
www.facebook.com/SarahFulk
www.sarahfulk.net

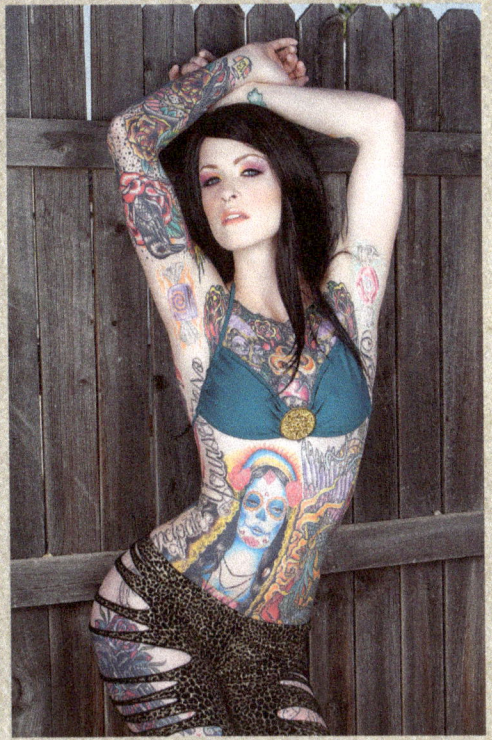
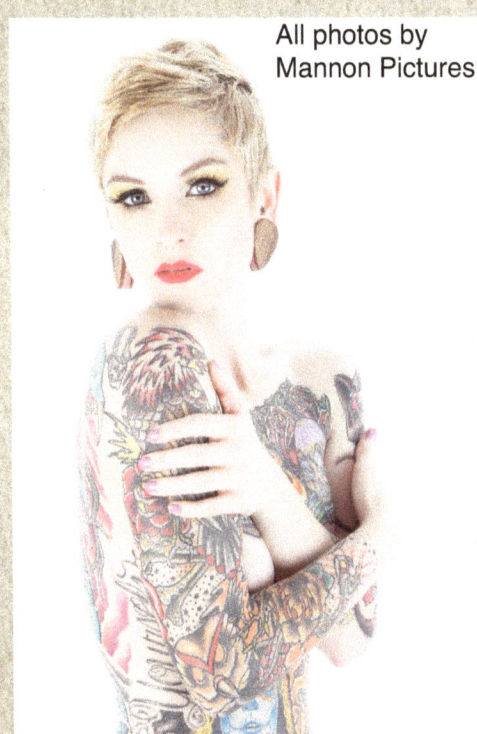

All photos by Mannon Pictures

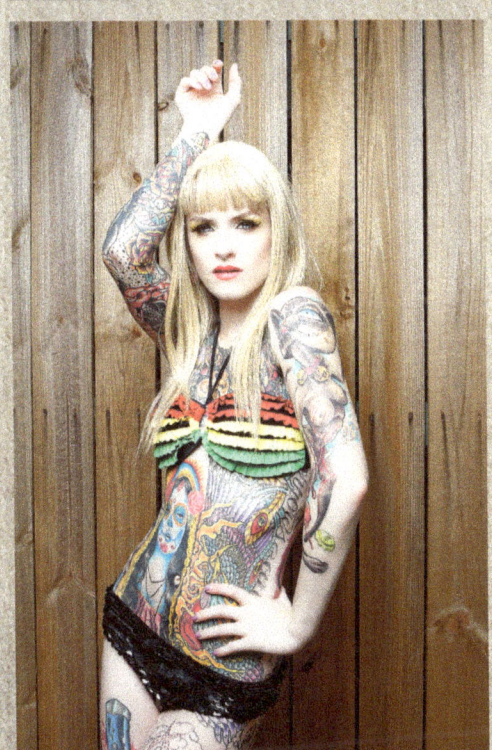
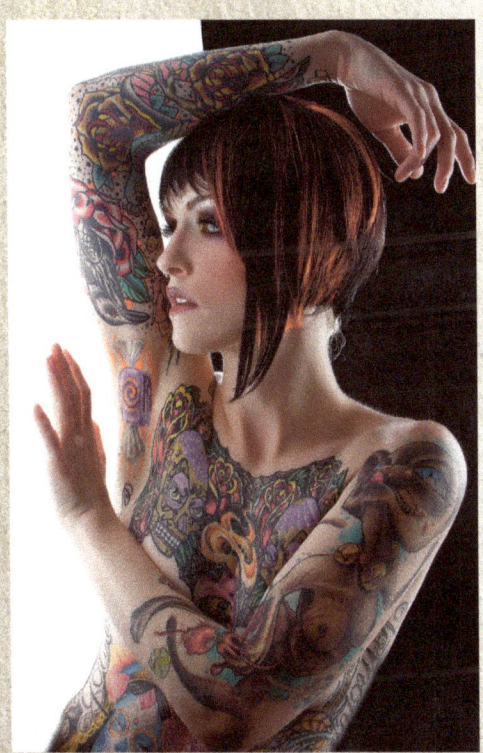

Ruca

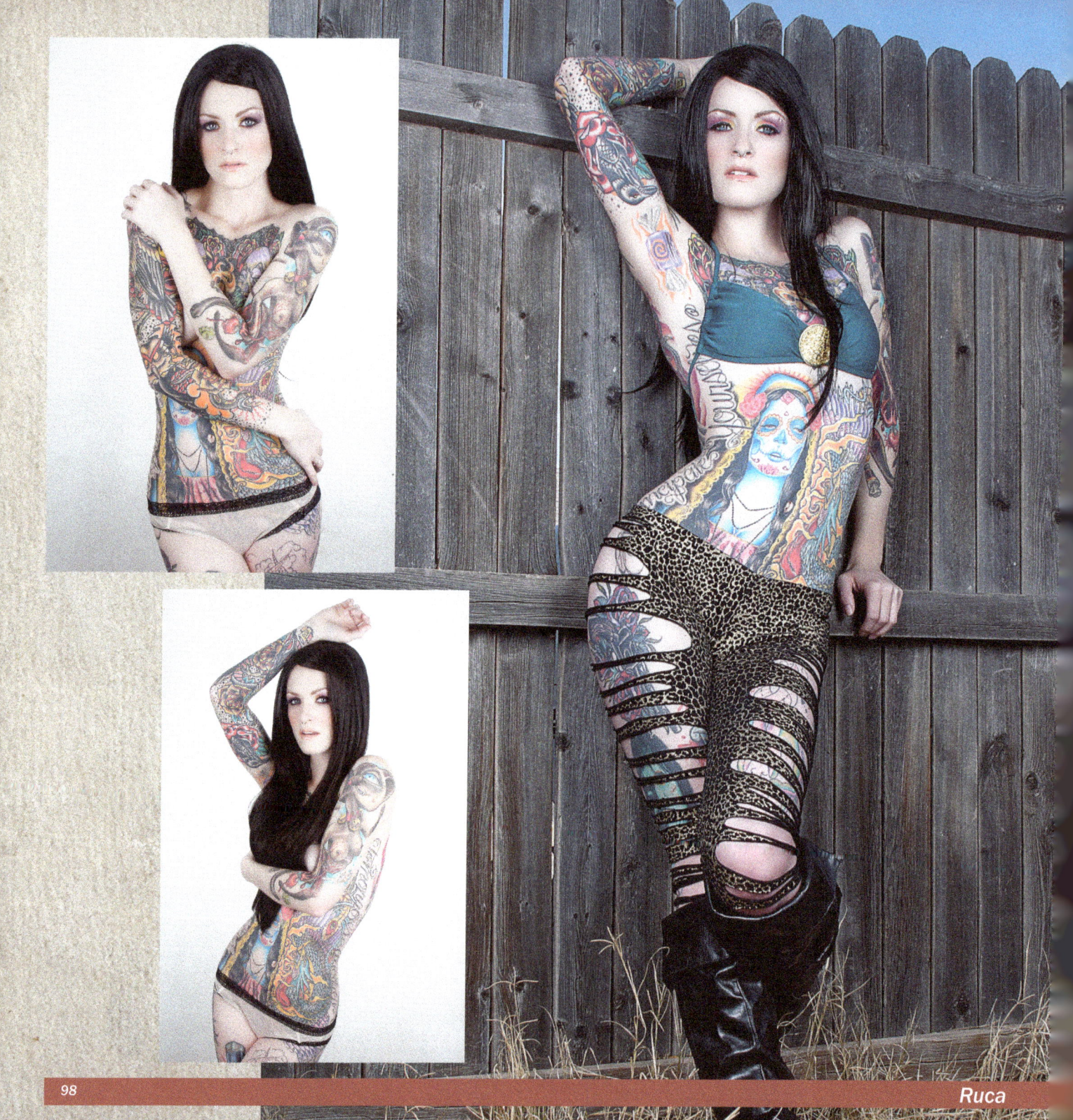

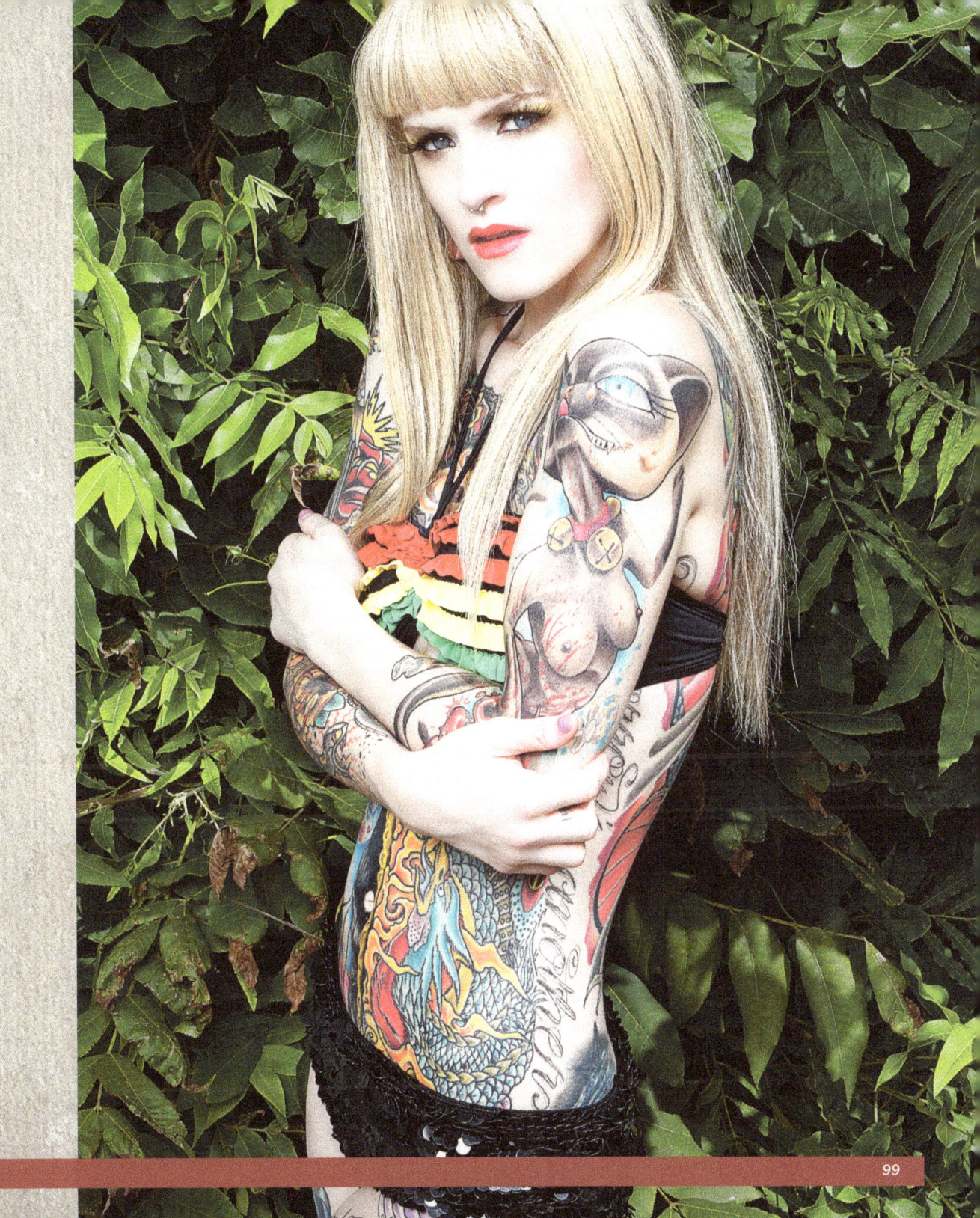

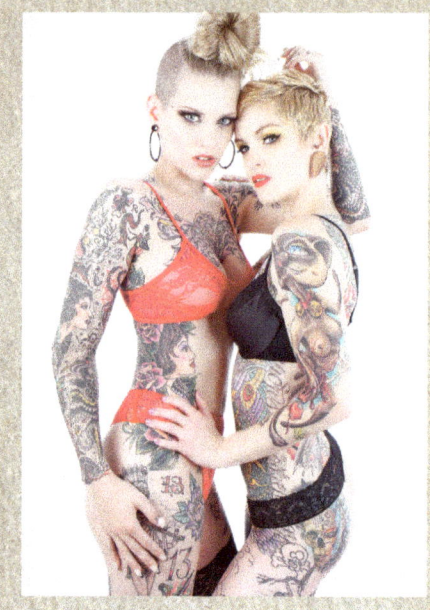
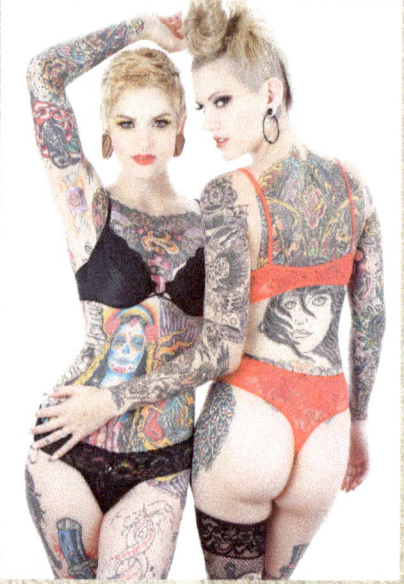
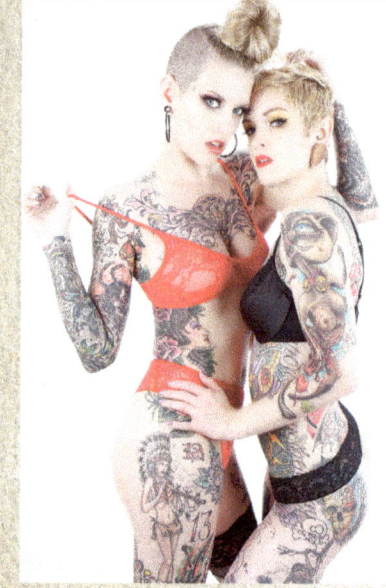

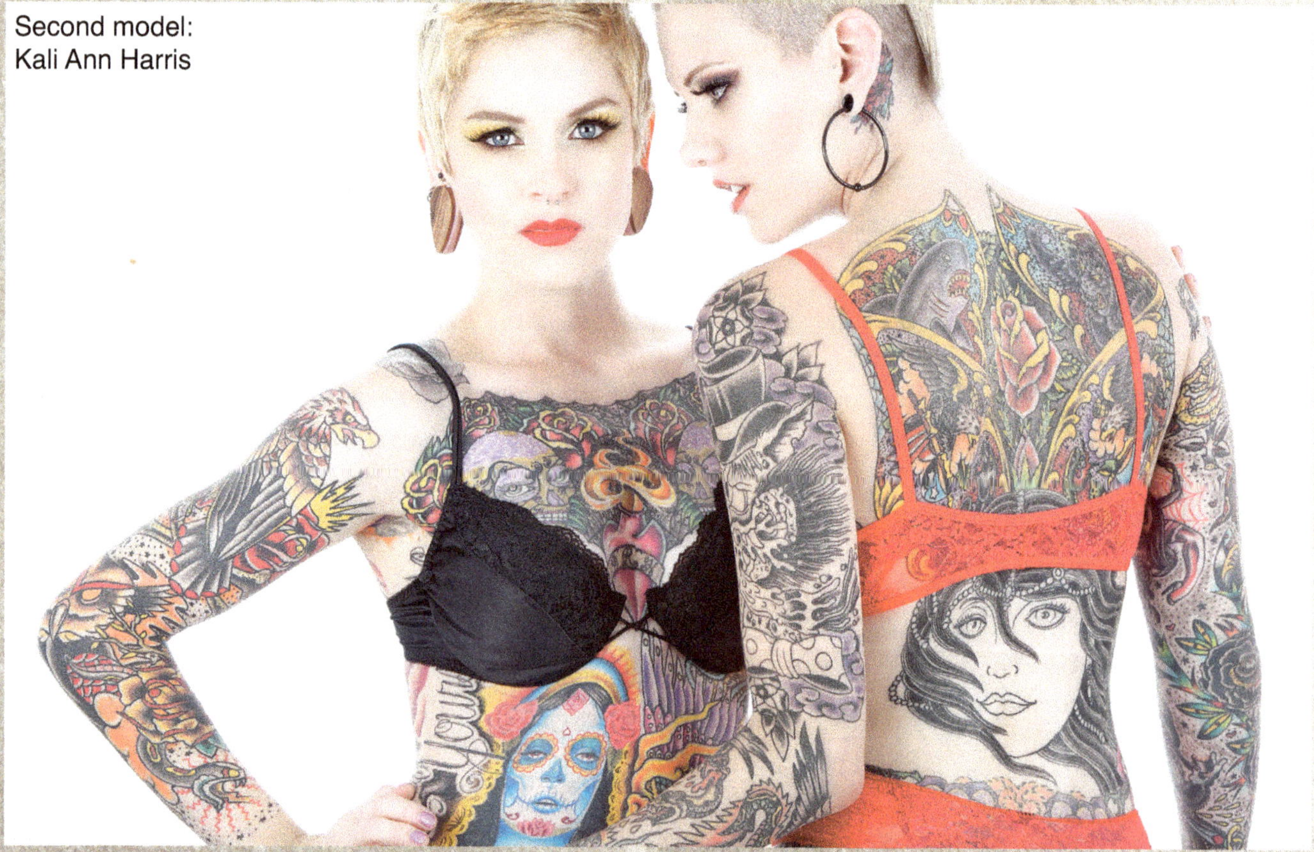

Second model:
Kali Ann Harris

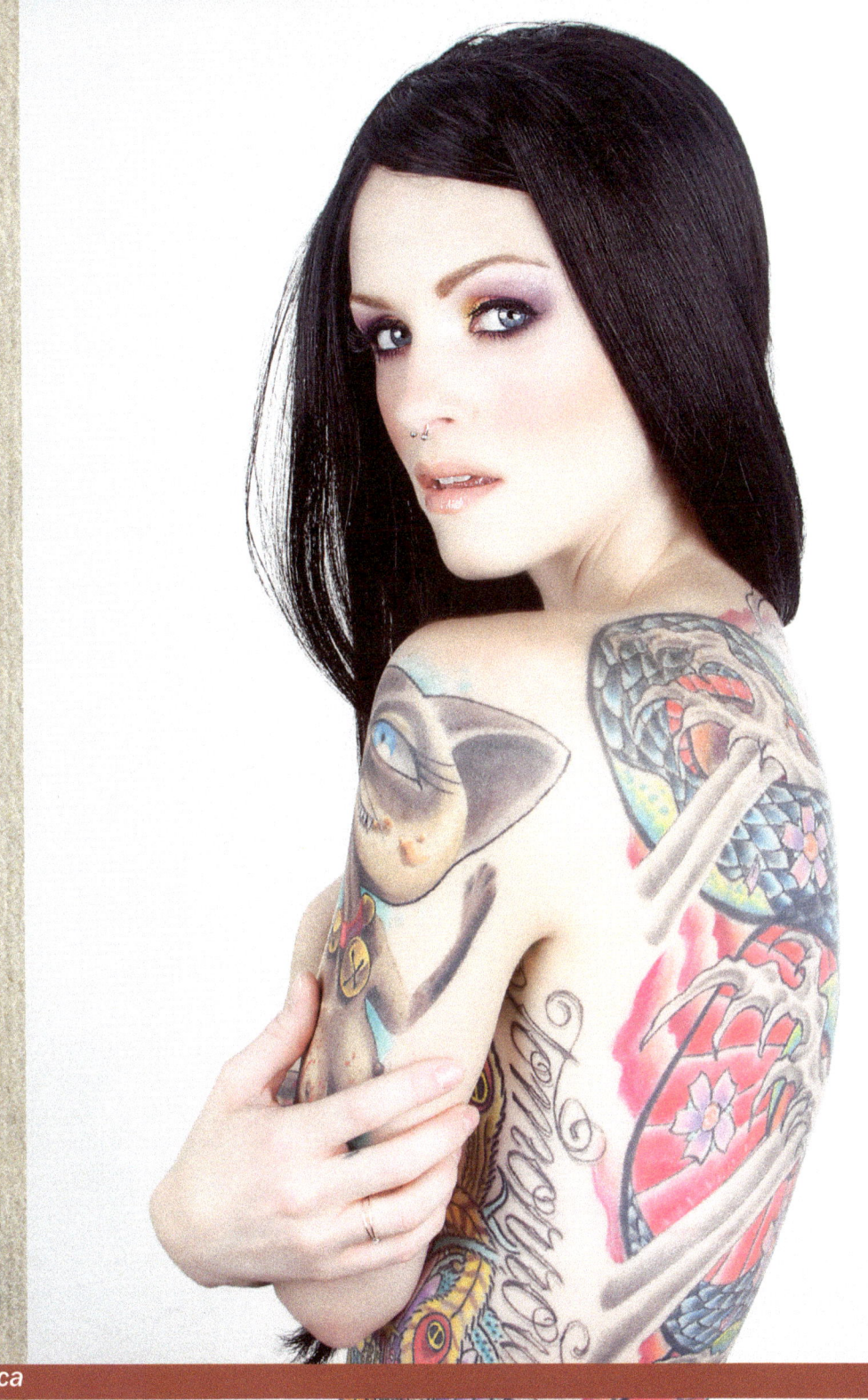

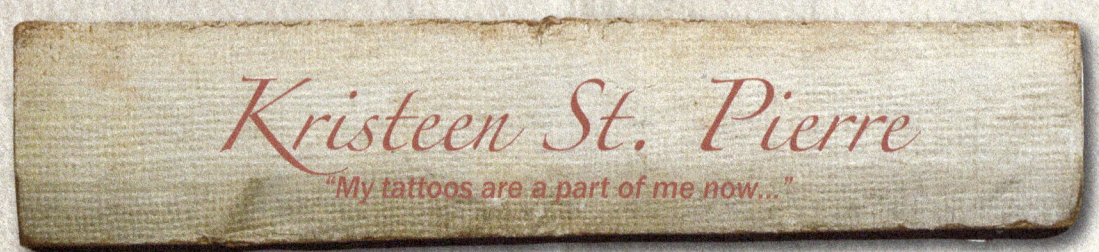

Kristeen St. Pierre
"My tattoos are a part of me now..."

I am Kristeen St. Pierre. I'm not your cookie cutter lady. I was born and raised in Roseville CA, surrounded by stuck up snobs and goodie two-shoes. Finally, at age 21, a new chapter – modeling - began.

How did you get your start in modeling?

I never really had the opportunity to explore the field of modeling, but after a rocky breakup, Jessie DeVille took me under her wing as a Diamond Doll, and introduced me to Keith Selle. And that is where the magic began.

How long have you been a model, and what do you enjoy the most about it?

I am a relative rookie, but I love getting dolled up and being the center of attention for sure. Not accustomed to acting like a modeling, but I am blessed to get this opportunity and to work with so many wonderful people. I owe it all to Jessie D. and Keith for their support and the time they've invested in me.

When did your interest in tattoos begin? And how long was it from then until you got your first one?

I was 16 when I started dating David, 6'7 and blasted. And ever since then, I have been fascinated about the tattoo culture and industry. Not more than six months into our relationship I decided to get my first piece.

Which was your first one? And why did you choose it?

Foolishly, I choose my left side to receive my first piece. I knew I wanted bright traditional style flowers curving to my body and a Bible verse. Jessie from The Studio had her hands full with me. I briefly passed out while she was free handing my side. I believe I was the worst client she had ever had. All said and done, she did an awesome job, and I couldn't be happier.

Among all your tattoos, which one do you prefer and why?

Honestly, my chest piece. Some people may live their whole lives wondering, what if? I don't want to blend in with the crowd and float by in life without taking risks. I want to make a name for myself, be proud to be different, and do it all with a "suck it" attitude. The center of my chest piece is a heart shaped diamond locket, and on each side are two mismatching keys tucked inside blue roses. It's apparent, no one has the key to my heart, and I want to keep it that way. Kerry "KR" Rossi put solid work and his own creative touch into my chest piece. Without him as my main artist, I wouldn't be where I am now.

Please talk us through some of your tattoos and the reason behind them.

The back of my neck is a matching tattoo with my ex. At the time, it was a wonderful gift for our anniversary. His tattoo was smack center of his chest, but we had the same design of a treble clef and a bass clef that formed the shape of a heart. Definitely the least painful tattoo. As for my side, the Bible verse Psalm 37:3-7 basically says to live right, do good, be righteous, and have faith. And in that you will be fulfilled inside, and your life's purpose will reveal. Something about the passage hit home, because I have definitely fallen hard, and it reminds me to just keep positive and that if I am a good person, good things will come.

Do you regret any of your tattoos?

100% No. You can't live your life with regrets. We all mess up, but I embrace my mistakes, I grow and become stronger from each of them. I think about the art I want on my body, so I can be pleased with it five or ten years from now.

What's the next step for Kristeen St. Pierre?

I am hoping to find a cure for cancer, run a marathon, and battle world hunger, but we'll see how modeling and college go first.

www.myspace.com/feisty_n_finicky
www.facebook.com/profile.php?id=100000115563785
keithselle.tumblr.com/post/.../the-feature-of-kristeen-st-pierre-in-the

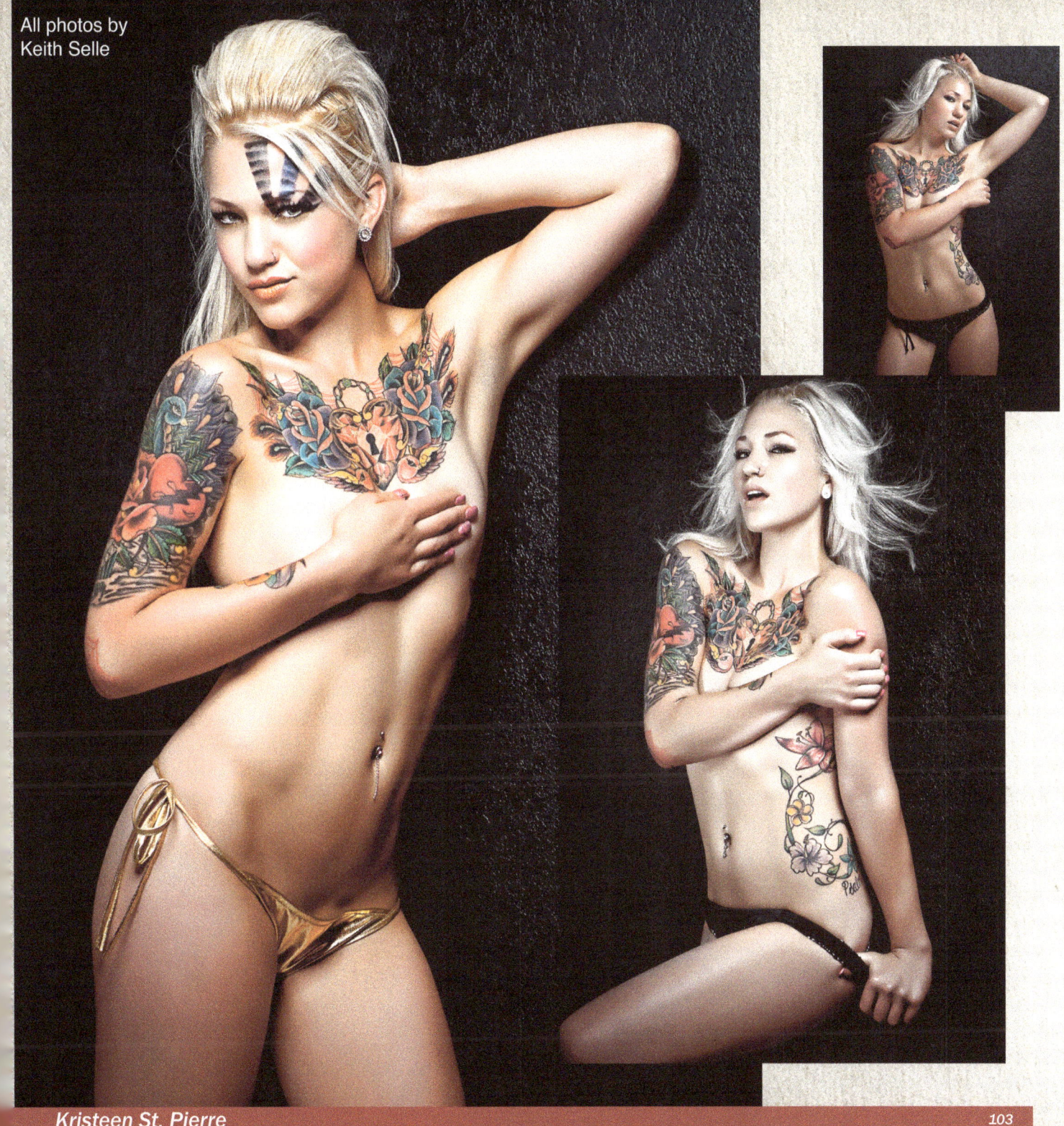

All photos by Keith Selle

Kristeen St. Pierre

103

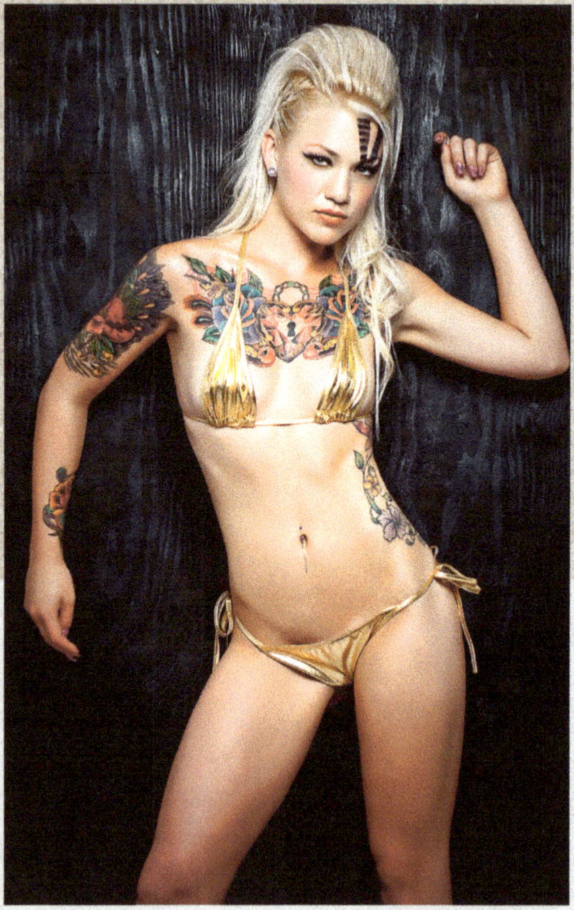

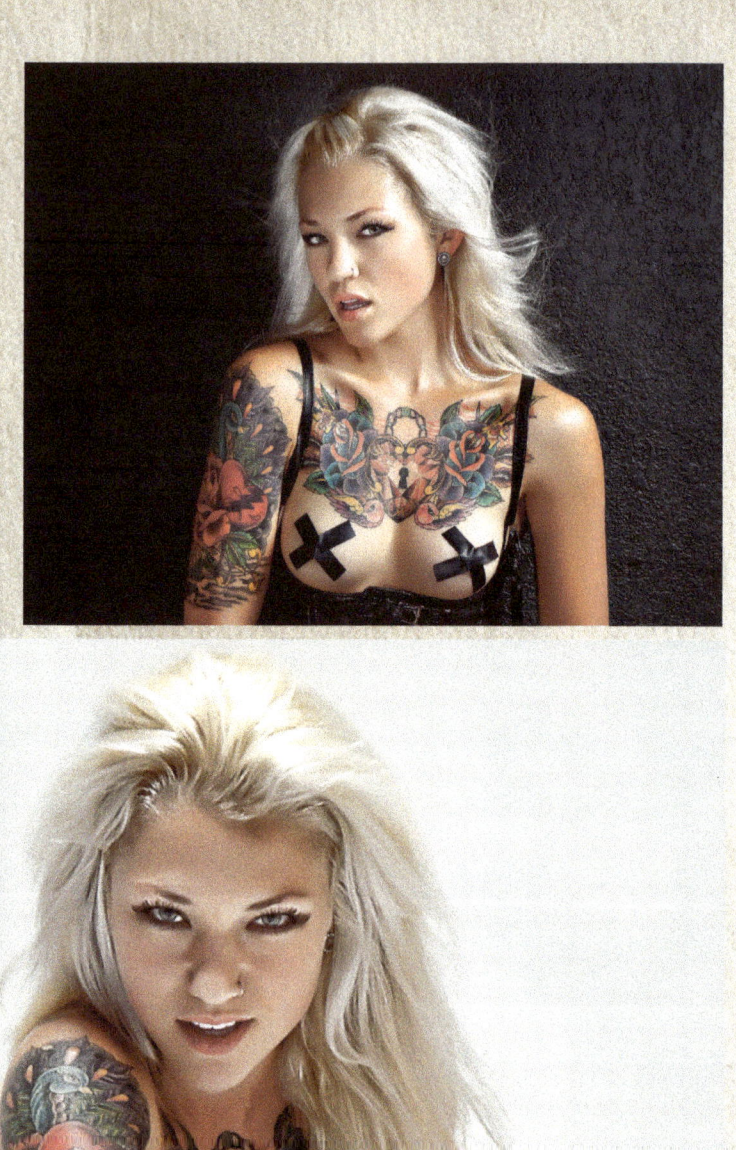

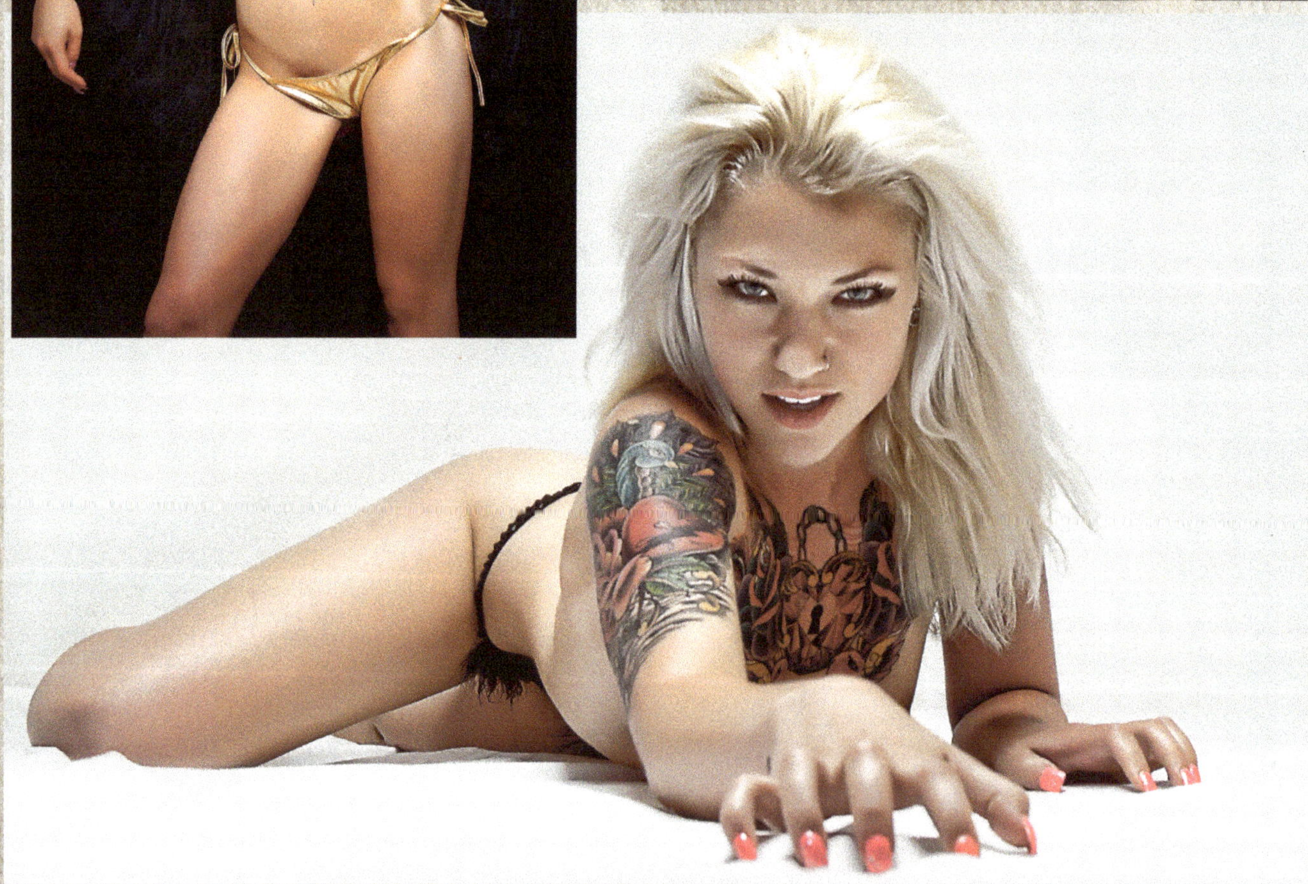

Kristeen St. Pierre

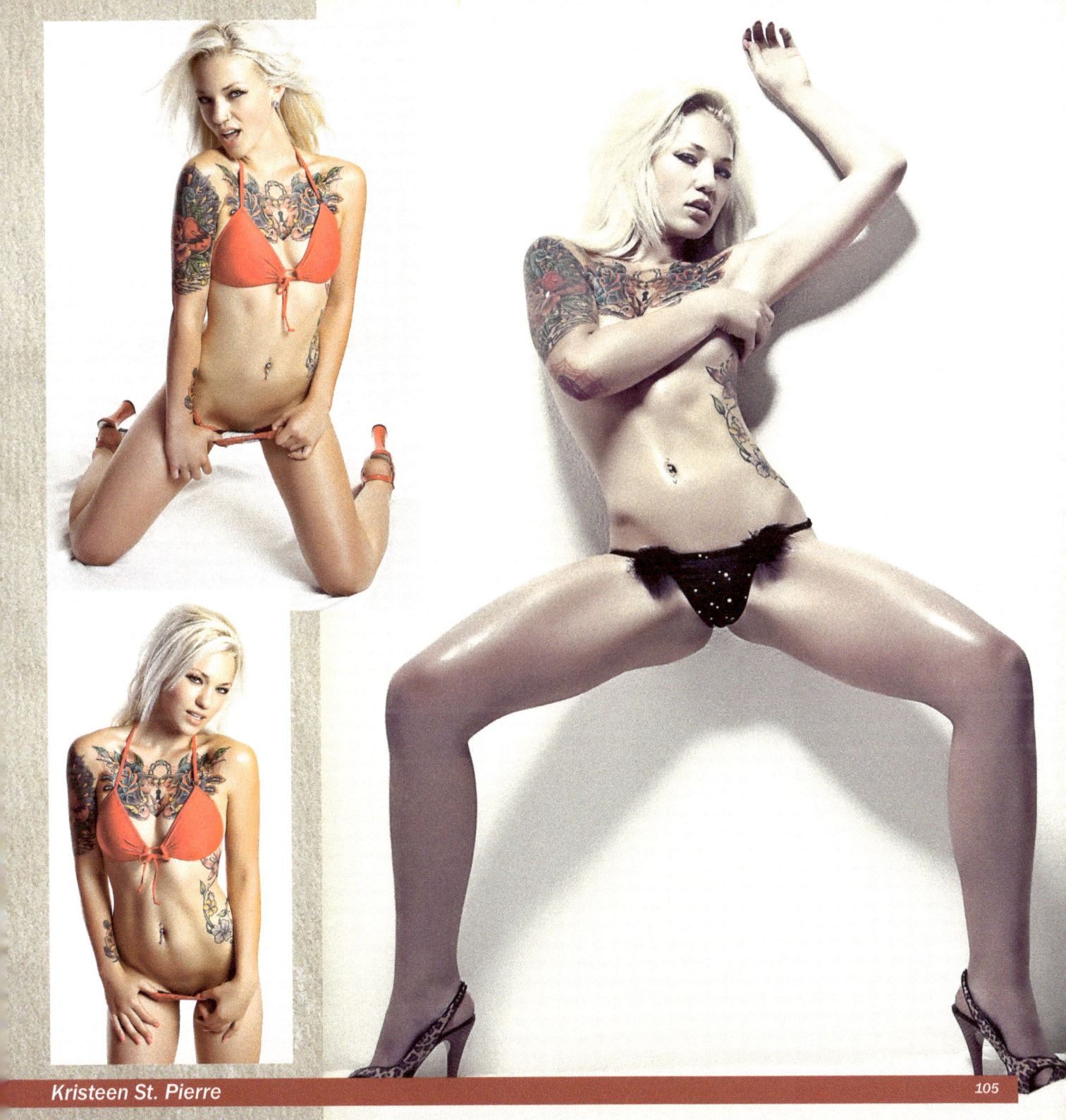

Kristeen St. Pierre

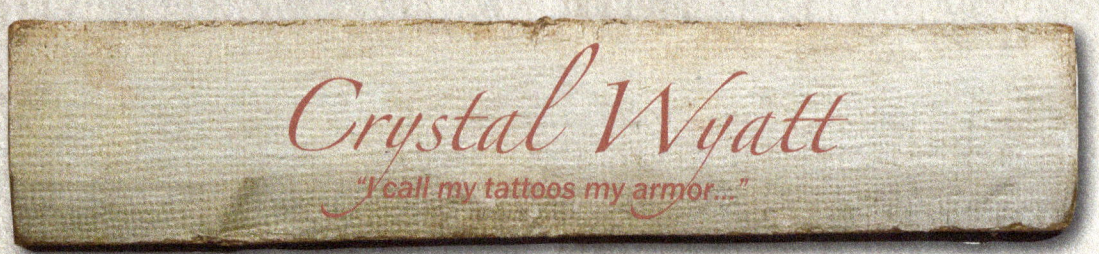

Crystal Wyatt
"I call my tattoos my armor..."

My name is Crystal Wyatt and I am the singer for the rock band Moxie. We are southern California based rock/pop band and I love being on stage. I am also a model, and love collaborating with different artists and photographers to create beautiful images.

How did you get your start in modeling?

It started out as promotion for my solo music, I was shooting to promote myself on the internet. I didn't realize how much I would love it, but it stuck with me so I started doing more shoots and working with some local companies. I did a few runway shows as well, but I am much more into the creative photo shoots.

Do you work with any special photographers on a regular basis?

Yes, Justice Howard is my absolute favorite photographer to work with. She is so amazing, I prefer her to anyone else. I have worked with several other good photographers, but Justice and I have a comfort and an artistic element that can't easily be duplicated.

How did your love for tattoos start? And how old were you when you got your first one?

I have always been fascinated with tattoos! My older sister got me into it and took me to get my first tattoo when I turned 18. My mom actually agreed to pay for it if I promised to never pierce my tongue! I wasn't really interested in piercings so it was a good deal.

What is your favorite tattoo so far, and why?

My back piece. The dragon set against the flowers is really special to me, and I got it as a guardian. It is my favorite because it represents a lot about me, with the Japanese imagery coming from my childhood, the cherry blossoms which are so delicate and pretty, and the dragon which represents strength. It is about balance, and I think that life is about balance.

How do you come up with the ideas for your pieces?

I just come up with things that have meaning to me, and then the imagery comes. It is great to have a tattoo artist that understands my vision, so they can easily translate my ideas to art.

What do your tattoos mean to you?

I call my tattoos my armor. They each have a significant back story and meaning to me, and I think of them as armor because they protect me from where I have been, and remind me of the direction I need to be going.

Have you gotten any new work done?

The last work I got was finishing up my right sleeve. I am debating a full sleeve on the left arm because I find that with modeling, I like the contrast of one of my arms being heavily tattooed and the other naked. I think it's beautiful.

Do you like to stick to one artist, or try a number of different ones?

I have been to a few since I started getting tattooed, but I have been loyal to Bill Canales for about six years now.

Do you think people treat you differently for being heavily tattooed?

It depends. Some do, and some don't. It is definitely getting more and more common, especially in southern California for women and people in general to be heavily tattooed. It can be a bit of a challenge in the corporate office world. But I have learned that if I rock at my job, the real people who matter don't see the tattoos as an issue. Unfortunately not everyone is as open minded.

What is your favorite part about your body?

I love my curves! All of them, top and bottom, and I love my eyes.

www.myspace.com/crystalwyatt
www.facebook.com/crystal.wyatt2
www.modelmayhem.com/1118053

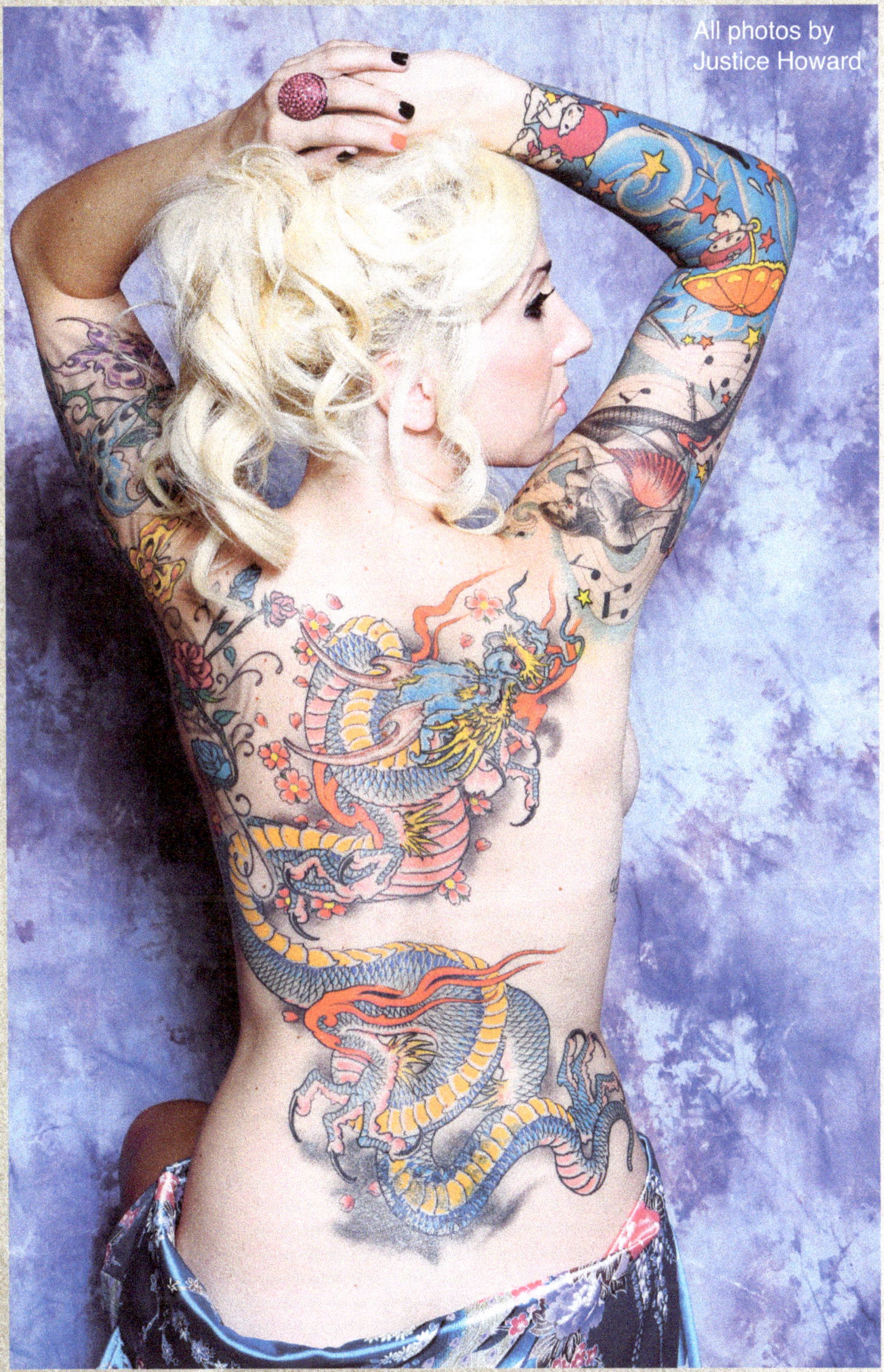

All photos by Justice Howard

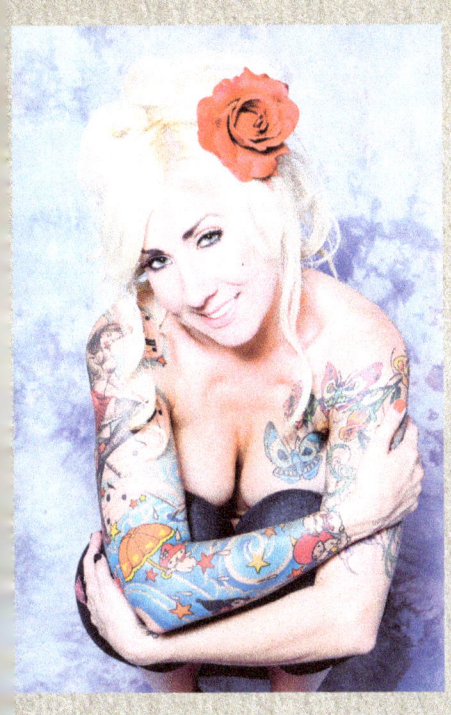

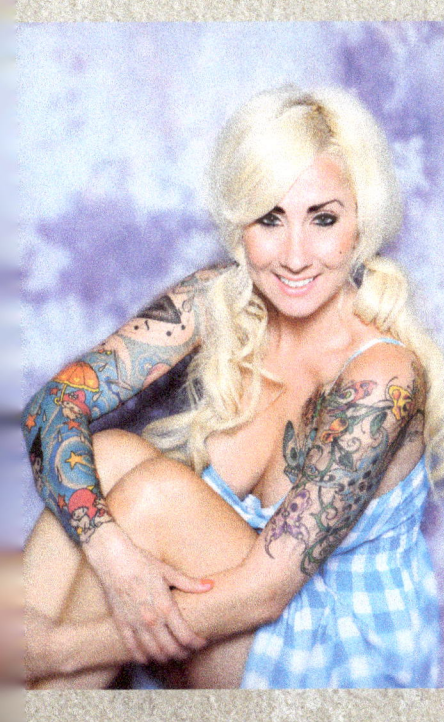

Crystal Wyatt

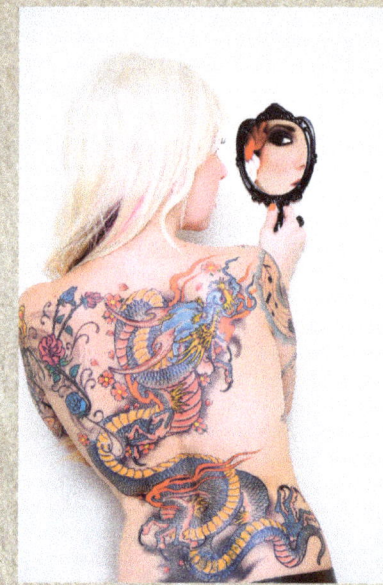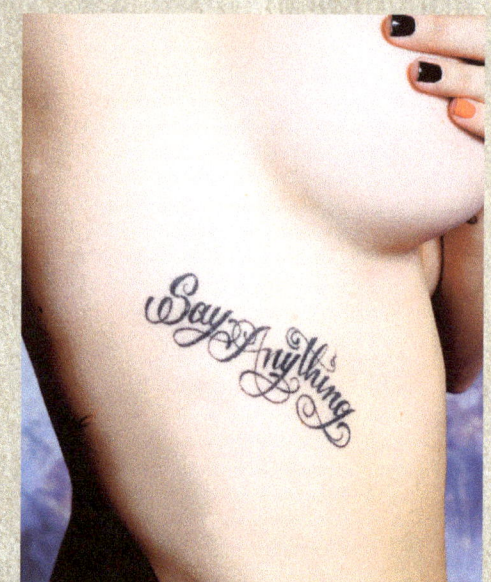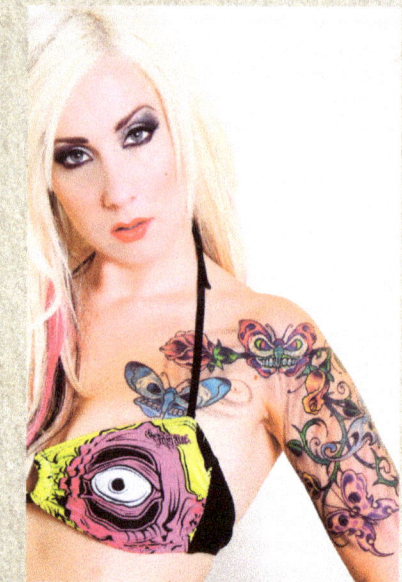

Crystal Wyatt

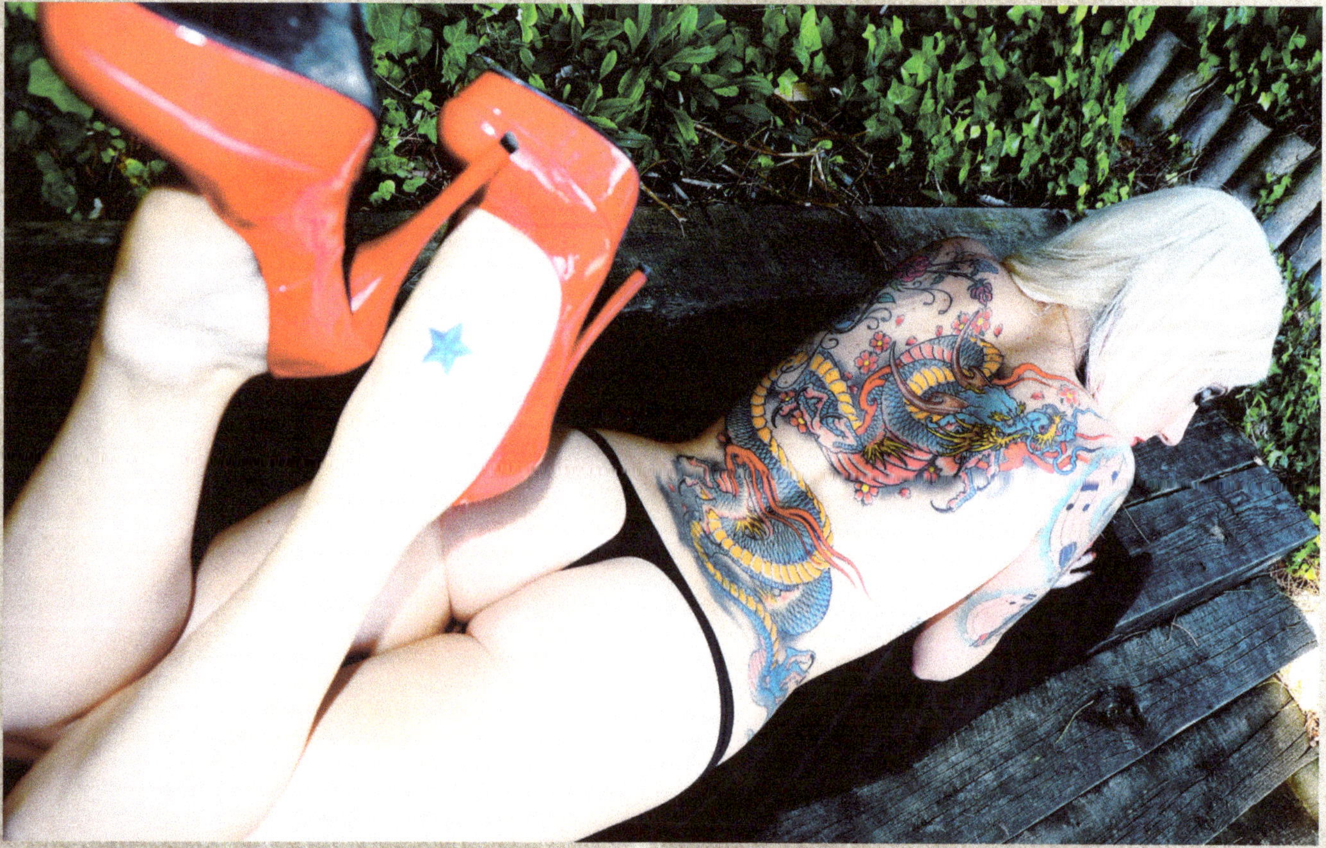

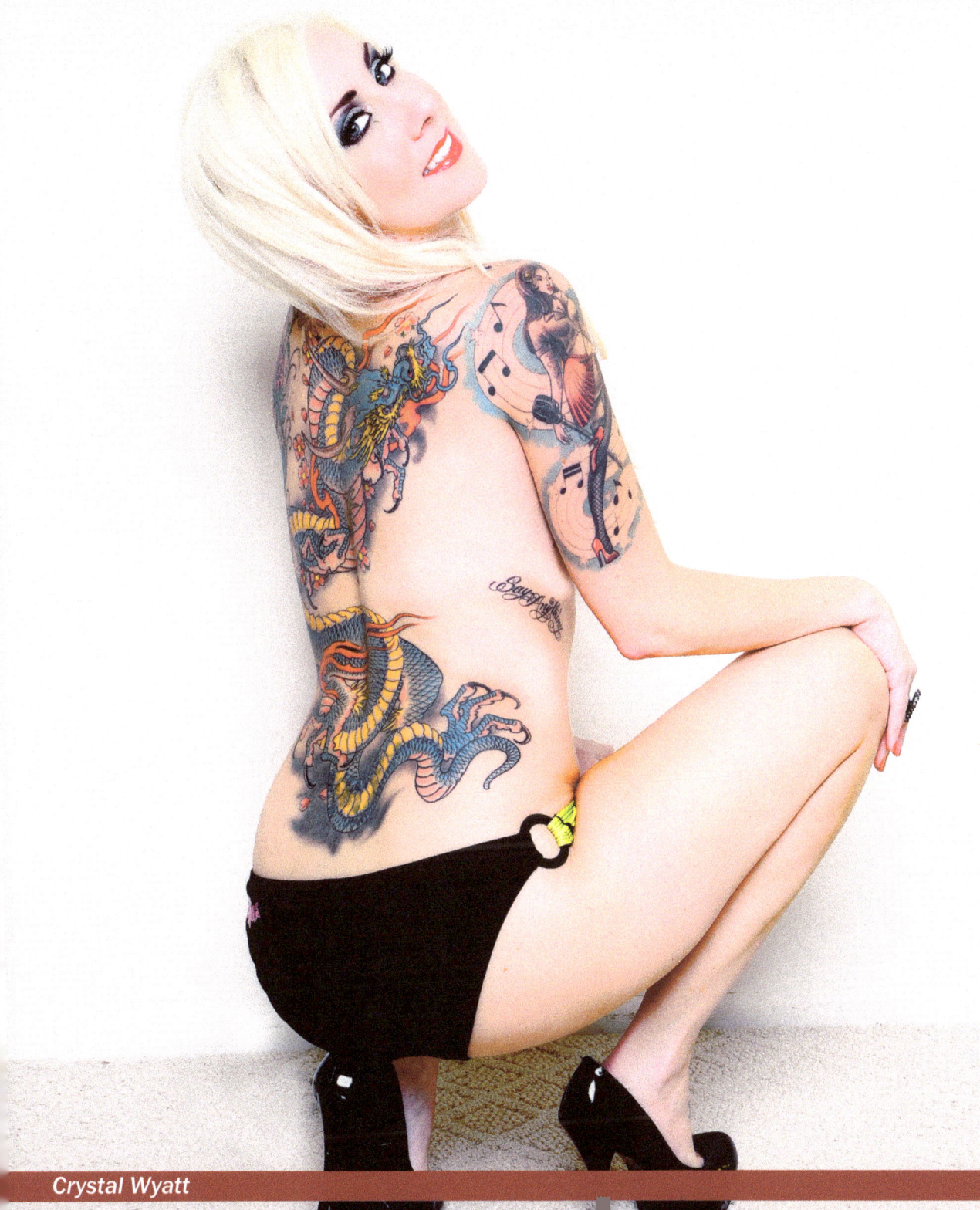

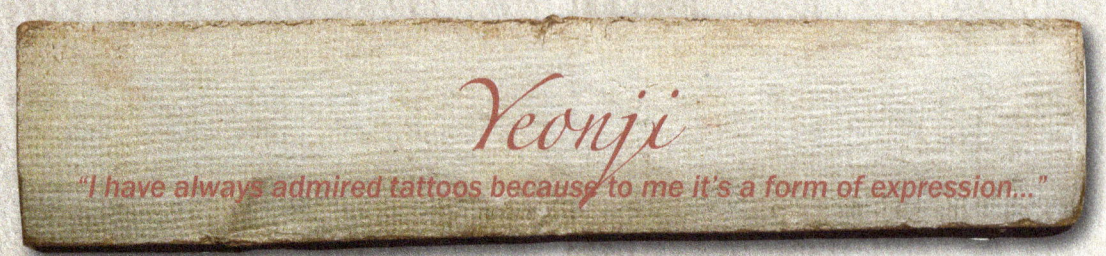

Yeonji

"I have always admired tattoos because to me it's a form of expression..."

I am Yeonji, born in Seoul, South Korea, but a resident of the San Francisco Bay area since I was two years old. I am a retail manage for a cosmetics company, and of course a tattoo model as well.

How long have you been a model, and what do you enjoy the most about it?

I have been modeling since August 2010 and I love being in front of the camera. I feel empowered and free when I'm modeling. I have been fortunate enough to meet and work with a lot of amazing and talented people. So far I have been on the cover of five tattoo magazines and hopefully I will have many more to come. I love every aspect of modeling and can't wait to see what will be in store for me in the near future.

How did you get your start in modeling?

My first official photo shoot was with Keith Selle. To be honest, everything took off from there. I haven't been modeling for very long, but I was bitten by the modeling bug ever since. I am very grateful to Keith for helping me out when I first got started and I look forward to what's to come.

When did your interest in tattoos begin? And how long was it from then until you got your first one?

I have always admired tattoos because to me it's a form of expression. I got my first tattoo when I was 18 years old and I have been hooked ever since. I plan on finishing and covering both my arms and possibly my entire back.

Which is your first one? And why did you choose it?

My first tattoo was my name in Korean on my left shoulder. I am very proud of my heritage and felt at the time it was best to express it that way.

What do your tattoos mean to you? Are they symbolic or do you just dig the art?

All of my tattoos have a symbolic meaning to them whether it's religion, family or love.

Among all your tattoos, which one do you prefer and why?

Among all my tattoos my favorite one would have to be the one on my left forearm. It is a broken rosary with my grandmother's birthday and the day that she passed away. I was able to take care of her before she passed away in 2005. Her passing really changed my outlook on life in a positive way.

Please talk us through some of your tattoos and the reason behind them.

Left side: Tropical flowers around a message in Portuguese for my husband which symbolizes our love and marriage. This huge piece is still in the works by my close friend who is more like my brother, Steve Nguyen. Right Side: My favorite verse from the bible. Matthews 5:8 "Blessed are those who are pure in heart for they shall see God," surrounded by anime style flowers blowing in the wind. Right forearm: It says "Getaway" and my husband has the same exact one on his forearm. This was his nickname back in the days when he used to be a bad boy. Lol.

Of all the above mentioned things that you've accomplished in your relatively short career what would you pick as your biggest achievements in your career?

My biggest achievements have been the various tattoo magazines I have been featured in.

What's the next step for you?

This is just the beginning for me and I have many more exciting projects in the works. I am a firm believer in the saying "you only live once" and am determined to make it in the modeling scene. So for more updates please follow my fan page on Facebook at: www.facebook.com/loveyeonji to view all my recent photos and stay updated on everything I do!

www.modelmayhem.com/1759365
www.tumblr.com/tagged/yeonji
www.h2oceanmodels.com/yeonji/

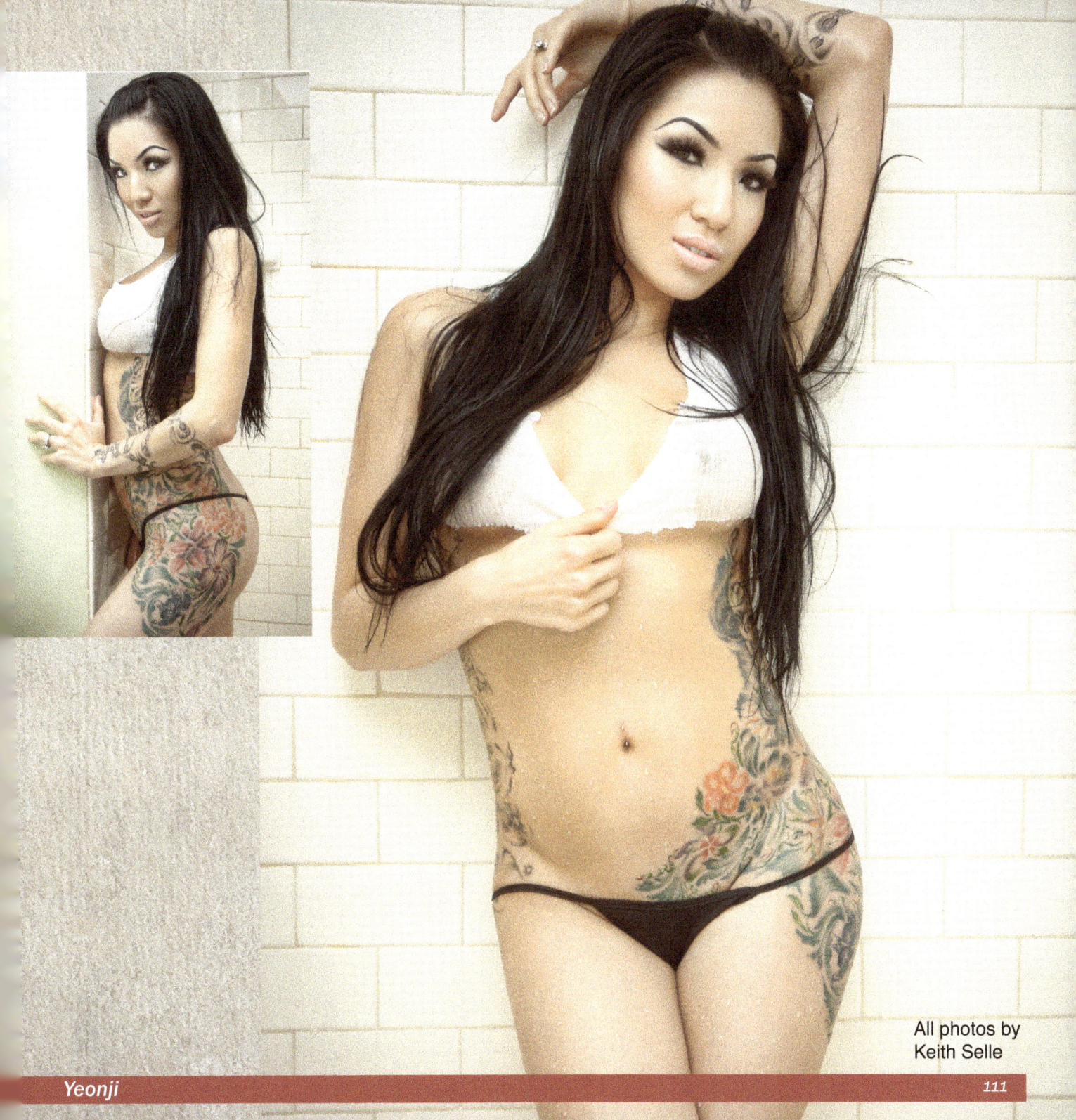

All photos by Keith Selle

Yeonji

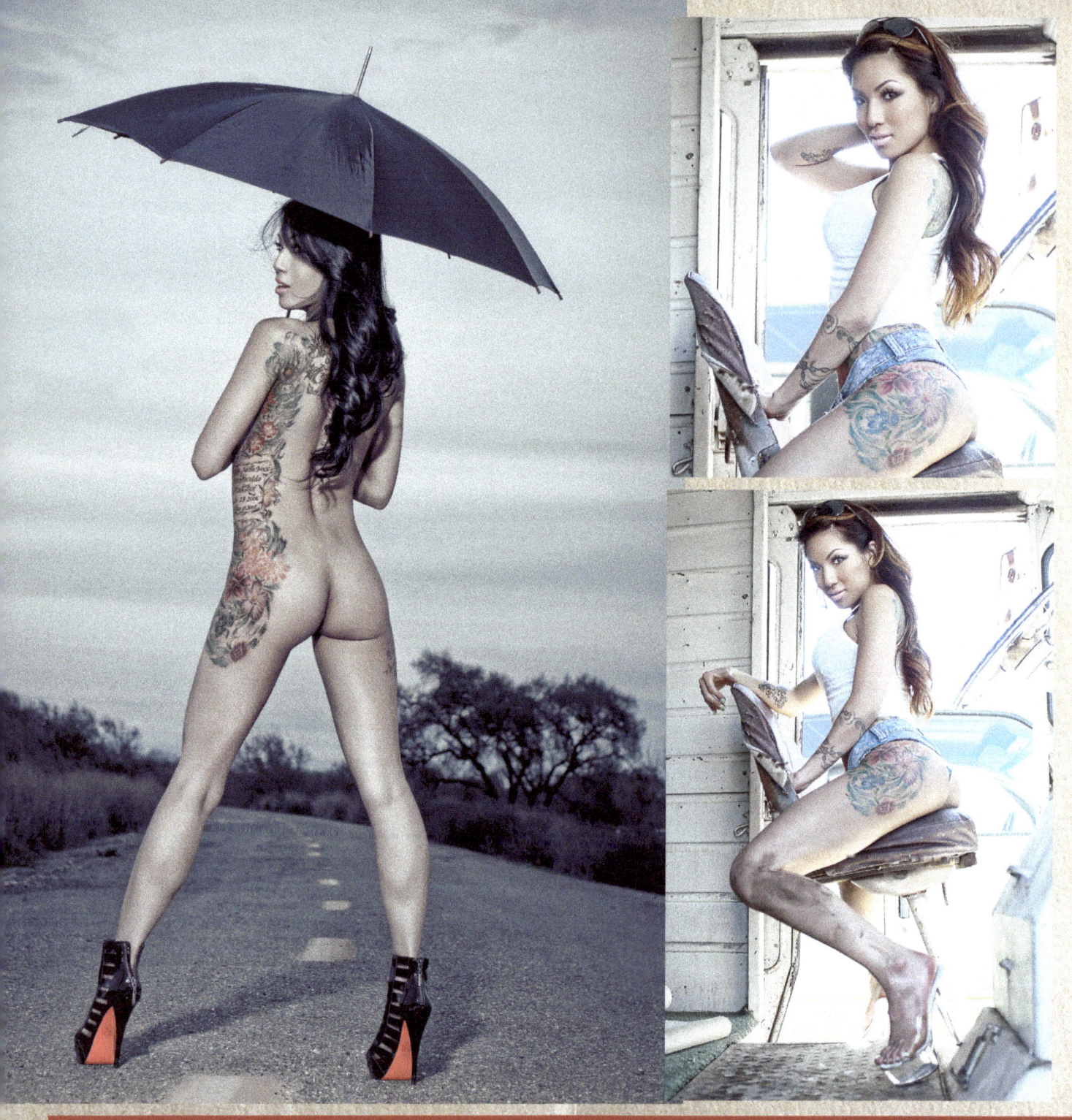

Yeonji

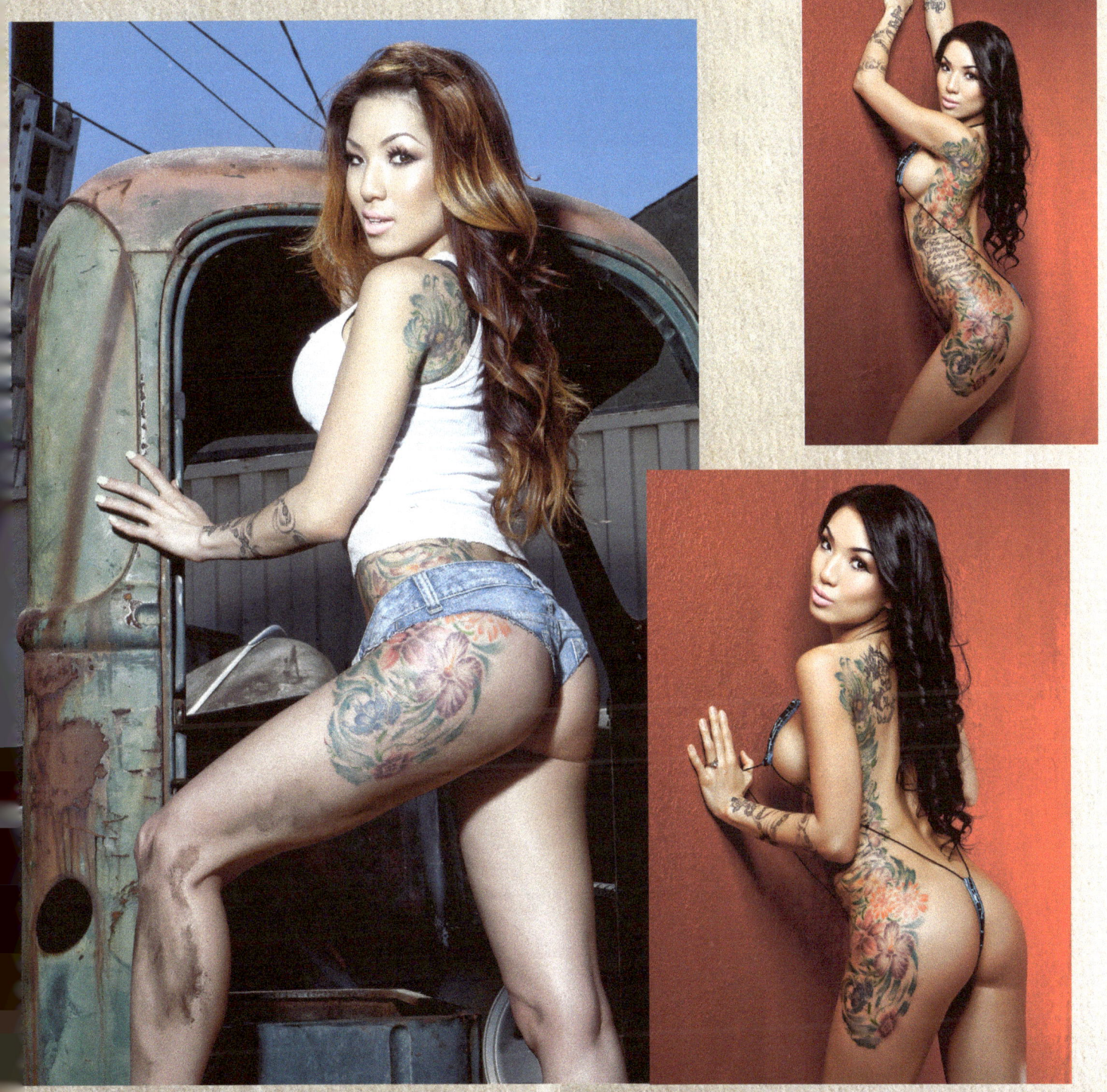

Yeonji

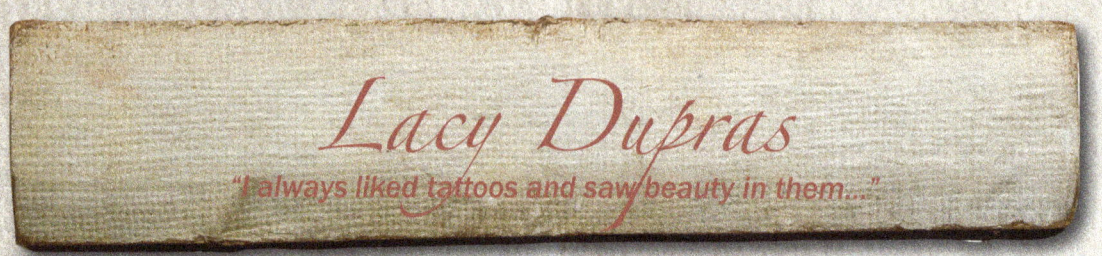

Lacy Dupras
"I always liked tattoos and saw beauty in them..."

I am Lacy Dupras, born and raised in Arizona. I'm a wife and a mother to three beautiful babies. In addition to modeling, I co-own a cake business called Tatt'd Cakes and I'm going to school to be a respiratory therapist.

How did you get your start in modeling? Have you always wanted to be a model?

I have always wanted to model, even when I was little I would make my grandma take me to model searches. Then if I got picked they would tell her how much money it was going to be and she would tell them if they were choosing me they could pay me. Lol. Needless to say that went no where. Then when I started getting more tattoo's I met fellow model Heather Moss and she just threw me in the mix.

Where do you draw your influences? Who are your role models?

Honestly, I am most influenced by my children. Whenever someone is wanting to set up a shoot I always think of them first and ask myself if this is something that they would ever be embarrassed of. So I pride myself on portraying myself well because I am not only representing myself but my family.

What would you say, in your opinion, is the biggest misconception about modeling?

That it's all glam and glitz. Modeling takes a lot of time and a lot of work... just like anything else, practice makes perfect.

How old were you and how did you decide you wanted to get your first tattoo – were you inspired by other people's art?

I was 21 when I got my first tattoo, I grew up in a super strict house and definitely wasn't allowed to have a tattoo. But I always liked tattoos and thought they were beautiful.

How did you find the guy who does your tattoos?

He was my friend on MySpace, lol.

You've had plenty of tattoos done, but how do you go from the initial idea to the finished design?

I just brainstorm everything with my artist, Bobby Moss, then he takes my ideas and turns it into artwork.

Please talk us through some of your tattoos and the reason behind them.

Well my left sleeve is definitely one of the most significant and meaningful tattoos on my body. It is dedicated to my Mom. She is portrayed as an angel with a wing covering her face, and I have unconditional love written beside her because that is all I ever had for her! No matter what I loved my mom unconditionally. She passed away in 2007 giving birth to Triplets and that is the reason for the three sunflowers. Sunflowers where her favorite flower and the three boys where the last thing she ever gave us. The elephant on my right sleeve is one of my favorites along with the evil eye on my right side.

What do your tattoos mean to you?

They represent me and who I am, so they mean everything to me.

What is it about tattoos that appeals to you?

Tattoos are art that you can wear and that you can put your emotions into. They are memorials, reminders, dedications that you carry with you for life!

Which areas have been the most painful to tattoo?

Definitely the inner parts of my upper arm, ouch.

What is your definition of beauty?

Beauty comes from within, if the insides are ugly so is the outside!

Any words of advice for a young lady who aspires to be a model?

Always stay humble and never forget where you came from - the crazy road to where you are going!

www.facebook.com/lacydupras
www.modelmayhem.com/2336344
www.theinkonme.com/2012/05/ink-on-lacy-dupras.html
www.tumblr.com/tagged/lacy-dupras

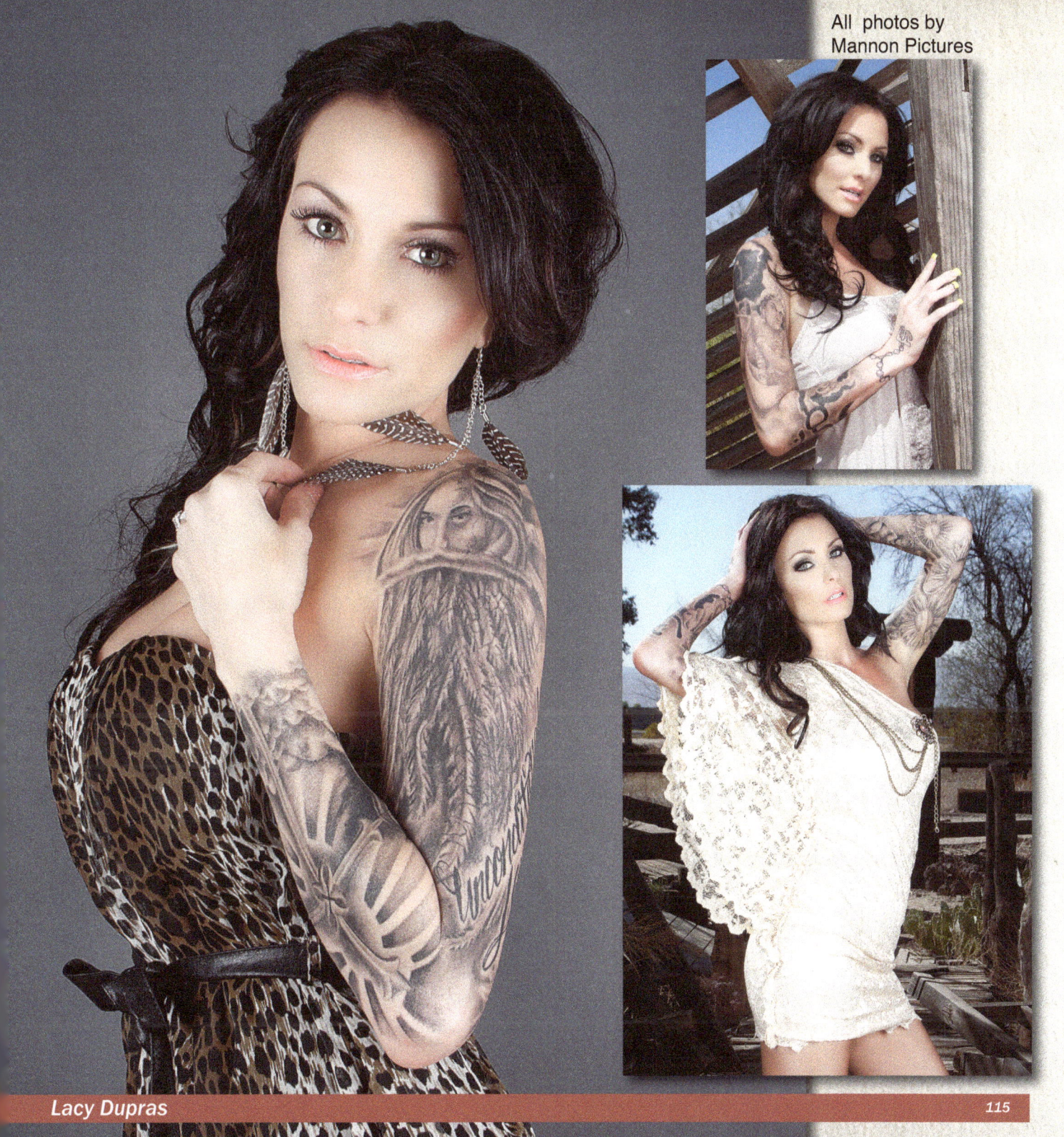

All photos by Mannon Pictures

Lacy Dupras

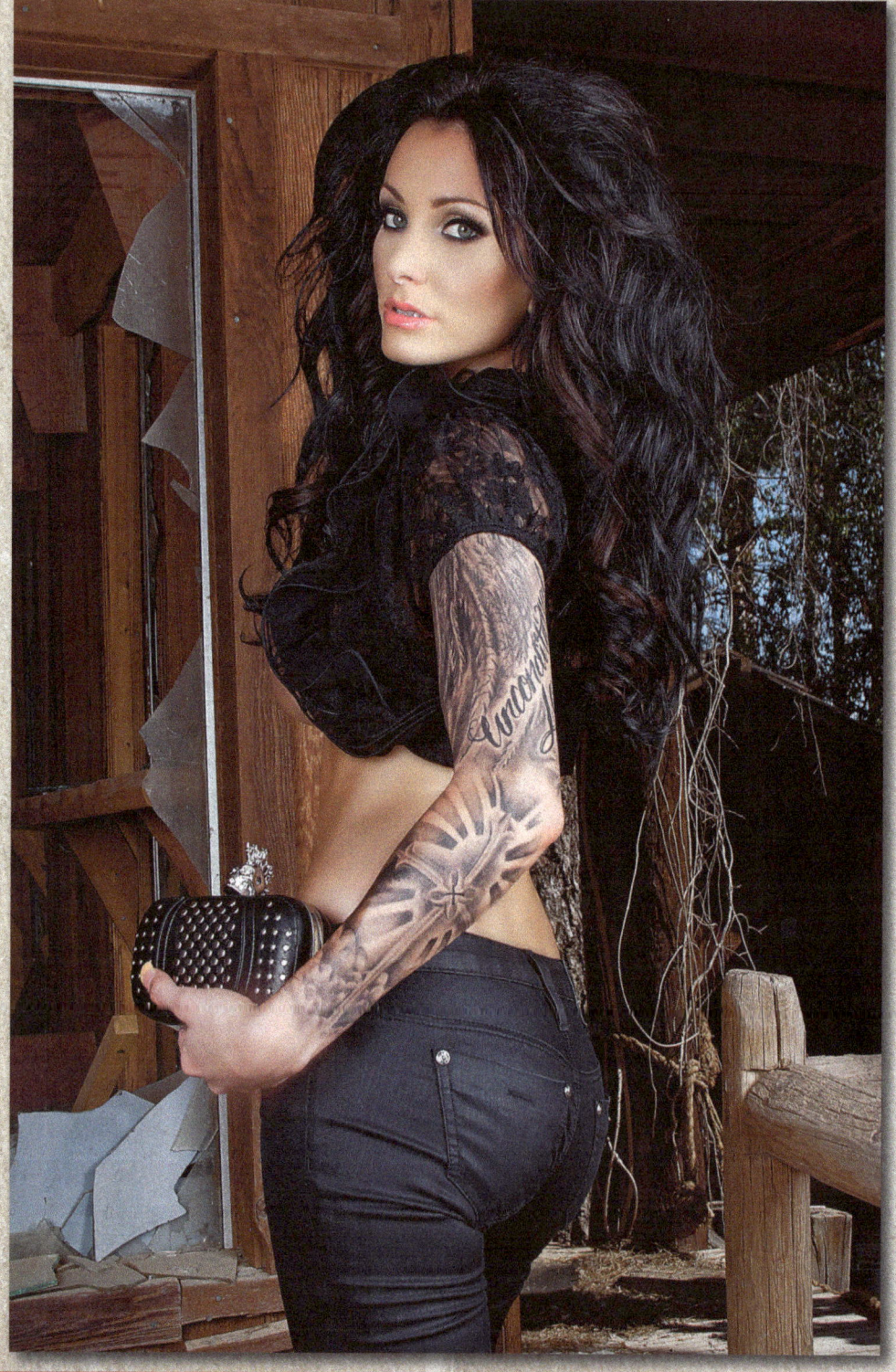

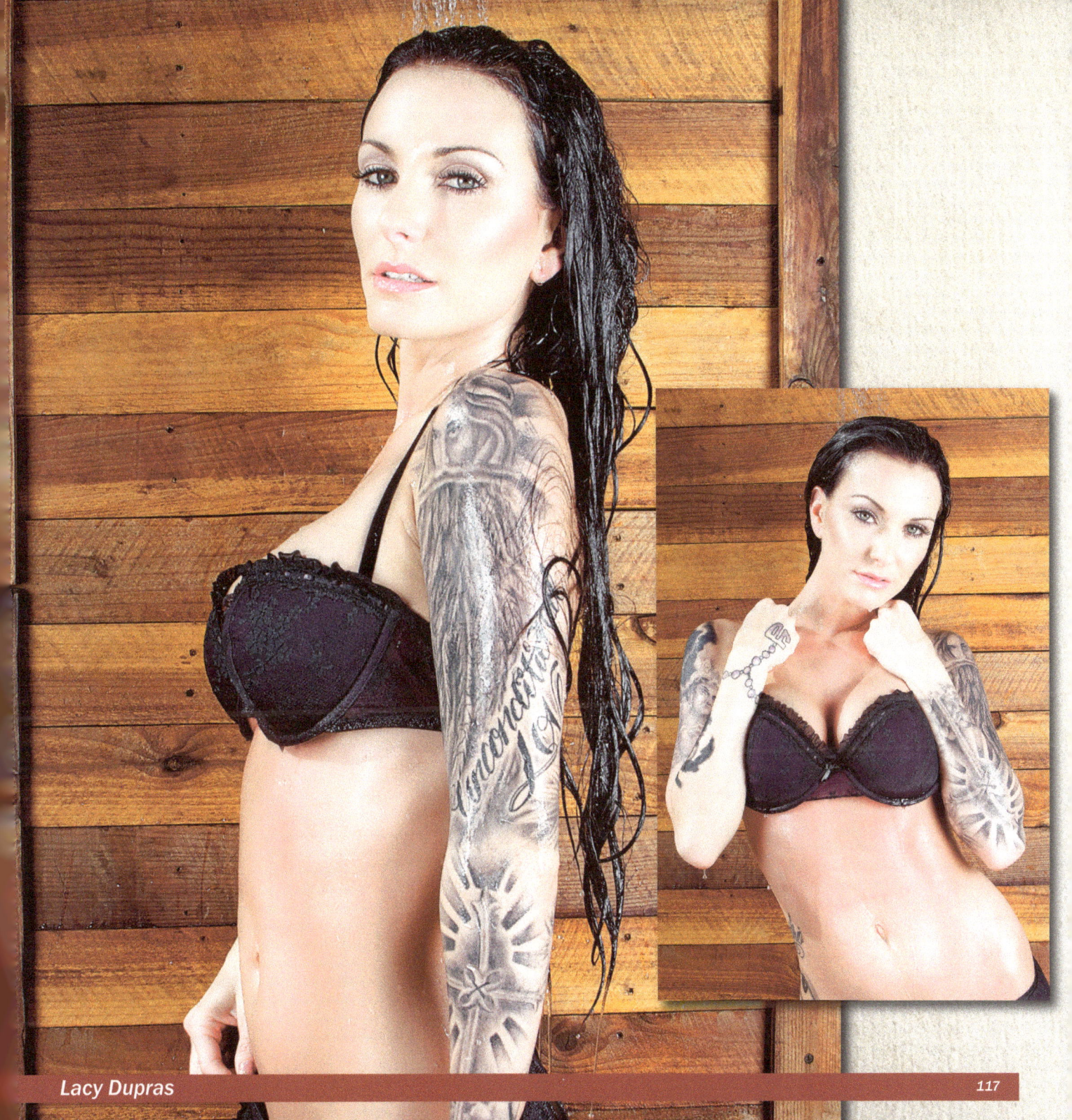

Lacy Dupras

Jennifer Groblebe
"I get treated differently by some people..."

I am Jennifer Groblebe from Sacramento, California. Tattoo modeling was never actually one of my goals, I sort of fell into it through some photographer friends. Eventually I had the opportunity to join Diamond Dolls. Along the way I have been fortunate enough to be involved in some amazing photoshoots and meet some great photographers.

How long have you been a model, and what do you enjoy the most about it?
I have been doing tattoo modeling for a couple of years. I would have to say that the thing I enjoy the most is the amazing people I've met along the way. My friends at Diamond Dolls Ink are incredible!

Do you work with any special photographers on a regular basis?
I have worked a lot with Gary Roberts and Keith Selle.

Tell us about your photo shoot with Keith Selle. Were you nervous?
No I wasn't nervous at all, Keith is great at making his models feel at ease. He's very professional and has a great sense of humor!

How did you decide you wanted to get your first tattoo – were you inspired by other people's art?
I decided to get a tattoo when I was 17. I was kind of a rebollious teen.

Were you nervous the first time?
Yes, I think I was pretty nervous the first time I got tattooed.

How did you find the guy who does your tattoos?
I mostly get tattooed by Miguel "Uzi" Montgomery, out of northern California. He's absolutely amazing. I heard about his work from a friend, found him on Facebook, then tracked him down at American Graffiti in Sacramento He was well worth the effort I put into stalking him.

Could you tell us about your first tattoo and the reason behind it, please?
I got a butterfly on my right lower stomach, I got it because my friend had drawn the picture and talked my mother into allowing it because she also has a tattoo of a butterfly on her stomach, haha!

You've had plenty of tattoos done, but how do you go from the initial idea to the finished design?
Well, I guess I get an idea, then present it to the tattoo artist, then they sort of take it from there and put their own artistic spin on it.

What do your tattoos mean to you? Are they symbolic or do you just dig the art?
Most of my tattoos mean something special, but some are just something silly or fun.

What is it about tattoos that appeals to you?
I enjoy the whole process, coming up with the idea, the actual tattooing, and then having the decoration on me forever.

Among all your tattoos, which one do you prefer and why?
My favorite tattoo is definitely my Indian princess head on my right thigh. It symbolizes my Indian heritage.

Do you think people treat you differently for being heavily tattooed?
Yes, I definitely think I get treated differently by some people. I think some people can be a bit judgmental and try to stereotype me.

Any final words?
Just want to shout out to my beautiful Diamond Dolls and my friends at American Graffiti Tattoo in Sacramento!

www.facebook.com/jgroblebe
www.myspace.com/nursejen26
www.modelmayhem.com/portfolio/pic/22524268

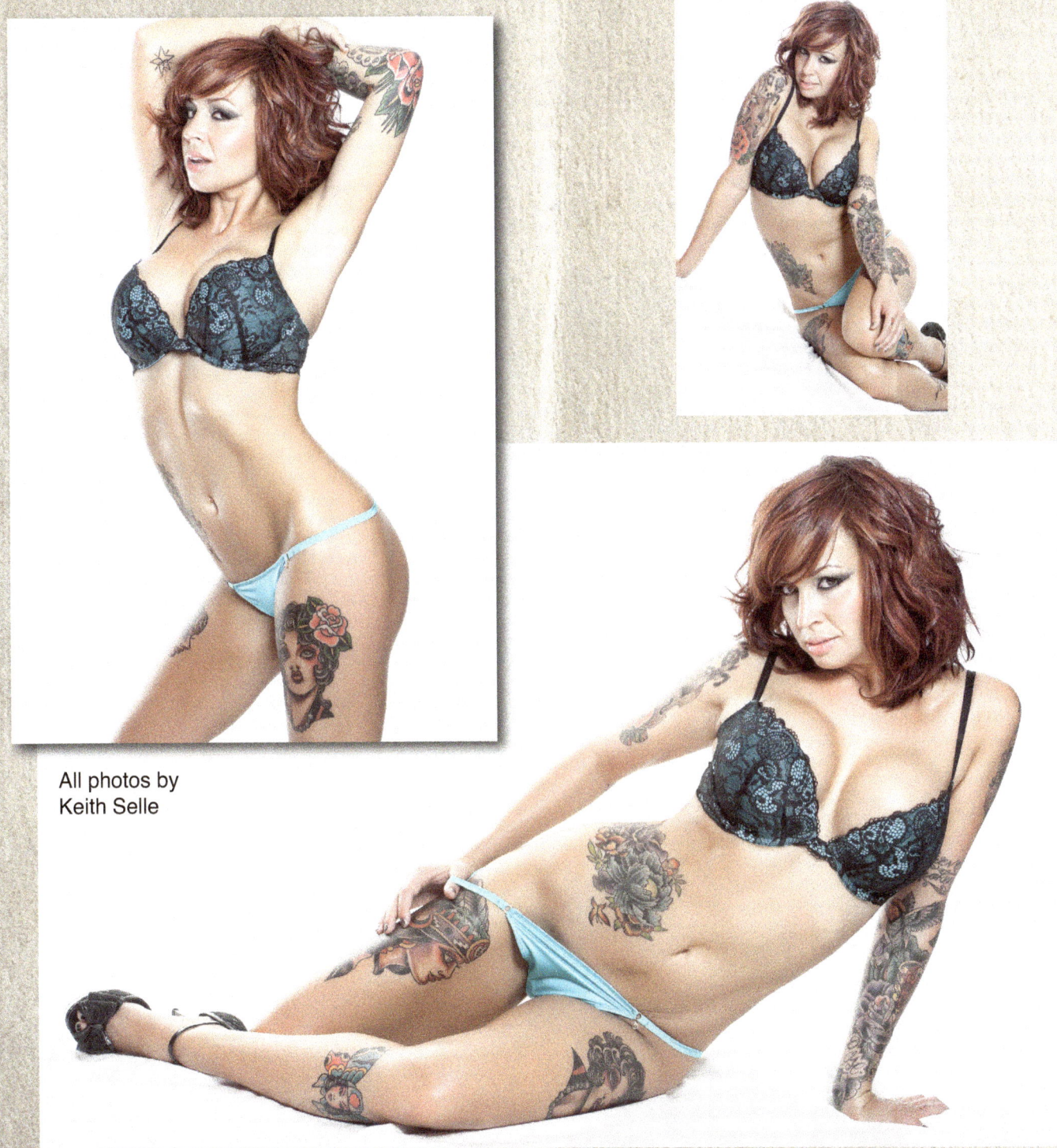

All photos by Keith Selle

Jennifer Groblebe

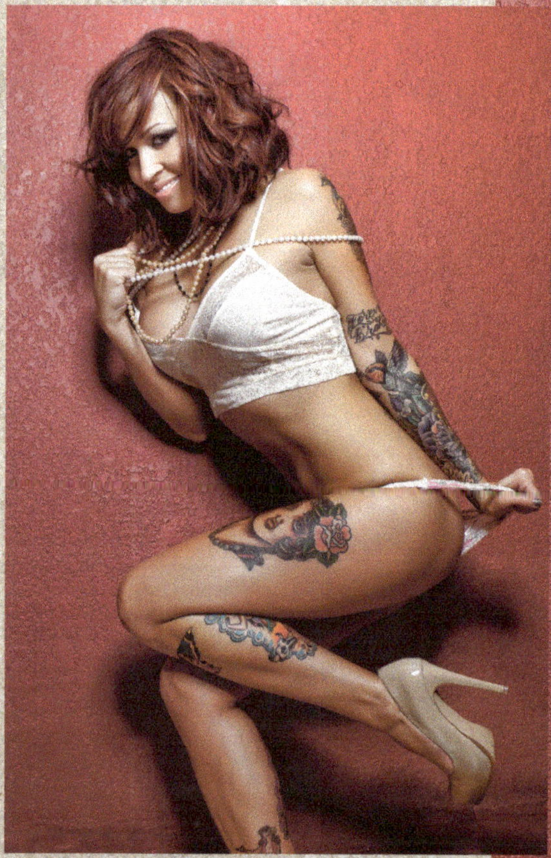

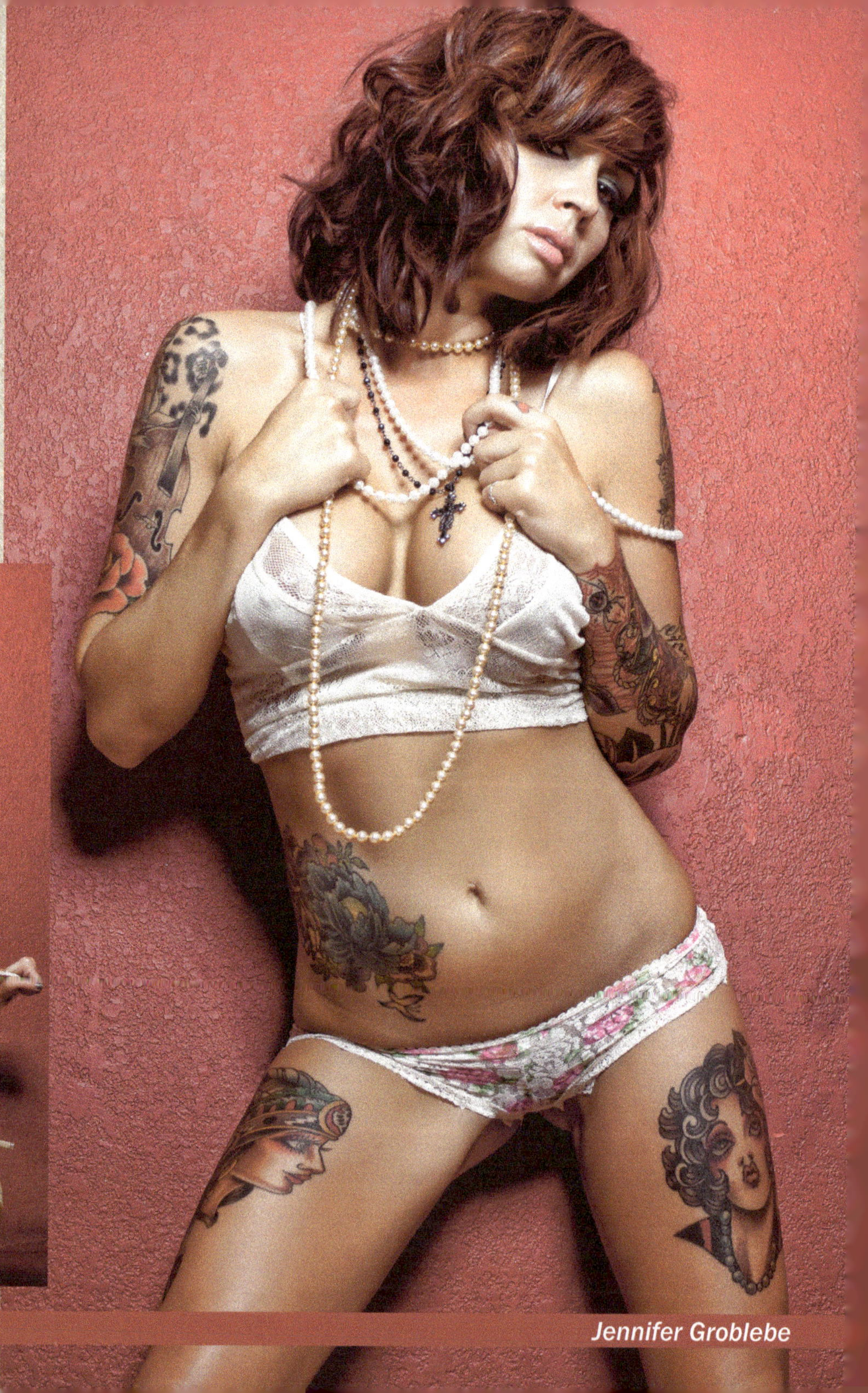

Jennifer Groblebe

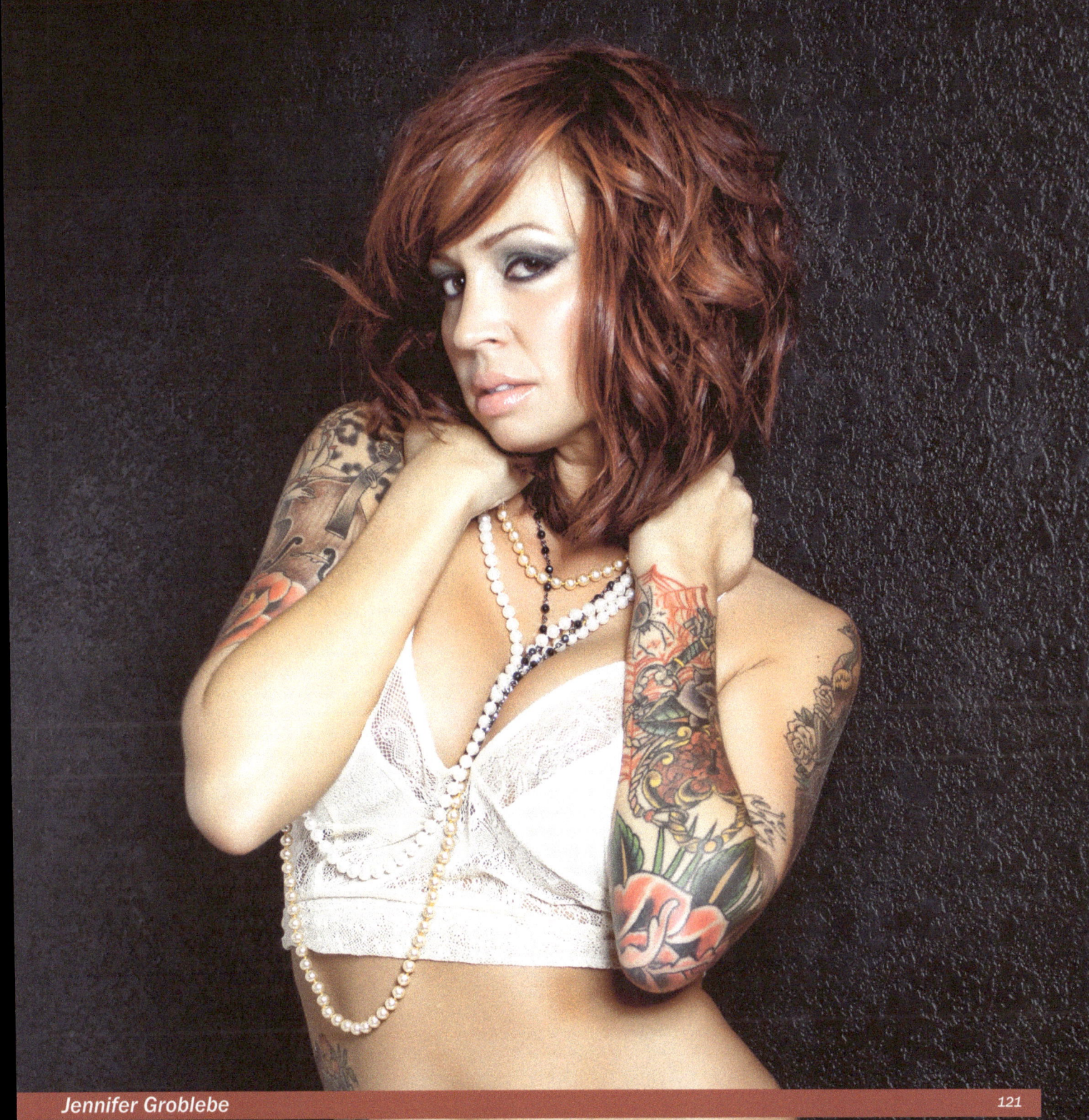
Jennifer Groblebe

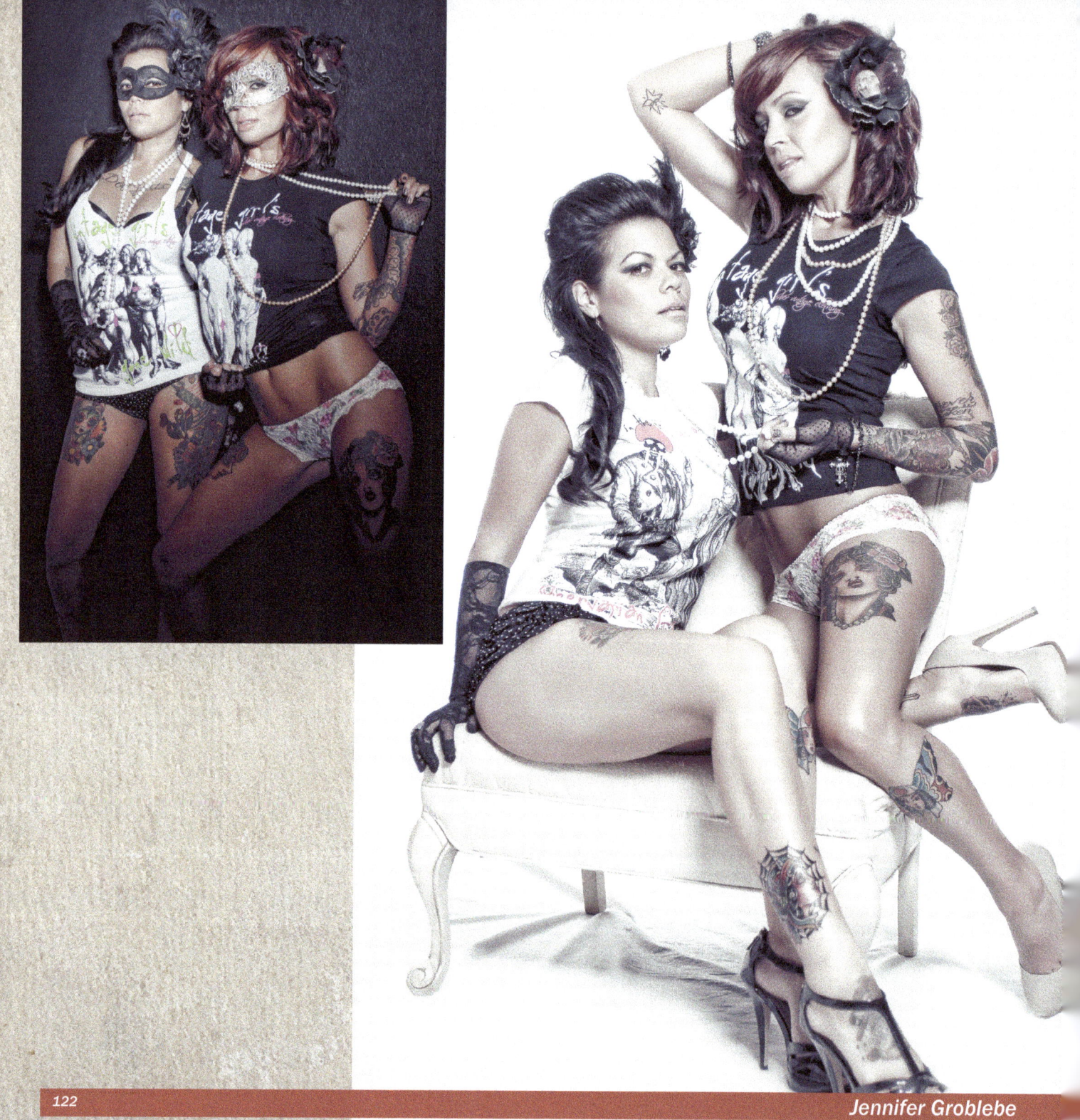

Jennifer Groblebe

Second model:
Krissy Logan

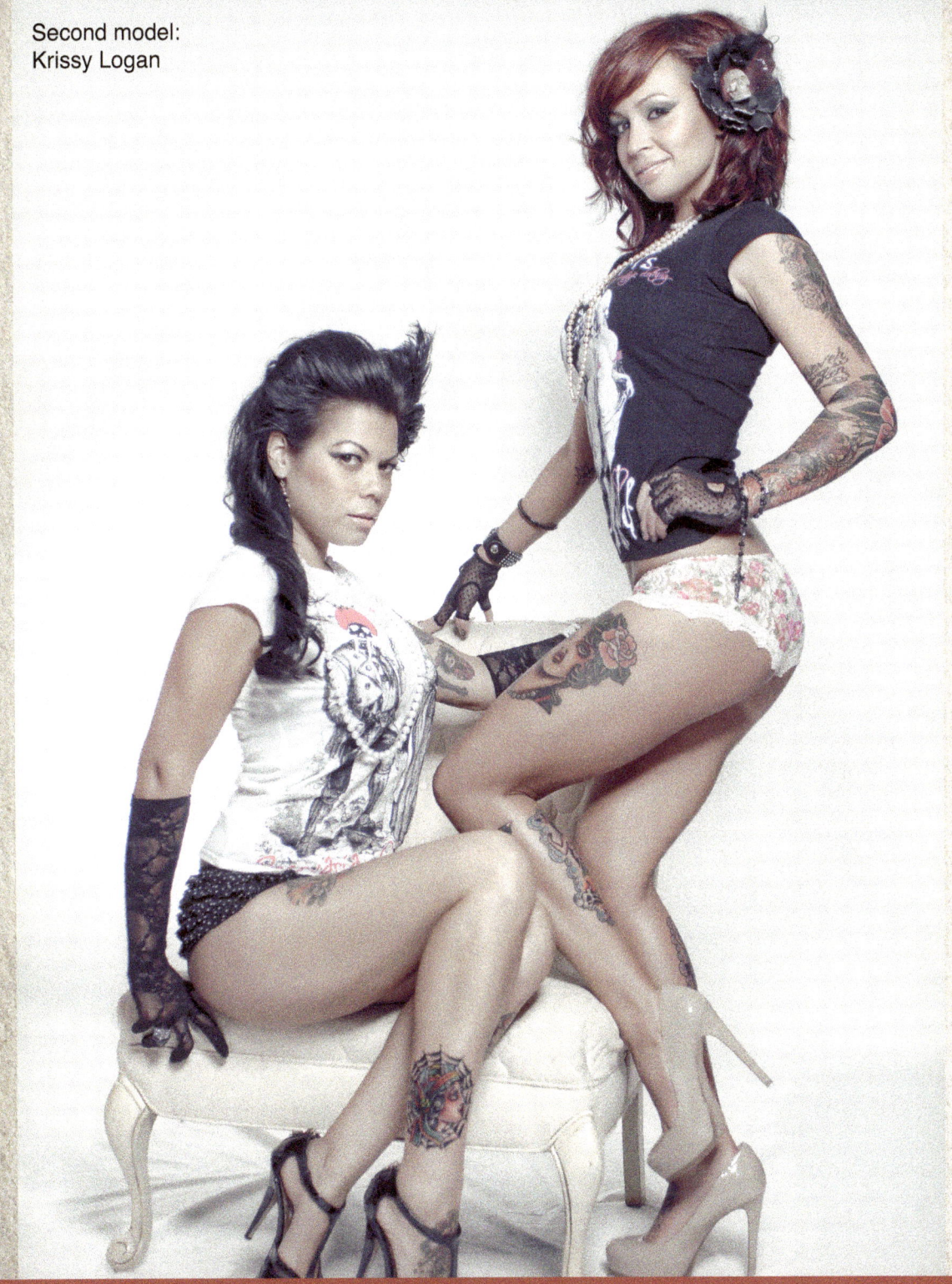

Jennifer Groblebe

Krissy Logan
"My tattoos tell my life story..."

I am Krissy Logan, mother and nurse. I am also a member of Diamond Dolls and a tattoo model. Though I was born in England, I finished growing up in California and now live in Oregon.

How did you get your start in modeling? Have you always wanted to be a model? What made you say yes?

I am a very late bloomer when it comes to modeling. I started after all of my children were born and after my divorce. I always wanted to model and had a great interest in it, but was told by people in my life that I couldn't do it. Once I found myself on my own, answering to no one but myself, I decided to venture out and try all the things I had once aspired to do. Modeling was the first thing I set out to do. And I haven't stopped since.

How long have you been a model, and what do you enjoy the most about it?

I have been modeling for three years now. It is strictly a hobby. I love the creativity that goes into shooting a set. I normally design all my outfits, and tend to do more Alt shoots than glamour. With Alt, you can have extravagant hair, make up, and wardrobe.

Do you work with any photographers on a regular basis?

I work with Keith Selle on a regular basis. I think he could make a homeless woman look like a super model. His technique is flawless, the lights and the angles he uses. No one could duplicate him. I also work with Gary Roberts and Yellowbubbles Photography. Those three photographers are the ones I trust to get the best images, and we always get published.

How did you decide you wanted to get your first tattoo – were you inspired by other people's art?

My first tattoo was not glamorous. In fact, I no longer have it. I was such a hippie chic when I was younger, so I decided to get a Bob Marley Rasta lion on my bikini line. It has since been covered up. My choice in tattoos has definitely gotten better as I got older. I no longer get what I think "looks cool." Instead, all my tattoos tell a story about me and my life. My history is written on my body.

Were you nervous the first time?

I was nervous and excited. Then hooked.

How did you find the guy who does your tattoos?

I have a circle of friends who are all tattooed. Everyone knows someone that tattoos. I have had the privilege of being tattooed by amazing artists because I have seen their work on friends first. KR Rossi did my favorite thigh piece, my zombie "our lady of Guadalupe" complete with syringes and pills. It pays homage to my nursing background. Uzi is another tattoo artist in Sacramento who has done a lot of my work. With my skin tone, he is the only one who can make colors pop. And his work is impeccable. Traditional tattoos are my favorite.

What do your tattoos mean to you? Are they symbolic or do you just dig the art?

My tattoos tell my life story from my kids, to love, to my career, to my friends - me and my bestie have eight matching tattoos. All my tattoos represent me.

What is it about tattoos that appeals to you?

Tattoos are permanent wardrobe we wear, for all to see. I probably learn more about someone from their tattoos than anything else.

Among all your tattoos, which one do you prefer and why?

My absolute favorite tattoo is a Joy Lessposh image of a nurse on my thigh.

Any final words?

Everyone should visit us at Diamond Dolls Ink on Facebook. A group of unbelievably hot tattooed ladies, all on one page. Pictures by Keith Selle. Enough said. Shout out to all my Diamond Doll sisters!

www.facebook.com/profile.php?id=1234953978
www.facebook.com/diamonddollsink
www.modelmayhem.com/1189682 www.pinuplifestyle.com/profile/KrissyLogan

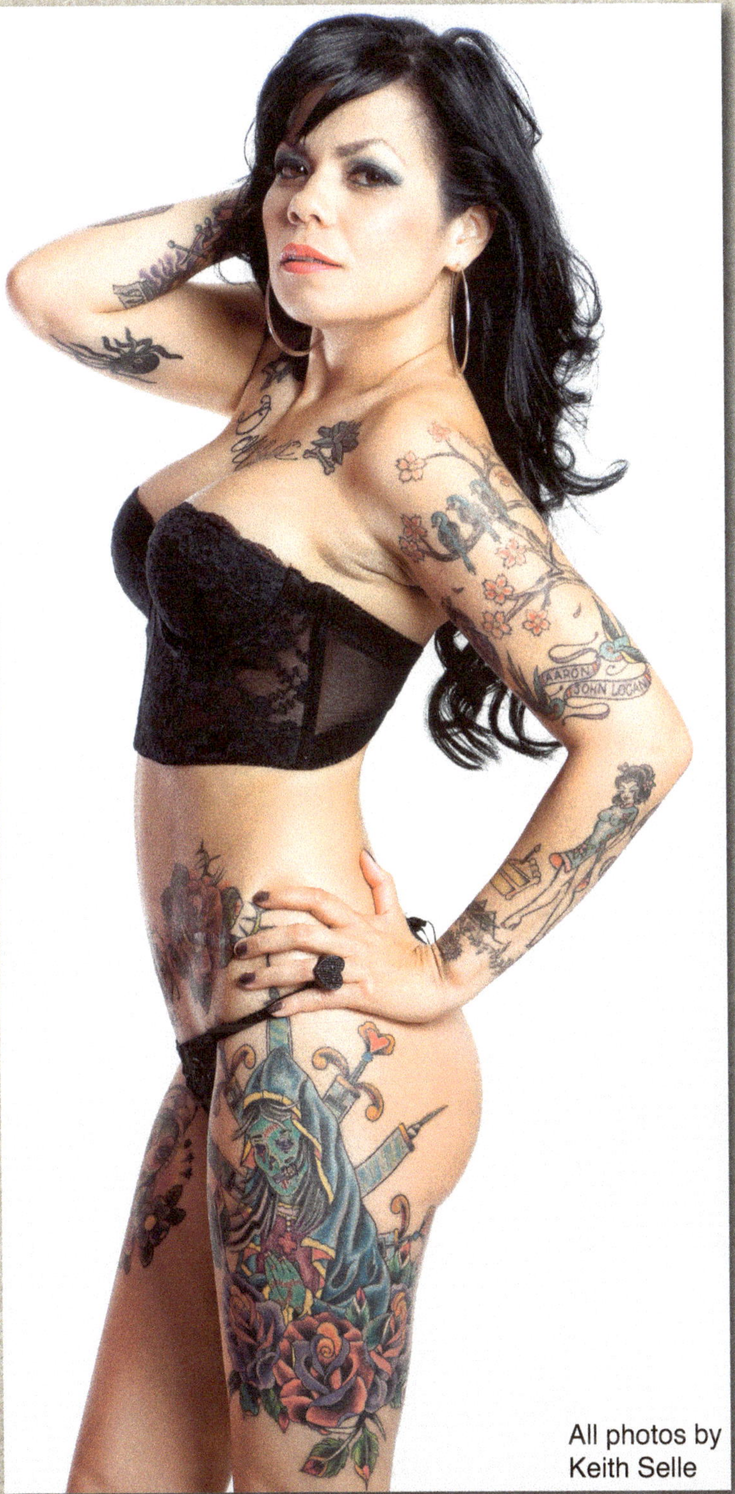

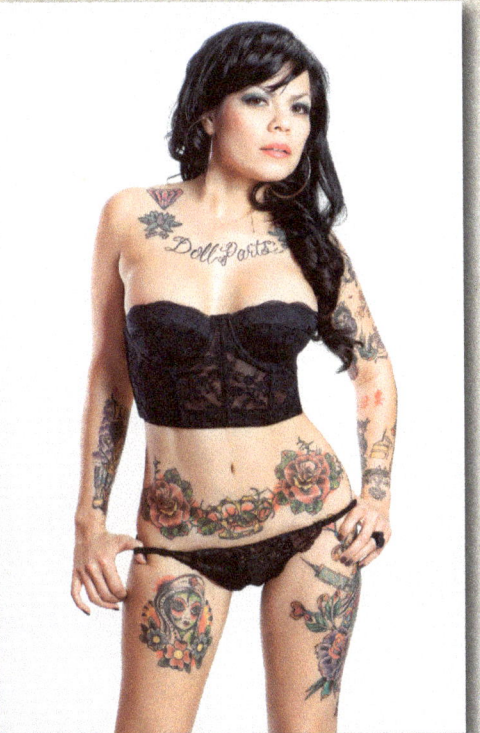
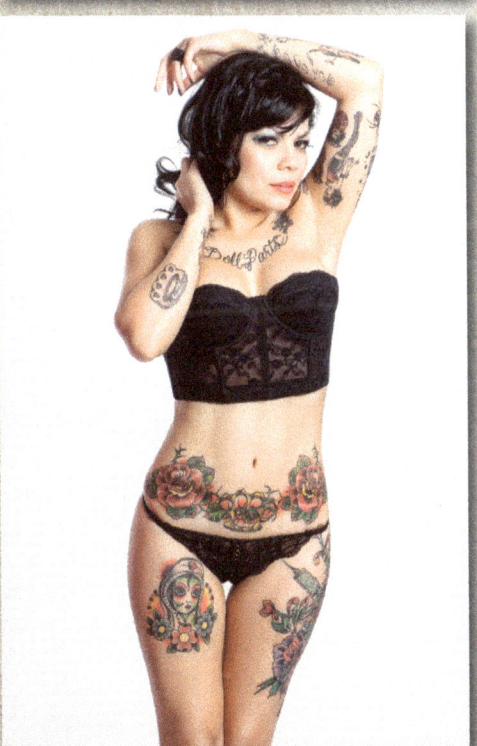

All photos by Keith Selle

Krissy Logan

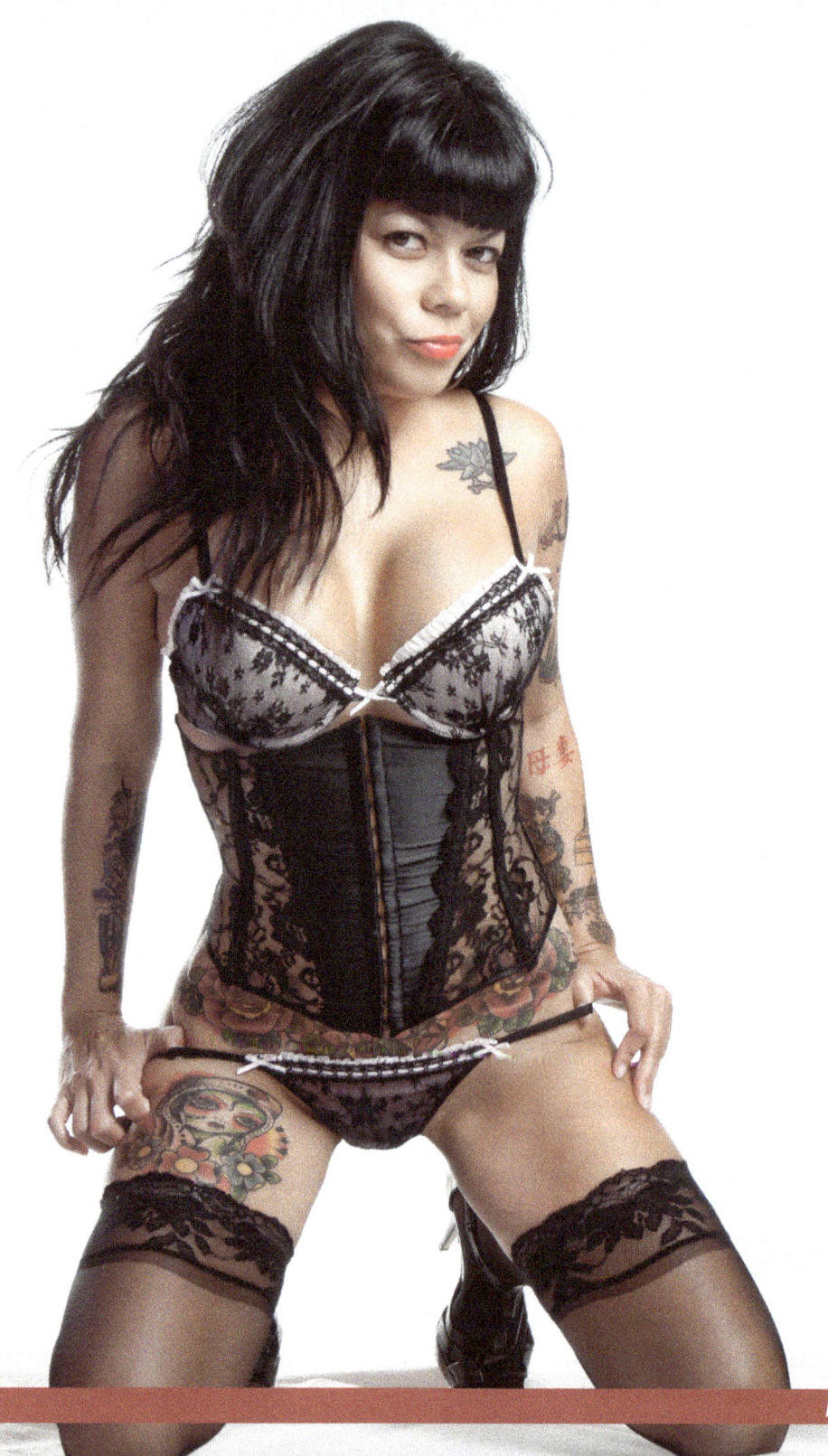

Krissy Logan

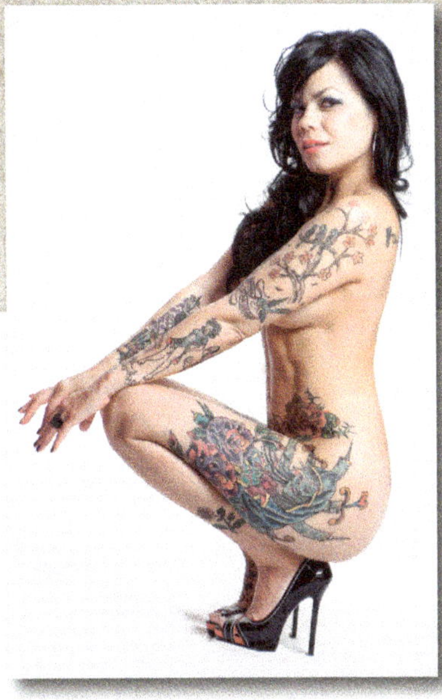

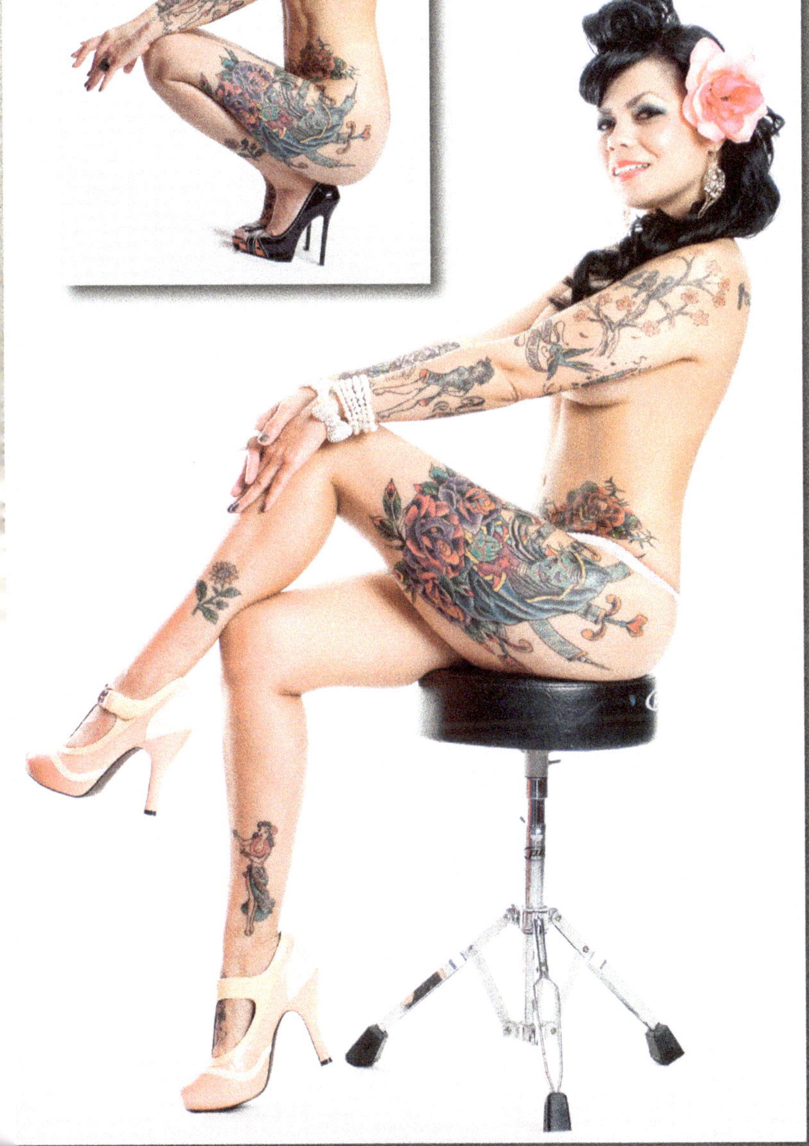

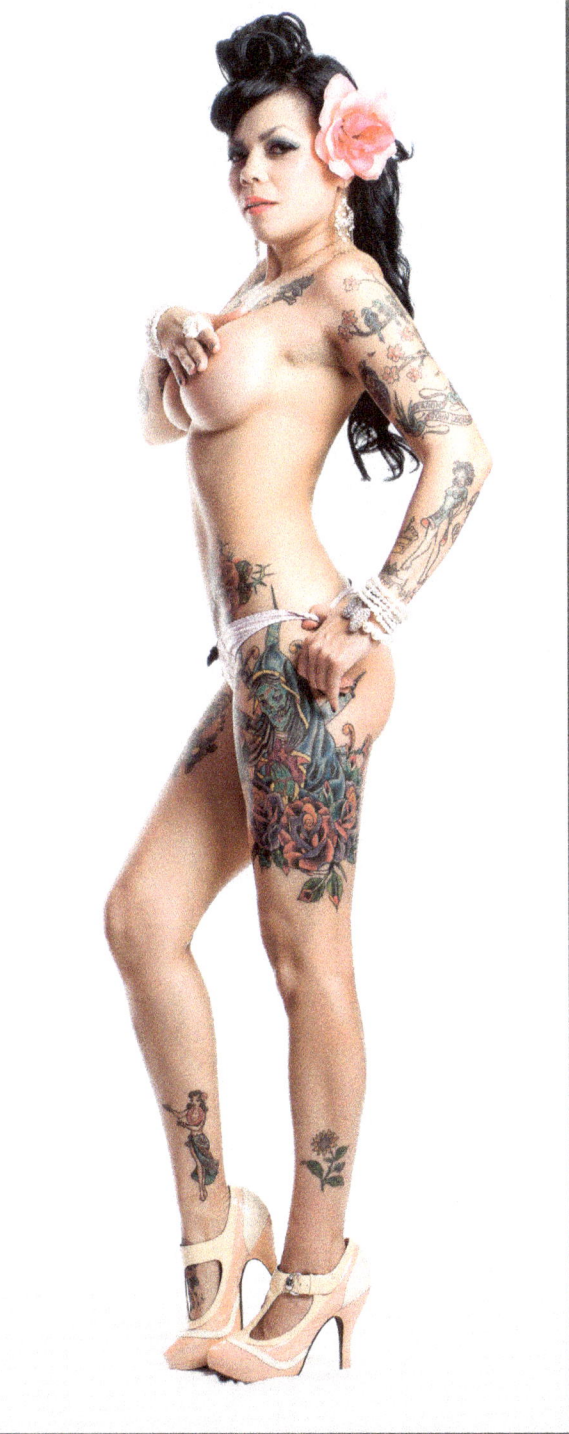

Krissy Logan

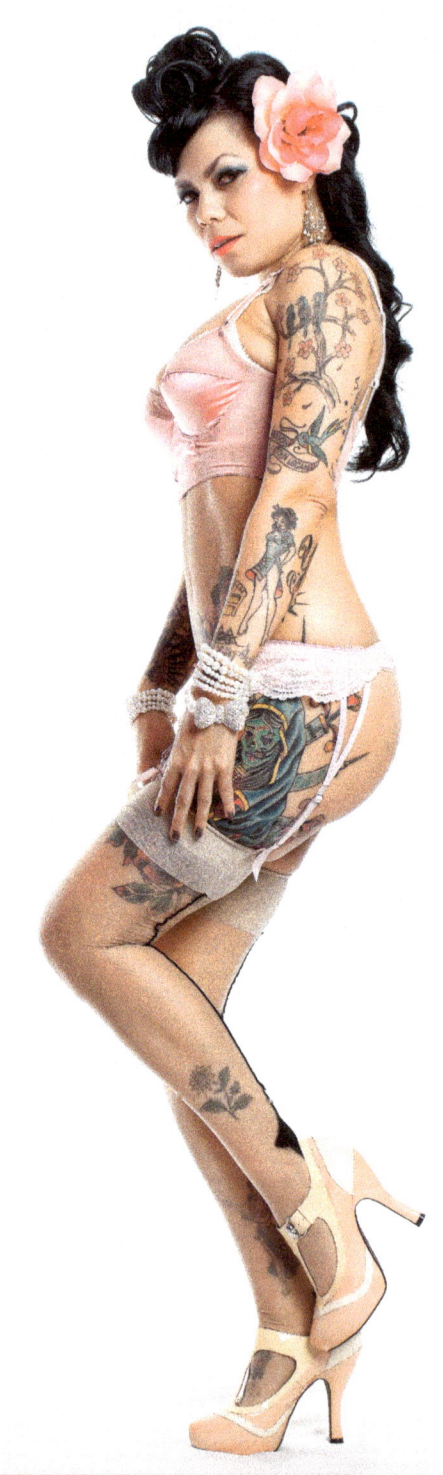

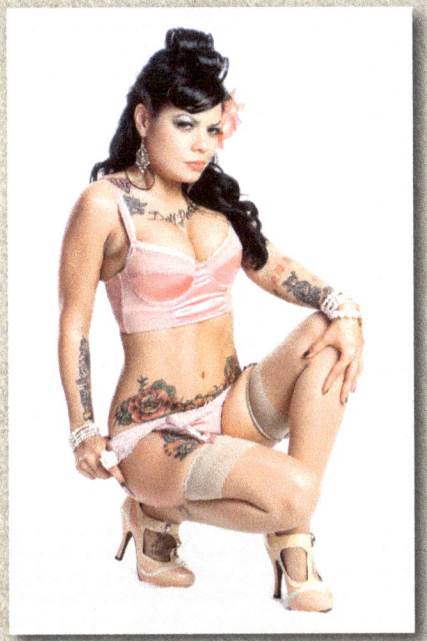
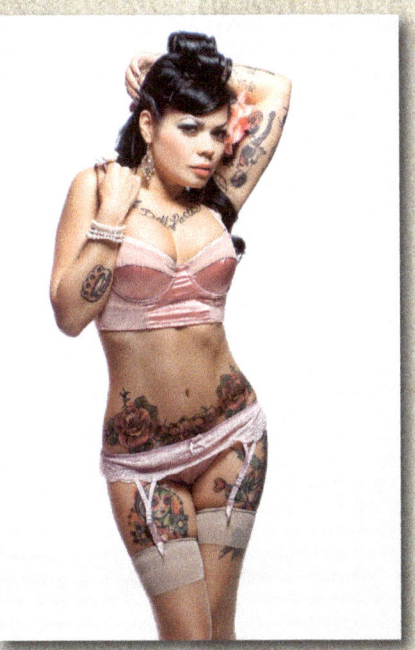
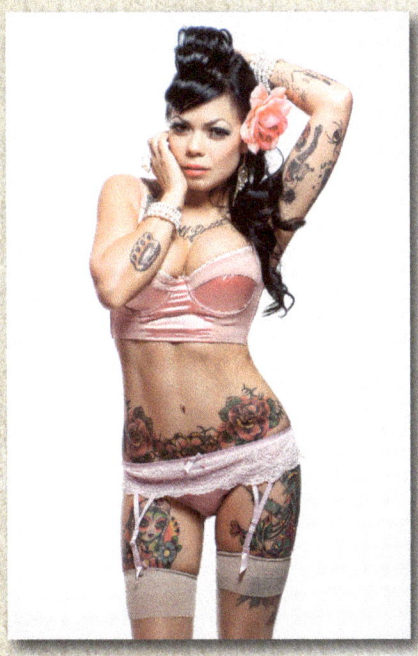
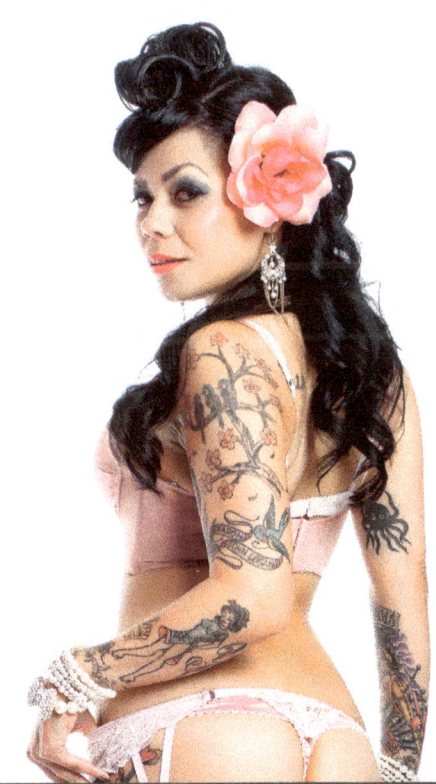

Krissy Logan

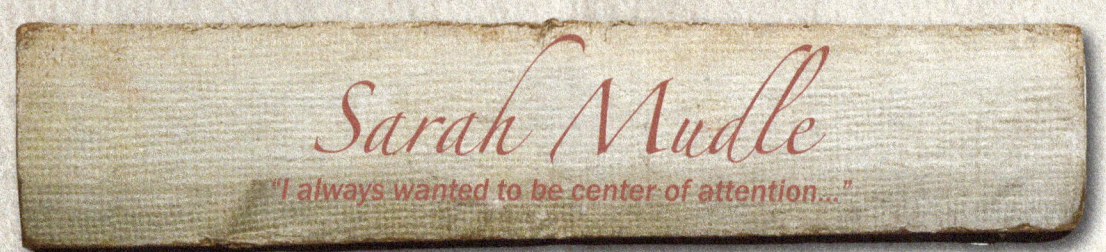

Sarah Mudle

"I always wanted to be center of attention..."

I am Sarah Mudle, aka the Pink Pirate. I was born and raised on Australia's Gold Coast, though I do get to the US now and then. In addition to modeling I also work in a childcare center educating children.

How did you get your start in modeling? Have you always wanted to be a model?
I always wanted to be center of attention somehow so I started modeling. Luckily I was picked up by a magazine and everything rolled from there.

How long have you been a model, and what do you enjoy the most about it?
About five years, and the most enjoyable part is the creative people you meet and/or the fans response to the photos I produce.

What are your influences? Who are your role models?
My role models are all beautiful women. For example, Gwen Stefani is my fav chick.

What goes through your head when you are in front of the camera?
What can I do to blow peoples' minds.

What are your thoughts on the tattooed model scene in Australia?
It's growing over here and becoming very popular nowadays.

Tell us about your photo shoot with Keith Selle. What is it like to work with him?
He is a great photographer and a nice guy. Keith is very professional and made me feel comfortable while we shot.

How old were you and how did you decide you wanted to get your first tattoo – were you inspired by other people's art?
I was 20. And I wanted to see how it felt first, then loved having it on me and wanted more.

How did you find the guy who does your tattoos? Do you like to stick to one artist, or try a number of different ones?
I've had a few artists work on me. I just get to know tattooists' styles and their artistic approach to tattooing.

You've had plenty of tattoos done, but how do you go from the initial idea to the finished design?
I inhale the idea in my head. I get the tattooist to draw it up, and then change things as we go if need be.

What do your tattoos mean to you?
They mean expression and creativity. It's how I share my artwork and show the world who I am.

What is it about tattoos that appeals to you?
To decorate a body is a beautiful thing. I love art.

Have you gotten any new work done?
Yes, Frank Ball in Melrose Hollywood did my hand and arm and knees during my adventure in America.

Which areas have been the most painful to tattoo?
Behind my knee and my sternum both hurt so bad.

You have a great body, how do you stay healthy?
I exercise on my pink exercise ball and I'm always moving.

What do you rather drink in the morning, coffee or tea?
Coffee all the way.

What's in your bag?
Two small monkey toys, gloss, camera, wallet, bouncy ball, phone, hair clips, (I actually looked).

What is on your iPod play list?
Chiodos, Incubus, Architects, The Devil Wears Prada, Katy Perry.

Diamonds or pearls?
Can't I have both?

What is your definition of beauty?
To have people not be able to take there eyes off you!

www.facebook.com/TheRealPinkPirate
www.facebook.com/xPink.Piratex
www.modelmayhem.com/pinkpiratexxx
www.myspace.com/sarahmudle
twitter.com/#!/realpinkpirate
www.tumblr.com/tagged/sarah-mudle

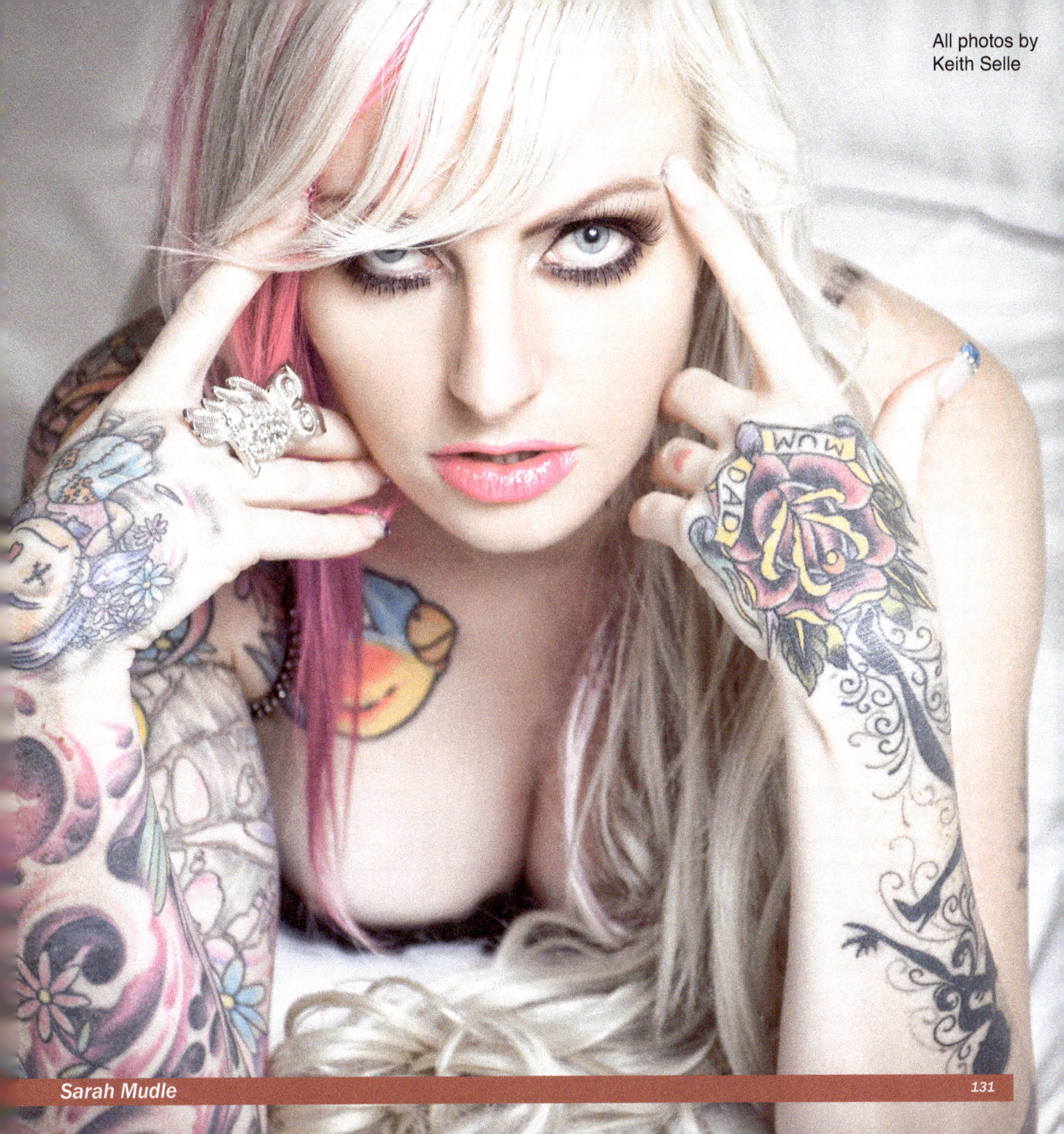

All photos by Keith Selle

Sarah Mudle

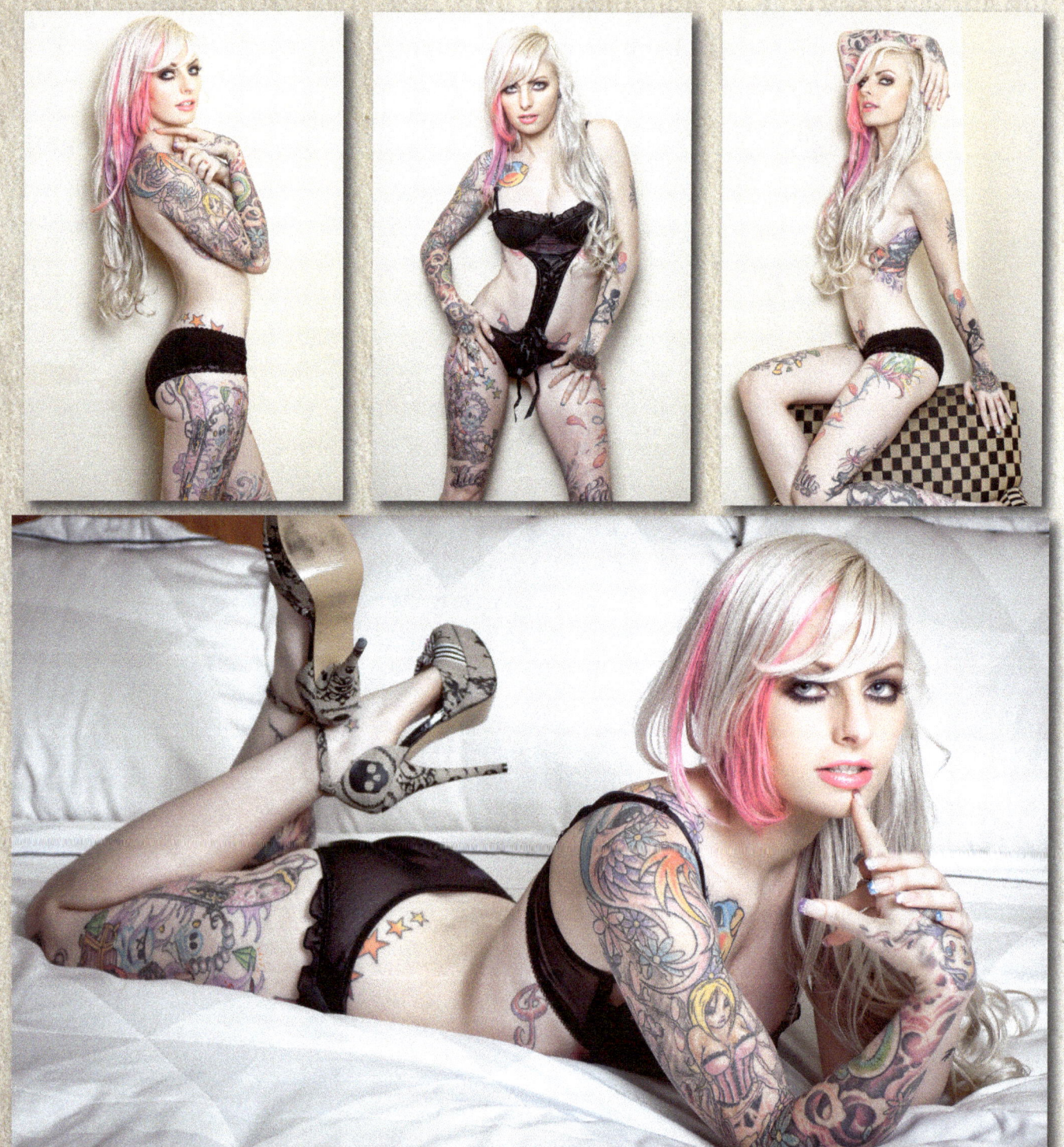

Sarah Mudle

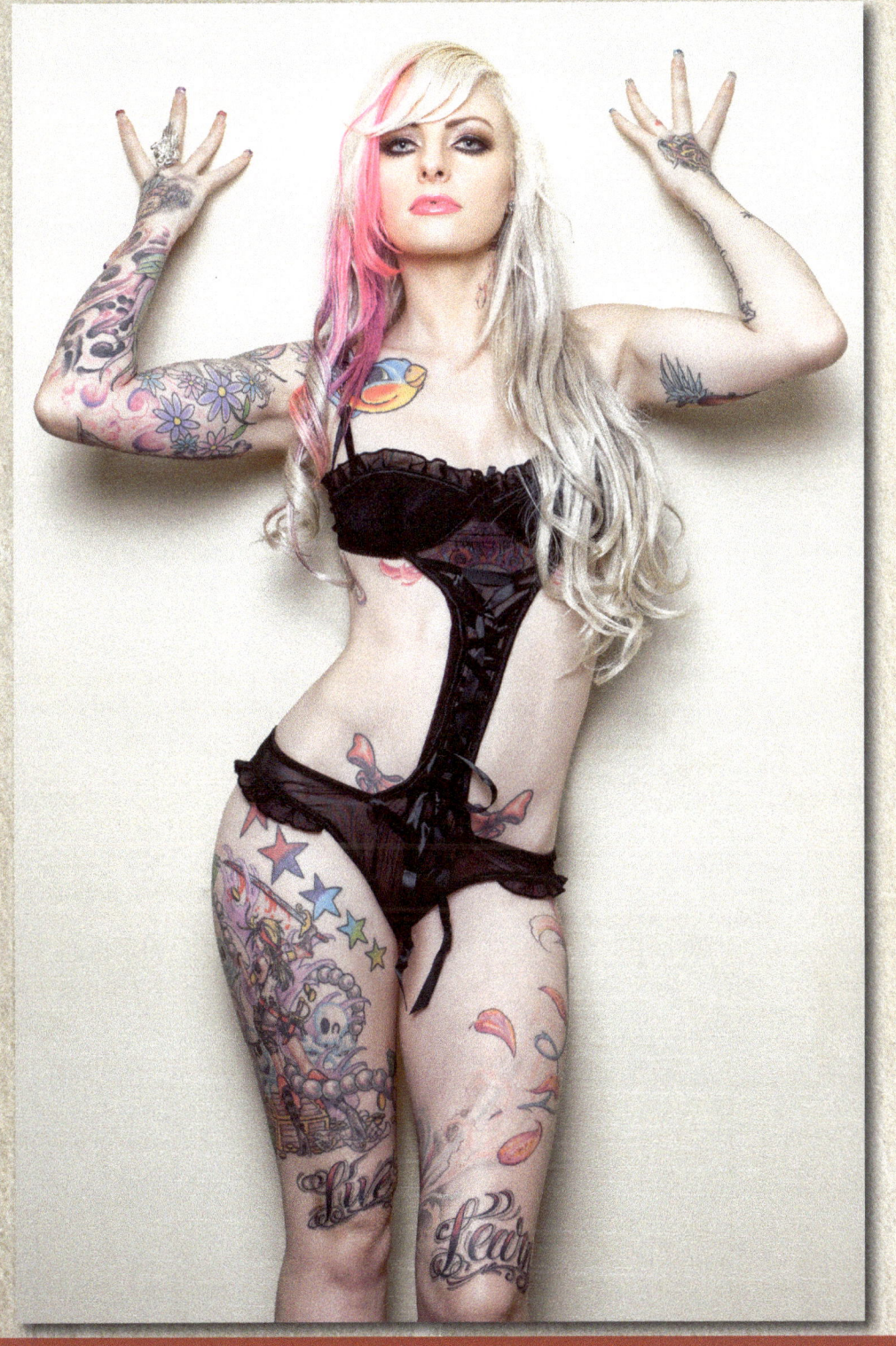

Sarah Mudle

Jacque Oh Murphy

"I'm a fan of my whole body..."

I am Jacque Oh, tattoo model, artist and bartender from Northern California. I'm a huge fan of billiards, spray paint and a gorgeous group of tattooed ladies called the Diamond Dolls.

How did you get your start in modeling? What made you say yes?
I did a few shoots with friends prior to shooting with Keith Selle. After shooting with Keith, I knew I wanted to pursue it a bit more. I love being able to tell a story or spark a little controversy in my pictures.

How long have you been a model, and what do you enjoy the most about it?
I'm in my second year and it's been such an amazing adventure. I love meeting new motivated people who make me want to try harder to do things I'm passionate about.

Do you work with any special photographers on a regular basis?
I have a few photographers that I consider quite dear to me. Keith Selle, Gary Roberts, Quroscuro and Badbonesphotography.

Tell us about your photo shoot with Keith Selle. Were you nervous?
The first shoot with Keith, I was a little nervous. However, within minutes I was in the groove of things.

Tell us a little bit about the Diamond Dolls.
We are like a little family. A sexy, motivated, positive family. I have been a bartender since I was bright eyed and bushy tailed at age 21. I'm really enjoying the alternative path in life.

How did you decide you wanted to get your first tattoo – were you inspired by other people's art?
I did exactly what you do not want to do when you get a tattoo. I picked out some tribal flash and had the tattoo done in a shed in a backyard in Tennessee at age 17. Luckily, with age, I also acquired a brain.

How did you find the guy who does your tattoos?
I get tattooed by Ronnie Grizzard and he is a friend of a friend. I really enjoy his work and his company so that made it easy.

You've had plenty of tattoos done, but how do you go from the initial idea to the finished design?
Since my artist and I are friends, it is really easy for me to tell him what I am thinking and we discuss and brainstorm ideas. I have no problem telling him I'm not digging his idea and he has no problem telling me my idea might not look correct. I love that relationship.

What do your tattoos mean to you? Are they symbolic or do you just dig the art?
It's a mixture of both. Many of them reflect a time in my life that I try to keep fresh on my memory and some are pieces from a favorite artist or concepts that I favor.

What is it about tattoos that appeals to you?
A lot of my pieces are positive and I like looking down and seeing the constant reminders.

Among all your tattoos, which one do you prefer and why?
I love them all, but I really love my stomach tattoo done by Gary Burton at the Exotic Body in Sacramento. The skull in front of the roses signifies the idea that there is beauty behind everything.

What is your definition of beauty?
Beauty, it's a positive reflection about the meaning of one's own existence.

Of all above mentioned things that you've accomplished in your relatively short career what would you pick as your biggest achievements in your career?
Being a Diamond Doll. I love my group of ladies.

www.facebook.com/profile.php?id=100002144170426
www.facebook.com/pages/Jacque-OH-Kennedy/168100216590185
inkedgirls.tumblr.com/post/14863494806

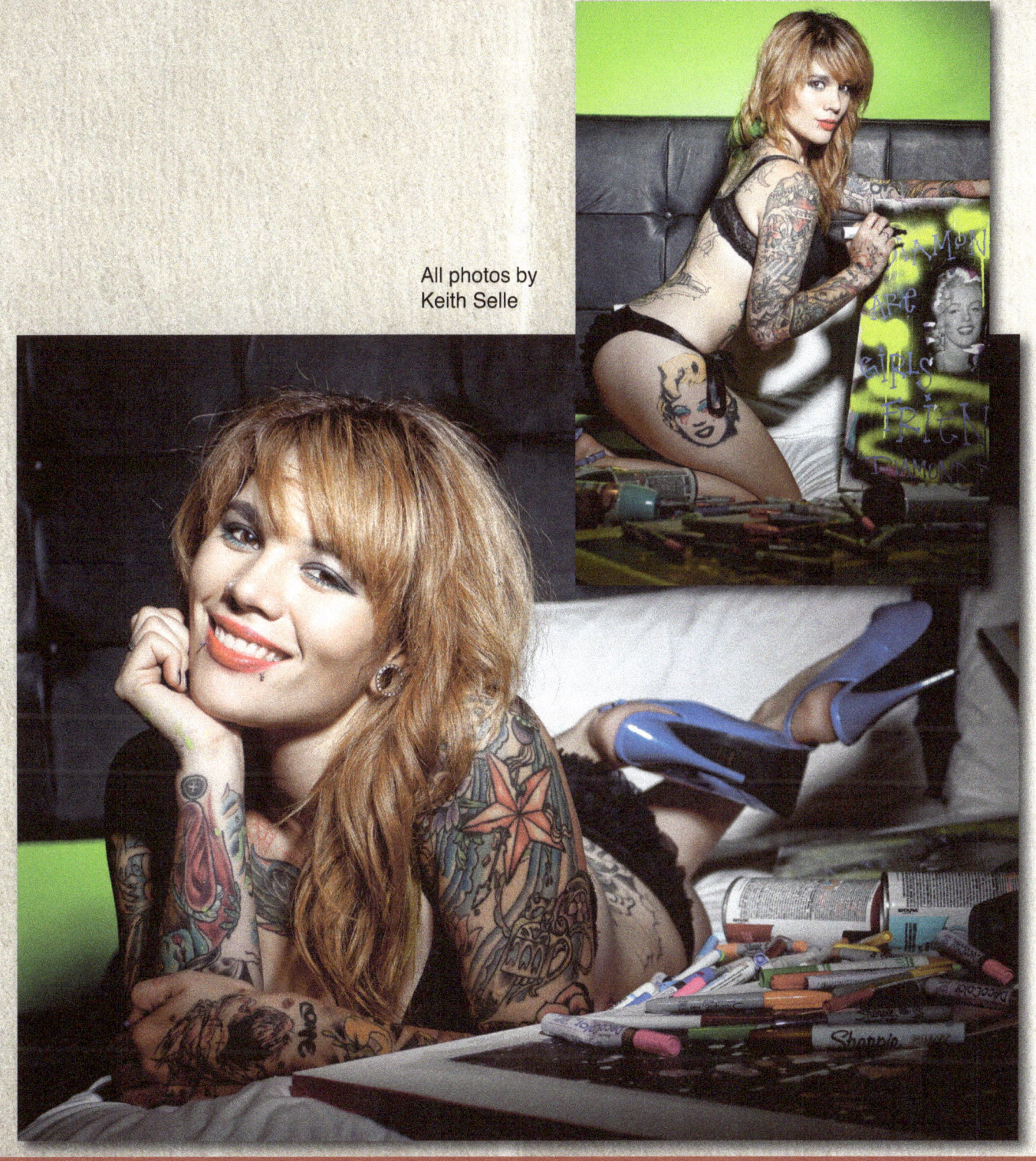

All photos by Keith Selle

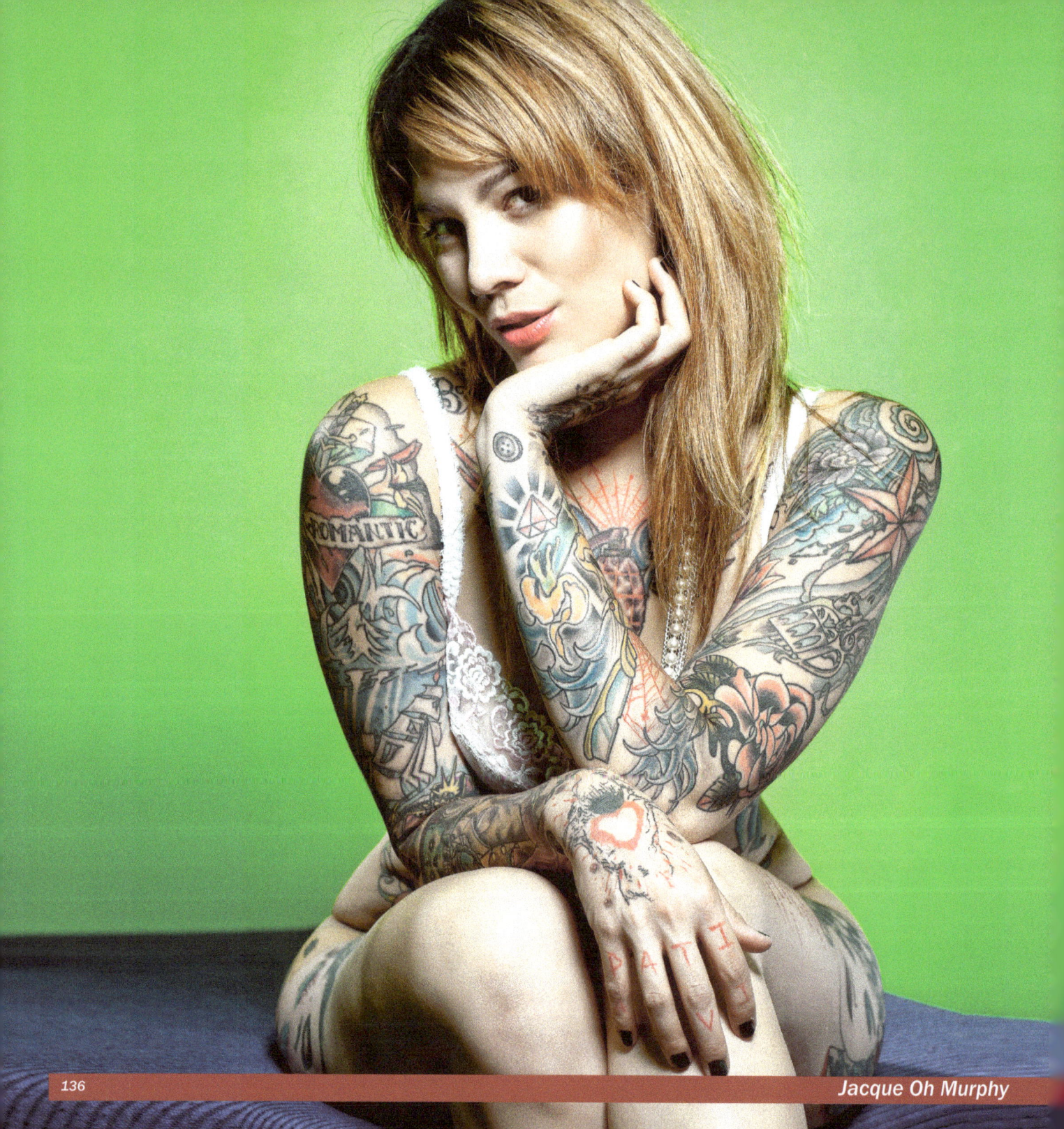
Jacque Oh Murphy

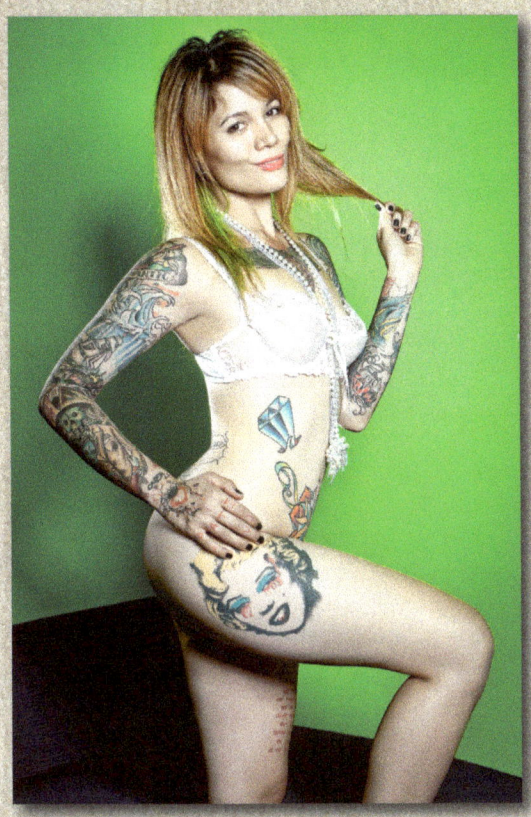
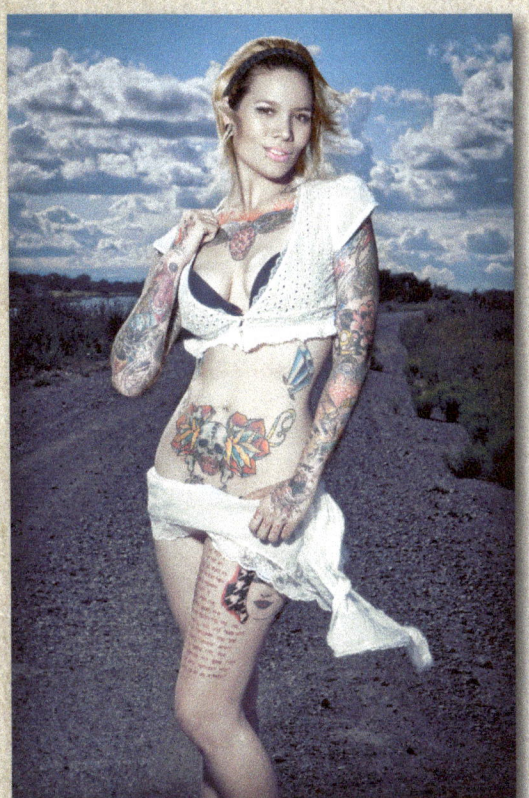
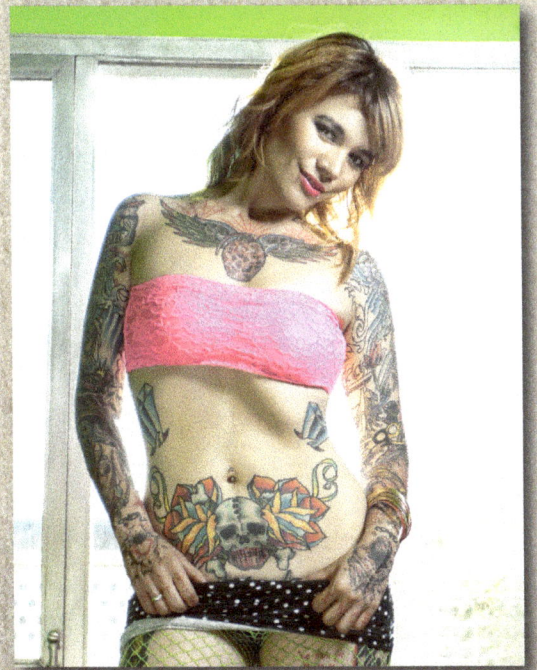
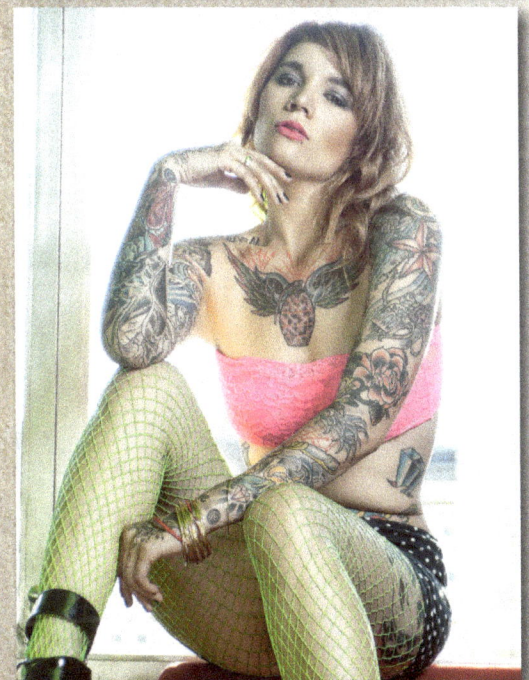

Jacque Oh Murphy

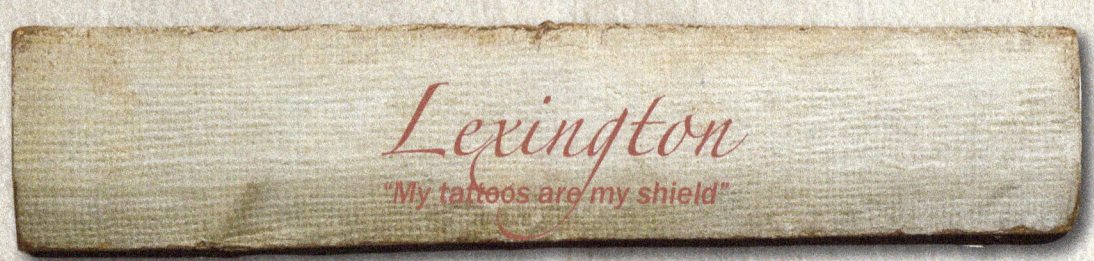

Lexington
"My tattoos are my shield"

I am Lexington. I'm a mother, a model and a "barber" - I do hair for the rock stars and elite of L.A. I love my life!

How did you get your start in modeling?

I started modeling at the suggestion of friends. In today's world, everyone is a model. Especially after the boom of social networking sites. So I never really cared, because my life is so busy with work, being a single mom, keeping up with friends and family. But as more and more opportunities came up, I decided to start taking it a bit more seriously. And now look where I am!

When did your interest in tattoos begin? And how long was it from then until you got your first one?

I started to get interested in tattoos when I was about 16. A friend I was working with suggested that if I ever wanted a tattoo that he knew someone who would do it. And what a good choice that was, because Gay "Sawdust" Ellsworth has done about 80% of my tattoos. So it got me thinking a lot about what I wanted and where I would get it. I didn't start out knowing that I would be completely covered in tattoos. This was before the whole Kat von D / LA Ink craze. So I started, and kind of never stopped.

What do your tattoos mean to you? Are they symbolic or do you just dig the art?

My tattoos are my shield. A "social filter" if you will. I think people who conform to society and live their lives hiding everything in are boring and cowardly. I wear my heart on my sleeve and I am not afraid to express who I truly am. Some people turn their noses up at heavily tattooed people. It takes more courage to walk around every day like this than to walk around with your nose in the air. And hello, do you know how much these tattoos cost!? Hahaha.

Which is your first one? And why did you get it?

The first tattoo I got was two swallows on my stomach. The swallows were a biblical reference. I got them on my 18th birthday. It hurt more than I expected! Funny how people in school thought it was so crazy at the time. Now I am sure most of them all have a tattoo, or 100. Oh if they can see me now!

Among all your tattoos, which one do you prefer and why?

Hmmm, that's a hard question. So many of them are meaningful, or from a point in my life that was cherished. I think I'll go with my son's name, Londyn, written in New York Dolls writing. Since he's definitely my favorite thing in the world.

Please talk us through some of your tattoos and the reason behind them.

Well, I have a lot of silly tattoos. I have a cupcake on one thumb and a chili pepper on the other, because I'm "sweet and spicy"! Or I have the KISS logo on my butt. Like "KISS my a**!" I also have a bible verse on my chest in memory of my grandparents. They meant the world to me. Oh, and the crown on my neck, that's because I am the queen!

Did you enjoy working with Amber? What was it like to work with her?

Ummm, YEAH! Amber and Levi are fun yet professional. They truly capture their models in such a comfortable level that it is easy to get the correct image the first time around.

Do you think people treat you differently for being heavily tattooed?

Like I said before, it is a social filter. If people are shallow enough to judge you based on appearance alone, then what's the point of getting to know them?

Finally, any future plans you would like to share with us?

Lots of travel, work, play, and FUN!

www.facebook.com/alycialex
www.myspace.com/xucci
www.modelmayhem.com/1046366

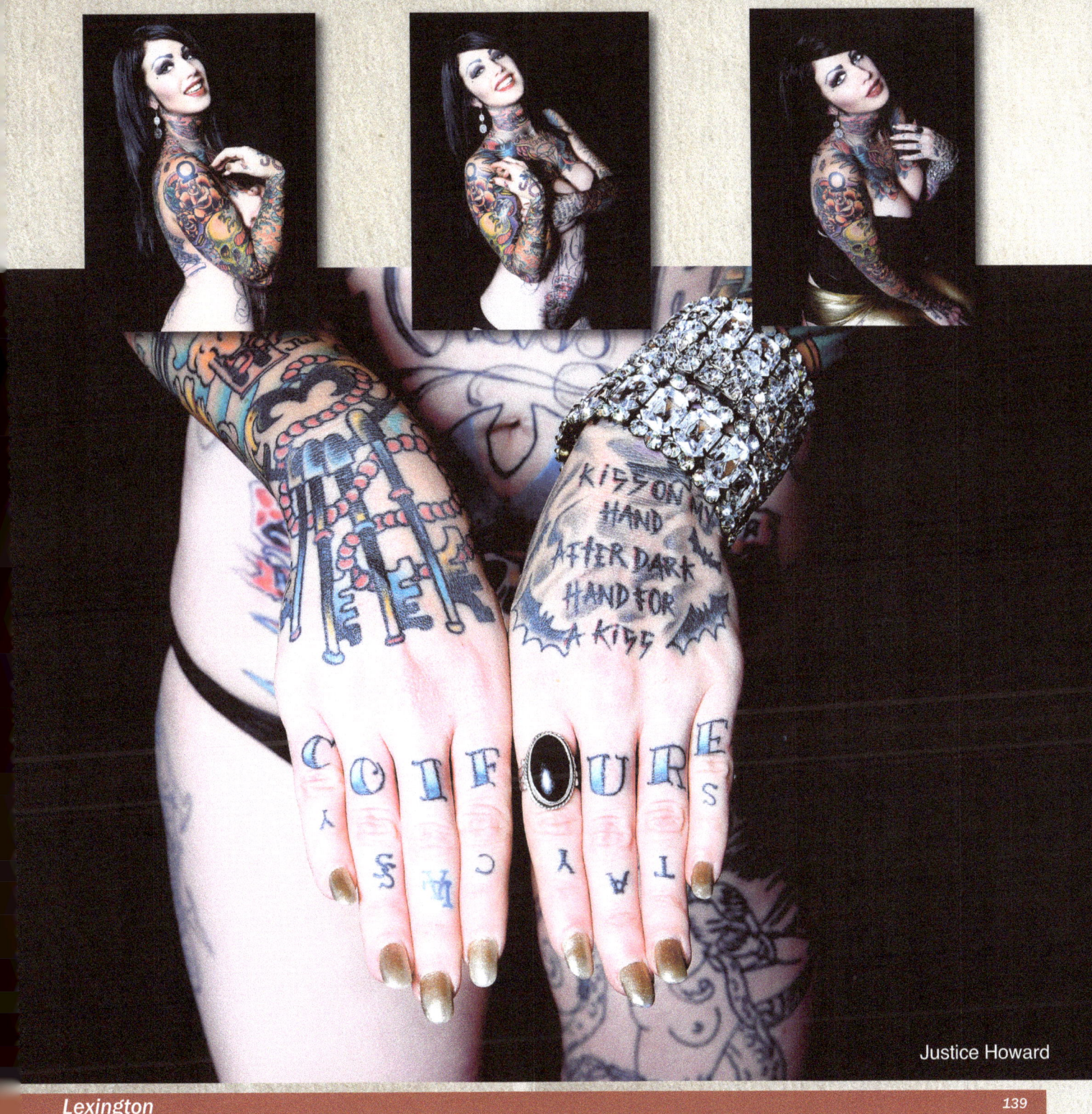

Justice Howard

Lexington

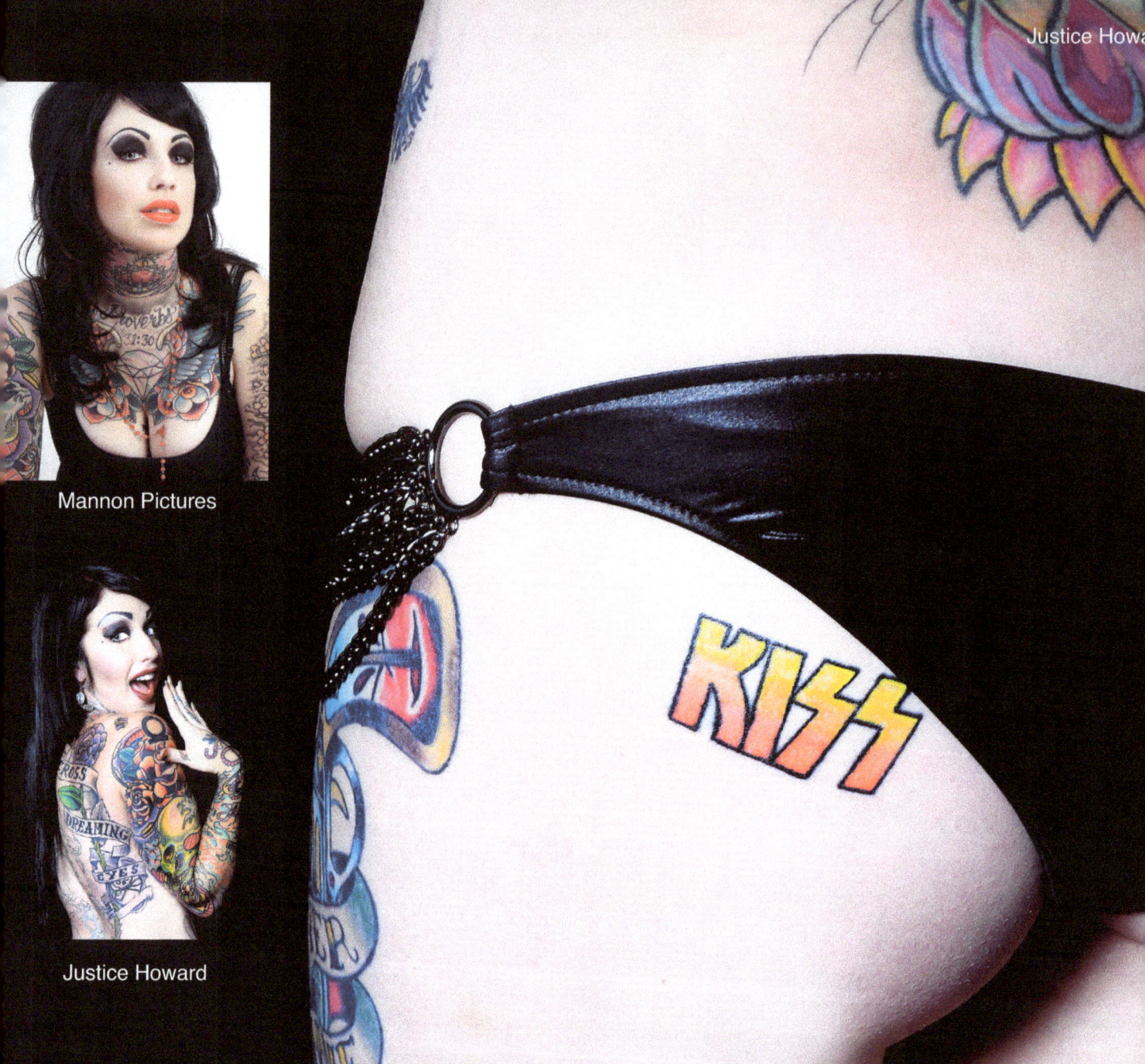

Justice Howard

Mannon Pictures

Justice Howard

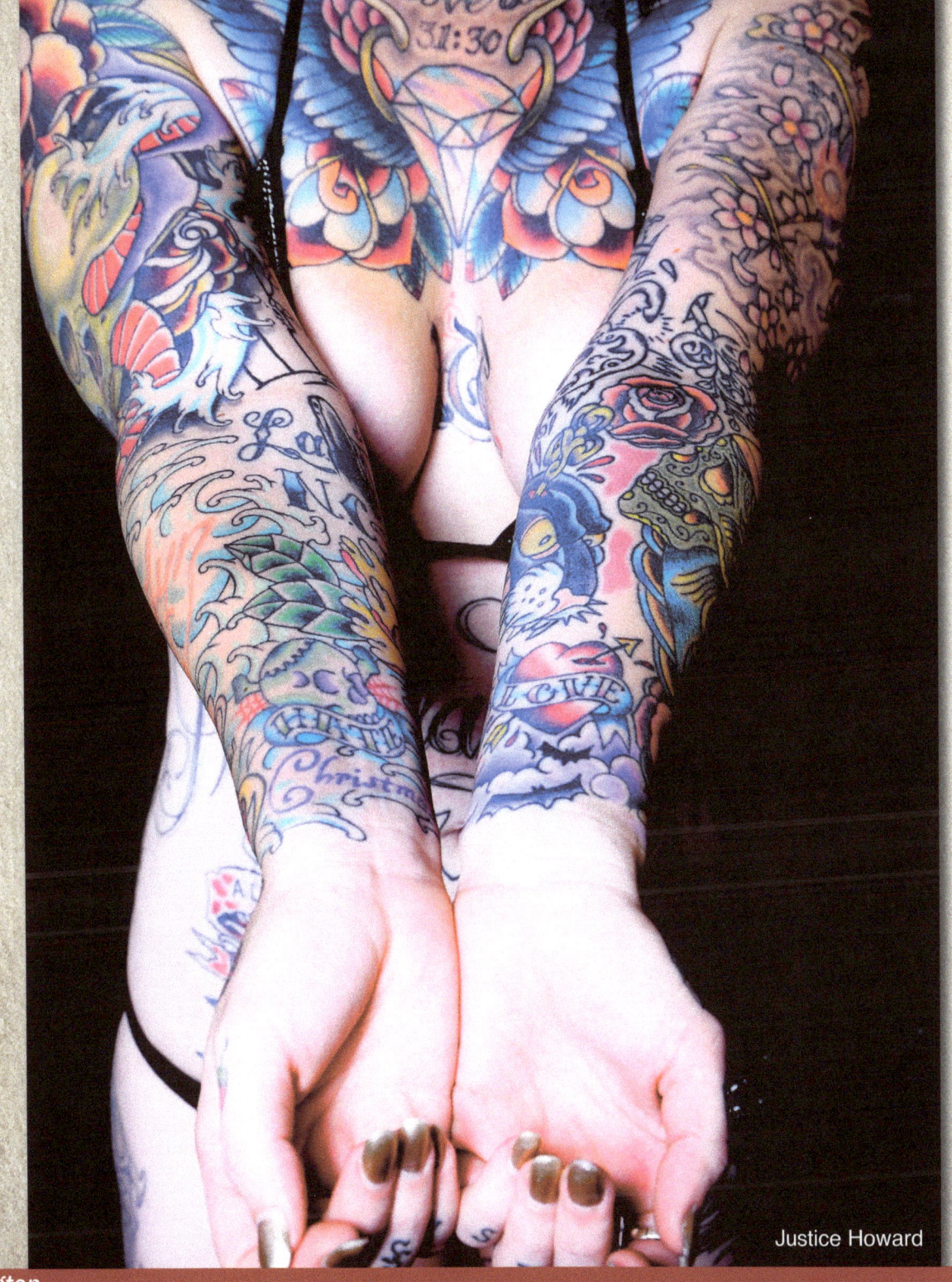
Justice Howard

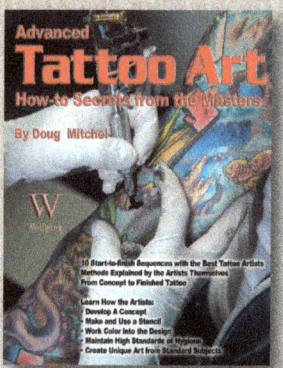

Advanced Tattoo Art
How to Secrets from the Masters
Author: Doug Mitchel $27.95

The art of the tattoo has emerged from the garage to the parlor, from the local bar to the boardroom. With interest in tattoos at a high point, the time is right for a detailed look at the art, and the artists, who create the elaborate designs.

Wolfgang Publications and Doug Mitchel take the reader inside the shops of ten well-known and very experienced artists spread across the country. Both a how-to book and a photo-intense look the world or tattoos; Advanced Tattoo Art includes interviews with the artists that explain not only how they do what they do, but also their personal preference for materials and methods.

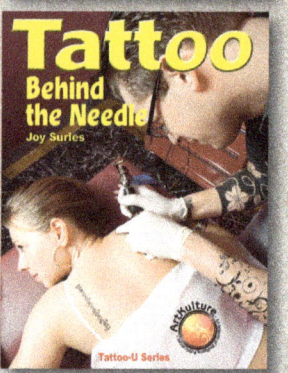

Tattoo - Behind the Needle
Author: Joy Surles $27.95

Tattoo – Behind the Needle, takes the reader into the shop of 12 talented young tattoo artists. This is an opportunity to learn how and where each artist learned his or her skills, who they turn to for inspiration, and exactly how they create bright, colorful, living tattoos.

Tattoo – Behind the Needle, includes interviews with well-known artists like Brandon Bond, Amanda Wachob, Shannon Schober and Nate Beavers. Each has a distinctive style, a unique philosophy, and a very personal approach to tattoo art.

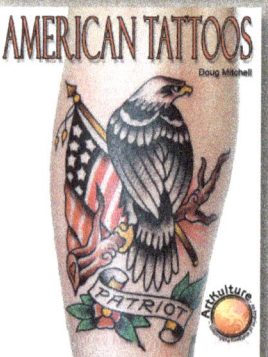

American Tattoos
Author: Doug Mitchel $27.95

Among the most visually powerful tattoos are those that can only be called American Tattoos. Whether it's Old Glory in red white and blue spread across a bicep, or the Harley-Davidson bar and shield done in orange with a black outline, these images are among the most compelling ever seen. Each step in the process is here, from the initial concept drawing to the last prick. The book also includes pictures of exceptional finished Tattoos, as well flash art of the highest quality.

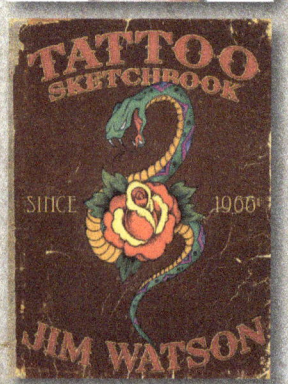

Tattoo Sketch Book
Author: Jim Watson $32.95

Although Jim Watson's tattoo style is normally recognized for being bright and colorful, these sketches show the reader the drawing technique and sketching process of a tattoo artist. The pages contain valuable reference sketches for tattoo artists, and is a great source for easy-to-perform tattoo designs. For anyone who needs to tattoo a "Mom" across a traditional heart, or "Harley-Davidson" down the arm, Jim provides a variety or simple and elaborate "fonts" so you're sure to have the correct type style for a given situation. This collection will help everyone from new artists to journeymen; as well as their clients, to select (and, if needed, modify) the tattoo that they want and need.

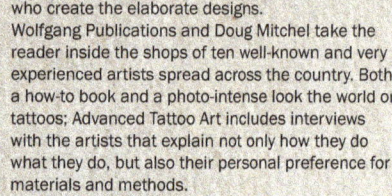

Into The Skin
Author: Superior Tattoo $34.95
(includes companion DVD)

Into the Skin is a true Tattoo How-To book. From choosing the tattoo machine to picking the best needles for a particular situation, the information that tattoo artists need to create their day-to-day art is included here.

Ten tattoos are covered from start to finish, from sketch to competed art. Each step in the process is photographed and explained in detail. The companion DVD covers the tattooing process with a video camera. Whether you've been tattooing for five years, or five minutes, there is information here that will help with choosing and using your machine, picking needles, and applying color.

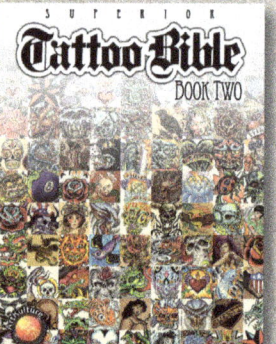

Tattoo Bible Book One
Author: Superior Tattoo $27.95

Whether you are preparing for your first tattoo or your twenty-seventh, you need artwork and designs that are just right. Tattoo Bible, authored by Superior Tattoo, provides well over 500 pieces of unique flash art - flash never before compiled into one single book.

While most tattoo books available today concentrate on one specific genre, this Tattoo Bible covers many different genres and the ideas are endless. This is not just a book to add to your collection - this is your collection. You can combine different pieces of art from within the book, or just take them as is. This book is for you and your imagination to do with as you wish.

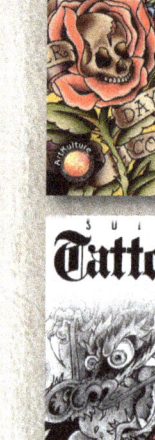

Tattoo Bible Book Two
Author: Superior Tattoo $27.95

Another unique and colorful collection of flash art. Everything is here, from Skulls to Tribal, Americana to the avant-garde.

Tattoo Bible includes flash images never before compiled in one single book. The artists included in this book include the very well known, and those artists who should be well known. The best known names include Kevin LeBlanc, Aaron Coleman, Bob Sims, Nate Powers and many, many more.

Tattoo Bible - Book Two, covers different styles and an endless supply of ideas. Make your own design by combining different pieces of art from within the book, or use one of the images as a stand-alone tattoo. A great supplement to your imagination.

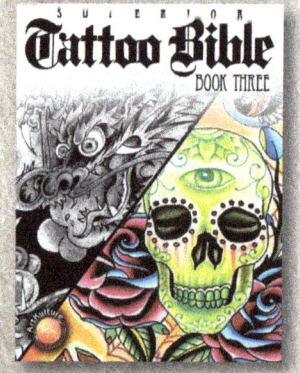

Tattoo Bible Book Three
Author: Superior Tattoo $27.95

Unlike the earlier Bibles, Tattoo Bible Book Three is a collection of designs from opposite ends of the spectrum. This new book contains images from both the old school and the new. Among this expanse of flash are colorful images of sacred hearts, and black and grey representations of Celtic knots. With over 350 images, this new book is the perfect companion for any tattooist, from the aspiring novice to the seasoned vet; and a useful resource for tattoo aficionados looking for the art they need to create the ultimate tattoo design. Book Three showcases artwork from some of the most-recognizable names in the tattoo world, as well as the coolest, trendiest designs from some of the newest, up-and-coming talent in the industry!

Wolfgang Books available at www.wolfpub.com

Photographers

Corbin Wade
Corbin Wade is a photographer who travels the world – and brings back images of everything from wildlife to the indigenous people he meets when far off the beaten path. Somehow he finds time to do some very nice studio and tattoo model work between all that globe trotting.
www.modelmayhem.com/855656
www.myspace.com/corbinwade
photo.net/photodb/user?user_id=2404365

Travis Haight
With a knack for poses, props and lighting, Travis produces images that are both provocative and just a little out of the ordinary. In addition to his work with models, Travis' web site shows a large portfolio of "wheels" images, hot rods and motorcycles, with and without lovely women, photographed – again – from very interesting angles.
www.myspace.com/haight
travishaightphotography.com
www.facebook.com/travishaightphotography
twitter.com/TravisHaight
travishaightphotography.tumblr.com

Greg Truelove
Greg is a photographer always looking for fresh models to satisfy a wide range of magazines and publishers. His credits include Playboy Special Editions, as well as a number of tattoo magazines, including Inked Girls, PRICK and TapouT. Greg is active on ModelMayhem, Facebook and Myspace.
www.facebook.com/gregtruelove
www.myspace.com/trueloveless
www.modelmayhem.com/312882

Colin Carrington
Colin isn't a photographer in the professional sense. As the husband of Brittany Casualty, however, he's in the perfect position to take some very nice pictures.

Justice Howard
Justice Howard's Tattoo and Erotic photography is simply in a class of it's own. Perhaps it's her ability to put the models at ease. Or her very creative use of backgrounds. Or her ability to pose her models. No matter. The net result is images that draws you eye and won't let go.
www.justicehoward.com
www.divadollart.com
www.spattergasm.com
www.facebook.com/JusticeHoward

Keith Selle
The man responsible for much of the photography in this book is well known in the tattoo community. Not only for taking pictures of high quality, that always get published, but also for creating a very model-friendly and relaxed environment in his Las Vegas studio. Experienced and beginning models can contact Keith through his web site or model mayhem.
www.keithselle.com
www.sellephotography.com
www.facebook.com/keithsellephotography
keithselle.tumblr.com

Mannon Pictures
Mannon Pictures is actually a team of two talented photographers: Amber Viktoria and Levi Mannon. In addition to their work with tattoo models, they cover everything from weddings to glamour. Their work for a large number of magazines and publications is shot both in their studio and on location.
www.mannonpictures.com
www.mannonpictures.webs.com
www.youtube.com/mannonpictures
www.facebook.com/mannon.pictures.5

Dennis Sprinkle
Dennis is another talented photographer with a varied portfolio. Though we know him for his work with tattoo models, Dennis also enjoys shooting landscapes, cityscapes and portraits – and often displays those images in fine-art galleries.
www.rocksolidphoto.net
www.myspace.com/rocksolidphoto
www.facebook.com/sprinklestudios

DiRado & Sons Photography
Owners Dave and Pam DiRado run a small photo studio and service serving their home town of Tehachapi, California. Their work includes everything from family and business portraits to photo shoots with various models.
www.dirado.net

Joseph Weisgerber
Joseph is another non-professional-photographer. He is, instead, an old friend of Jen Ashton, and was kind enough to supply some of the images found in this book.
www.facebook.com/joseph.weisgerber

Marcus Lopez
Trained as a fine-art painter, with a degree in film and video from Columbia College, Marcus works both in the studio and on location. It's been said that photographers paint with light, and that is certainly true of Marcus' over-the-top images of tattoo models.
www.marcuslopezphoto.com
www.facebook.com/marcuslopezphotography
www.modelmayhem.com/101240

Rick Wright
From southern Utah, Rick is another photographer comfortable using a full studio, or working outside under nature's own softbox. In addition to his work with tattoo models, Rick shoots musicians and celebrities in a variety of settings.
www.facebook.com/rickwrightphoto
www.supershoots.net/portfolio.cfm?ID=365
www.richardwrightphotography.com/

Dale Hannaford / Pictor
"I'm interested in edgy/erotic/fetish/quirky themes," explains Dale, "but I'm also prepared to shoot most anything especially if it is something I haven't done. Though Dale keeps a studio at his house, he prefers to work on location, "I seem to enjoy the uncertainty of it."
www.modelmayhem.com/46945
photo.net/photodb/user?user_id=1050563
www.profilekiss.com/picture/code-100/pictor.html

Chris LeBlanc
A little dark, a little edgy and a lot creative might best describe Chris' style when shooting models. In settings that lean toward gritty, his models always look sexy as hell.
www.flickr.com/people/chrisleblanc/
500px.com/TheUrbanPhotographer
www.facebook.com/chris.leblanc.58118

David MacKenzie/DMacStudios
David's images seen here, and his portfolio, show a tendency toward images that are well lit and varied. In addition to female models in a host of striking and unusual poses, there are cats and even birds.
twitter.com/DMacStudios
www.facebook.com/david.mackenzie.1029
dmacstudios.com/

Phoenix Taylor
Phoenix Taylor's portfolio might be called not-normal. The images should also be called arresting, intriguing, beautiful and sometimes erotic. After looking at the images on his web site, or tumblr, one gets the impression this is a photographer who definitely dances to his own drummer.
www.phoenixtphotography.com
phoenixtaylor.tumblr.com
www.facebook.com/PHOENIXTAYLOR
www.facebook.com/PHOENIXTSTUDIO

www.ingramcontent.com/pod-product-compliance
Lightning Source LLC
Chambersburg PA
CBHW040541220526
45473CB00016B/2996